1 MONTH OF
FREE
READING

at
www.ForgottenBooks.com

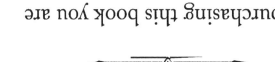

By purchasing this book you are eligible for one month membership to ForgottenBooks.com, giving you unlimited access to our entire collection of over 1,000,000 titles via our web site and mobile apps.

To claim your free month visit:
www.forgottenbooks.com/free8795591

ISBN 978-0-265-71422-5
PIBN 10879591

For support please visit www.forgottenbooks.com

TRAVELS

INTO

Several remote Nations of the World;

By LEMUEL GULLIVER,

First a Surgeon, and then a Captain of several Ships.

In FOUR PARTS.

PART I.

A Voyage to LILLIPUT.

PART II.

A Voyage to BROBDINGNAG.

PART III.

A Voyage to LAPUTA, BALNIBARBI, LUGG-NAGG, GLUBBDUBDRIB, and JAPAN.

PART IV.

A Voyage to the Country of the HOUYHNHNMS.

LONDON,

Printed for C. BATHURST.

MDCCLXVIII.

THE PUBLISHER TO THE READER.

THE author of these travels, Mr. *Lemuel Gulliver*, is my antient and intimate friend; there is likewise some relation between us on the mother's side. About three years ago Mr. *Gulliver*, growing weary of the concourse of curious people coming to him at his house in *Redriff*, made a small purchase of land with a convenient house near *Newark* in *Nottinghamshire*, his native country; where he now lives retired, yet in good esteem among his neighbours.

Although Mr. *Gulliver* was born in *Nottingham-shire*, where his father dwelt, yet I have heard him fay, his family came from *Oxfordshire*; to confirm which, I have observed in the church-yard at *Ban-bury* in that county feveral tombs and monuments of the *Gullivers*.

Before he quitted *Redriff*, he left the cuftody of the following papers in my hands, with the liberty to difpofe of them as I fhould think fit. I have carefully perufed them three times: The ftyle is very plain and fimple; and the only fault I find is, that the author, after the manner of travellers, is a little too circumftantial. There is an air of truth ap-parent through the whole; and indeed the author was fo diftinguifhed for his veracity, that it became a fort of a proverb among his neighbours at *Redriff*,

when

when any one affirmed a thing, to ſay it was as true as if Mr. *Gulliver* had ſpoken it.

By the advice of ſeveral worthy perſons, to whom with the author's permiſſion I communicated theſe papers, I now venture to ſend them into the world, hoping they may be, at leaſt for ſome time, a better entertainment to our young noblemen, than the common ſcribbles of politicks and party.

This volume would have been at leaſt twice as large, if I had not made bold to ſtrike out innumerable paſſages relating to the winds and tides, as well as to the variations and bearings in the ſeveral voyages, together with the minute deſcriptions of the management of the ſhip in ſtorms, in the ſtyle of ſailors; likewiſe the account of longitudes and latitudes; wherein I have reaſon to apprehend, that Mr. *Gulliver* may be a little diſſatisſied: But I was reſolved to fit the work as much as poſſible to the general capacity of readers. However, if my own ignorance in ſea affairs ſhall have led me to commit ſome miſtakes, I alone am anſwerable for them: And if any traveller hath a curioſity to ſee the whole work at large, as it came from the hand of the author, I will be ready to gratify him.

As for any further particulars relating to the author, the reader will receive ſatisfaction from the firſt pages of the book.

RICHARD SYMPSON.

LETTER

FROM

Captain *Gulliver* to his Cousin *Sympson.*

Written in the Year 1727.

I HOPE you will be ready to own publickly, whenever you shall be called to it, that by your great and frequent urgency you prevailed on me to publish a very loose and uncorrect account of my travels, with direction to hire some young gentleman of either university to put them in order, and correct the style, as my cousin *Dampier* did by my advice in his book called, *A Voyage round the World.* But I do not remember I gave you power to consent, that any thing should be omitted, and much less that any thing should be inserted: there-fore, as to the latter, I do here renounce every thing of that kind; particularly a paragraph about her majesty queen *Anne,* of most pious and glorious me-mory; although I did reverence and esteem her more than any of human species. But you, or your in-terpolator, ought to have considered, that as it was not my inclination, so it was not decent to praise any animal of our composition before my master *Houyhnhnm:* And besides, the fact was altogether false; for to my knowledge, being in *England* dur-ing some part of her majesty's reign, she did govern by a chief minister; nay even by two successively, the first whereof was the lord of *Godolphin,* and the second the lord of *Oxford;* so that you have made me say the thing that was not. Likewise in the ac-

count of the academy of projectors, and several
passages of my discourse to my master *Houyhnhnm*,
you have either omitted some material circumstances,
or minced or changed them in such a manner, that
I do hardly know mine own work   When I formerly hinted to you something of this in a letter,
you were pleased to answer, that you were afraid of
giving offence ; that people in power were very
watchful over the press, and apt not only to interpret, but to punish every thing which looked like
an *Inuendo* (as I think you call it.)   But, pray how
could that which I spoke so many years ago, and at
above five thousand leagues distance, in another
reign, be applied to any of the *Yahoos*, who now are
said to govern the herd ; especially at a time when I
little thought on, or feared, the unhappiness of living under them? have not I the most reason to
complain, when I see these very *Yahoos* carried
by *Houyhnhnms* in a vehicle, as if these were brutes
and those the rational creatures? And indeed to
avoid so monstrous and detestable a sight was one
principal motive of my retirement hither.

Thus much I thought proper to tell you in relation to yourself, and to the truth I reposed in
you.

I do in the next place complain of my own great
want of judgment in being prevailed upon by the
intreaties and false reasonings of you and some o-
thers, very much against my own opinion, to suffer
my travels to be published   Pray bring to your
mind how often I desired you to consider, when
you insisted on the motive of *Public Good*, that
the *Yahoos* were a species of animals utterly incapable

pable of amendment by precepts or example : And
fo it hath proved; for, inftead of feeing a full ftop
put to all abufes and corruptions, at leaft in this
little ifland, as I had reafon to expect ; behold, after
above fix months warning, I cannot learn that my
book has produced one fingle effect according to
mine intentions. I defired, you would let me
know by a letter, when party and faction were ex-
tinguifhed ; judges learned and upright ; pleaders
honeft and modeft with fome tincture of common
fenfe, and *Smithfield* blazing with pyramids of law-
books ; the young nobility's education entirely
changed ; the phyficians banifhed ; the female *Ya-*
boos abounding in virtue, honour, truth, and good
fenfe; courts and levees of great minifters thoroughly weeded and fwept ; wit, merit, and learning
rewarded ; all difgracers of the prefs in profe and
verfe condemned to eat nothing but their own cotton, and quench their thirft with their own ink.
Thefe, and a thoufand other reformations, I firmly
counted upon by your encouragement ; as indeed
they were plainly deducible from the precepts delivered in my book. And it muft be owned, that
feven months were a fufficient time to correct every
vice and folly to which *Yaboos* are fubject, if their
natures had been capable of the leaft difpofition to
virtue or wifdom : Yet, fo far have you been from
anfwering mine expectation in any of your letters ;
that on the contrary you are loading our carrier
every week with libels, and keys, and reflections,
and memoirs, and fecond parts ; wherein I fee myfelf accufed of reflecting upon great ftates-folk ; of
degrading human nature (for fo they have ftill the
con-

confidence to ftile it) and of abufing the female fex.
I find likewife, that the writers of thofe bundles are
not agreed among themfelves; for fome of them
will not allow me to be the author of mine own
travels; and others make me author of books, to
which I am wholly a ftranger.

I find likewife, that your printer hath been fo
carelefs as to confound the times, and miftake the
dates of my feveral voyages and returns; neither
affigning the true year, nor the true month, nor
day of the month : And I hear the original manu-
fcript is all deftroyed fince the publication of my
book; neither have I any copy left; however, I
have fent you fome corrections, which you may in-
fert, if ever there fhould be a fecond edition : And
yet I cannot ftand to them; but fhall leave that
matter to my judicious and candid readers to adjuft
it as they pleafe.

I hear fome of our fea-*Yaboos* find fault with
my fea-language, as not proper in many parts, nor
now in ufe. I cannot help it. In my firft voyages,
while I was young, I was inftructed by the oldeft
mariners, and learned to fpeak as they did. But I
have fince found that the fea-*Yaboos* are apt, like
the land ones, to become newfangled in their words,
which the latter change every year; infomuch, as I
remember upon each return to mine own country,
their old dialect was fo altered, that I could hardly
underftand the new. And I obferve, when any *Yaboo* comes from *London* out of curiofity to vifit me
at mine own houfe, we neither of us are able to
deliver our conceptions in a manner intelligible to
the other.

If

If the cenfure of the *Taboos* could any way affect me, I fhould have great reafon to complain, that fome of them are fo bold as to think my book of travels a mere fiction out of mine own brain; and have gone fo far as to drop hints, that the *Houyhn-hnms* and *Taboos* have no more exiftence than the inhabitants of *Utopia*.

Indeed I muft confefs, that as to the people of *Lilliput*, *Brobdingrag* (for fo the word fhould have been fpelt, and not erroneoufly *Brobdingnag*) and *Laputa*, I have never yet heard of any *Taboo* fo prefumptuous as to difpute their being, or the facts I have related concerning them; becaufe the truth immediately ftrikes every reader with conviction. And is there lefs probability in my account of the *Houyhnhnms* or *Taboos*, when it is manifeft as to the latter, there are fo many thoufands, even in this city, who only differ from their brother brutes in *Houyhnhnm-land*, becaufe they ufe a fort of *Jabber*, and do not go naked? I wrote for their amendment, and not their approbation. The united praife of the whole race would be of lefs confequence to me, than the neighing of thofe two degenerate *Houyhn-hnms* I keep in my ftable; becaufe from thefe, degenerate as they are, I ftill improve in fome virtues without any mixture of vice.

Do thefe miferable animals prefume to think, that I am fo degenerated as to defend my veracity? *Taboo* as I am, it is well known through all *Houyhn-hnm-land*, that, by the inftructions and example of my illuftrious mafter, I was able in the compafs of two years (although I confefs with the utmoft difficulty) to remove that infernal habit of lying, fhuf-
fling,

fling, deceiving, and equivocating, so deeply rooted in the very souls of all my species ; especially the *Europeans.*

I have other complaints to make upon this vexatious occasion ; but I forbear troubling myself or you any further. I must freely confess, that since my last return some corruptions of my *Yaboo* nature have revived in me by conversing with a few of your species, and particularly those of mine own family, by an unavoidable necessity ; else I should never have attempted so absurd a project as that of reforming the *Yaboo* race in this kingdom : But I have now done with all such visionary schemes for ever.

April 2, 1727.

*** That the original copy of these travels was altered by the person, th ough whose hands it was conveyed to the press, is a fact ; but the passages, of which Mr. *Gulliver* complains in this letter, are to be found only in the first editions ; for the Dean having restored the text wherever it had been altered sent the copy to the late Mr. *Motte* by the hands of Mr. *Charles Ford.* This copy has been exactly followed in every subsequent edition, except that printed in *Ireland,* by *George Falkener* ; the editor of which, supposing the Dean to be serious when he mentioned the corruptions of dates, and yet finding them unaltered, thought fit to alter them himself ; there is however scarce one of these alterations, in which he has not committed a blunder : Though while he was thus busy in defacing the parts that were perfect, he suffered the accidental blemishes of others to remain : See the preface to this edition.

CONTENTS.

PART I.

A Voyage to LILLIPUT.

CHAP. I.

CHAP. II.

CHAP. III.

CHAP.

CHAP. IV.

CHAP. V.

CHAP. VI.

CHAP. VII.

CHAP. VIII.

PART

PART II.

A Voyage to BROBDINGNAG.

CHAP.

CHAP. IV.

CHAP. V.

CHAP. VI.

CHAP. VII.

CHAP. VIII.

PART

PART III.

A Voyage to LAPUTA, BALNIBARBI, LUGGNAGG, GLUBBDUBDRIB, and JAPAN.

CHAP.

CHAP. X.

CHAP. XI.

PART IV.

A Voyage to the country of the Houy-HNHNMS.

CHAP. I.

CHAP. II.

b 2   *relieved.*

CHAP. XII.

A VOYAGE

Hogs I.

SUMATRA

P. Mintaou

I. Good Fortune

I. Nassow

SUNDA

Sillabar

Straits of Sunda

Blefuscu

Lilliput

Mildendo

Discoverd A.D. 1699

Diemens Land

A
VOYAGE
TO
LILLIPUT.

CHAP. I.

The author gives some account of himself and family : his first inducements to travel. He is shipwrecked, and swims for his life ;. gets safe on shore in the country of Lilliput; *is made a prisoner, and carried up the country.*

MY father had a small estate in *Nottinghamshire*; I was the third of five sons. He sent me to *Emanuel* college in *Cambridge* at fourteen years old, where I resided three years, and applied myself close to my studies; but the charge of maintaining me, although I had a very scanty allowance, being too great for a narrow fortune, I was bound apprentice to Mr. *James Bates,* an eminent surgeon in *London,* with whom I continued four years; and my father now and then sending me small sums of money, I laid them out in learning navigation, and other parts of the mathematicks useful to those, who intend to travel, as I always be-

These voyages are intended as a moral political romance — to correct vice by shewing its deformity in opposition to the beauty of virtue, and to amend the false systems of philosophy by pointing out the errors, and applying salutary means to avoid them. ORRERY.

lieved it would be some time or other my fortune to do. When I left Mr. *Bates*, I went down to my father; where, by the assistance of him and my uncle *John*, and some other relations, I got forty pounds, and a promise of thirty pounds a year to maintain me at *Leyden:* there I studied physick two years and seven months, knowing it would be useful in long voyages.

Soon after my return from *Leyden*, I was recommended by my good master Mr. *Bates* to be surgeon to the *Swallow*, captain *Abraham Pannell*, commander; with whom I continued three years and a half, making a voyage or two into the *Levant*, and some other parts. When I came back, I resolved to settle in *London*, to which Mr. *Bates*, my master, encouraged me, and by him I was recommended to several patients. I took part of a small house in the *Old-Jury*; and being advised to alter my condition, I married Mrs. *Mary Burton*, second daughter to Mr. *Edmund Burton* hosier in *Newgate-street*, with whom I received four hundred pounds for a portion.

But, my good master *Bates* dying in two years after, and I having few friends, my business began to fail; for my conscience would not suffer me to imitate the bad practice of too many among my brethren. Having therefore consulted with my wife, and some of my acquaintance, I determined to go again to sea. I was surgeon successively in two ships, and made several voyages for six years to the *East* and *West Indies*, by which I got some addition to my fortune.

fortune. My hours of leifure I fpent in reading the beft authors, antient and modern, being always provided with a good number of books; and when I was afhore, in obferving the manners and difpofitions of the people, as well as learning their language, wherein I had a great facility by the ftrength of my memory.

The laft of thefe voyages not proving very fortunate, I grew weary of the fea, and intended to ftay at home with my wife and family. I removed from the *Old-Jury* to *Fetter-lane*, and from thence to *Wapping*, hoping to get bufinefs among the failors; but it would not turn to account. After three years expectation that things would mend, I accepted an advantageous offer from captain *William Prichard*, mafter of the *Antelope*, who was making a voyage to the *South-Sea*. We fet fail from *Briftol*, *May* 4th, 1699, and our voyage at firft was very profperous.

It would not be proper, for fome reafons, to trouble the reader with the particulars of our adventures in thofe feas: let it fuffice to inform him, that, in our paffage from thence to the *Eaft-Indies*, we were driven by a violent ftorm to the north-weft of *Van Diemen's land*. By an obfervation we found ourfelves in the latitude of 30 degrees 2 minutes fouth. Twelve of our crew were dead by immoderate labour, and ill food; the reft were in a very weak condition. On the fifth of *November*, which was the beginning of fummer in thofe parts, the weather being very hazy, the fea-

men

4

men spied a rock within half a cable's length of the ship; but the wind was so strong, that we were driven directly upon it, and immediately split. Six of the crew, of whom I was one, having let down the boat into the sea, made a shift to get clear of the ship and the rock. We rowed by my computation about three leagues, till we were able to work no longer, being already spent with labour while we were in the ship. We therefore trusted ourselves to the mercy of the waves, and in about half an hour the boat was overset by a sudden flurry from the north. What became of my companions in the boat, as well as of those who escaped on the rock, or were left in the vessel, I cannot tell; but conclude they were all lost. For my own part, I swam as fortune directed me, and was pushed forward by wind and tide. I often let my legs drop, and could feel no bottom: but when I was almost gone, and able to struggle no longer, I found myself within my depth; and by this time the storm was much abated. The declivity was so small, that I walked near a mile before I got to the shore, which I conjectured was about eight a clock in the evening. I then advanced forward near half a mile, but could not discover any sign of houses or inhabitants; at least I was in so weak a condition, that I did not observe them. I was extremely tired, and with that, and the heat of the weather, and about half a pint of brandy that I drank as I left the ship, I found myself much inclined to sleep. I lay down

on

on the grafs, which was very fhort and foft, where I flept founder than ever I remembered to have done in my life, and, as I reckoned, about nine hours; for when I awaked, it was juft day-light. I attempted to rife, but was not able to ftir: for as I happened to lie on my back, I found my arms and legs were ftrongly faftened on each fide to the ground; and my hair, which was long and thick, tied down in the fame manner. I likewife felt feveral flender ligatures acrofs my body, from my arm-pits to my thighs. I could only look upwards, the fun began to grow hot, and the light of-fended my eyes. I heard a confufed noife a-bout me; but, in the pofture I lay, could fee nothing except the fky. In a little time I felt fomething alive moving on my left leg, which advancing gently forward over my breaft came almoft up to my chin; when bending my eyes downward as much as I could, I perceived it to be a human creature not fix inches high, with a bow and arrow in his hands, and a quiver at his back. In the mean time, I felt at leaft forty more of the fame kind (as I con-jectured) following the firft. I was in the ut-moft aftonifhment, and roared fo loud, that they all ran back in a fright; and fome of them, as I was afterwards told, were hurt with the falls they got by leaping from my fides upon the ground. However, they foon re-turned, and one of them, who ventured fo far as to get a full fight of my face, lifting up his hands and eyes by way of admiration, cried

out

out in a fhrill but diftinct voice, *hekinah de-gul:* the others repeated the fame words feveral times, but I then knew not what they meant. I lay all this while, as the reader may believe, in great uneafinefs; at length, ftruggling to get loofe, I had the fortune to break the ftrings, and wrench out the pegs, that faftened my left arm to the ground; for, by lifting it up to my face, I difcovered the methods they had taken to bind me, and at the fame time with a violent pull, which gave me exceffive pain, I a little loofened the ftrings that tied down my hair on the left fide, fo that I was juft able to turn my head about two inches. But the crea-tures ran off a fecond time, before I could feize them; whereupon there was a great fhout in a very fhrill accent, and after it ceafed, I heard one of them cry aloud, *tolgo phonac;* when in an inftant I felt above an hundred ar-rows difcharged on my left hand, which pricked me like fo many needles; and befides, they fhot another flight into the air, as we do bombs in *Europe,* whereof many, I fuppofe, fell on my body, (though I felt them not) and fome on my face, which I immediately cover-ed with my left hand. When this fhower of arrows was over, I fell a groaning with grief and pain, and then ftriving again to get loofe, they difcharged another volley larger than the firft, and fome of them attempted with fpears to ftick me in the fides; but by good luck I had on me a buff jerkin, which they could not perce. I thought it the moft prudent
method

method to lie ftill, and my defign was to continue fo till night, when, my left hand being already loofe, I could eafily free myfelf: and as
for the inhabitants, I had reafon to beliĕve I
might be a match for the greateft army they
could bring againft me, if they were all of the
fame fize with him, that I faw. But fortune
difpofed otherwife of me. When the people
obferved I was quiet, they difcharged no more
arrows: but, by the noife I heard, I knew their
numbers increafed; and about four yards from
me, over-againft my right ear, I heard a
knocking for above an hour, like that of people at work; when turning my head that way,
as well as the pegs and ftrings would permit
me, I faw a ftage erected about a foot and half
from the ground, capable of holding four of
the inhabitants, with two or three ladders to
mount it: from whence one of them, who
feemed to be a perfon of quality, made me a
a long fpeech, whereof I underftood not one
fyllable. But I fhould have mentioned, that
before the principal perfon began his oration,
he cried out three times, *langro debul fan*; (thefe
words and the former were afterwards repeated
and explained to me). Whereupon immediately
about fifty of the inhabitants came and cut
the ftrings that faftened the left fide of my
head, which gave me the liberty of turning it
to the right, and of obferving the perfon and
gefture of him that was to fpeak. He appeared to be of a middle age, and taller than
any of the other three who attended him,

whereof

whereof one was a page that held up his train, and seemed to be somewhat longer than my middle finger; the other two stood one on each side to support him. He acted every part of an orator, and I could obferve many periods of threatnings, and others of promifes, pity, and kindnefs. I anfwered in a few words, but in the moft fubmiffive manner, lifting up my left hand and both my eyes to the fun, as calling him for a witnefs; and being almoft famifhed with hunger, having not eaten a morfel for fome hours before I left the fhip, I found the demands of nature fo ftrong upon me, that I could not forbear fhewing my impatience (perhaps againft the ftrict rules of decency) by putting my finger frequently to my mouth, to fignify that I wanted food. The *burgo* (for fo they call a great lord, as I afterwards learnt) underftood me very well. He defcended from the ftage, and commanded that feveral ladders fhould be applied to my fides, on which above an hundred of the inhabitants mounted, and walked towards my mouth, laden with bafkets full of meat, which had been provided and fent thither by the king's orders, upon the firft intelligence he received of me. I obferved there was the flefh of feveral animals, but could not diftinguifh them by the tafte. There were fhoulders, legs, and loins, fhaped like thofe of mutton, and very well dreffed, but fmaller than the wings of a lark. I eat them by two or three at a mouthful, and took three loaves at a time, about the bignefs of mufket

bullets.

bullets. They fupplied me as faft as they could, fhewing a thoufand marks of wonder and aftonifhment at my bulk and appetite. I then made another fign, that I wanted drink. They found by my eating, that a fmall quantity would not fuffice me, and being a moft ingenious people, they flung up with great dexterity one of their largeft hogfheads, then rolled it towards my hand, and beat out the top; I drank it off at a draught, which I might well do, for it did not hold half a pint, and tafted like a fmall wine of *Burgundy*, but much more delicious. They brought me a fecond hogfhead, which I drank in the fame manner, and made figns for more; but they had none to give me. When I had performed thefe wonders, they fhouted for joy, and danced upon my breaft, repeating feveral times as they did at firft, *bekinah degul*. They made me a fign that I fhould throw down the two hogfheads, but firft warning the people below to ftand out of the way, crying aloud, *borach mevola*, and when they faw the veffels in the air, there was an univerfal fhout of *bekinah degul*. I confefs, I was often tempted, while they were paffing backwards and forwards on my body, to feize forty or fifty of the firft that came in my reach, and dafh them againft the ground. But the remembrance of what I had felt, which probably might not be the worft they could do, and the promife of honour I made them, for fo I interpreted my fubmiffive behaviour, foon drove out thefe imaginations.

Befides,

Besides, I now confidered myfelf as bound by the laws of hofpitality to a people, who had treated me with fo much expence and magnificence. However, in my thoughts I could not fufficiently wonder at the intrepidity of thefe diminutive mortals, who durft venture to mount and walk upon my body, while one of my hands was at liberty, without trembling at the very fight of fo prodigious a creature, as I muft appear to them. After fome time, when they obferved that I made no more demands for meat, there appeared before me a perfon of high rank from his imperial majefty. His excellency, having mounted on the fmall of my right leg, advanced forwards up to my face, with about a dozen of his retinue. And producing his credentials under the fignet royal, which he applied clofe to my eyes, fpoke about ten minutes without any figns of anger, but with a kind of determinate refolution; often pointing forwards, which, as I afterwards found, was towards the capital city, about half a mile diftant, whither it was agreed by his majefty in council, that I muft be conveyed. I anfwered in few words, but to no purpofe, and made a fign with my hand that was loofe, putting it to the other (but over his excellency's head for fear of hurting him or his train) and then to my own head and body, to fignify that I defired my liberty. It appeared, that he underftood me well enough, for he fhook his head by way of difapprobation, and held his hand in a pofture to fhew, that I muft

be

be carried as a prifoner. However, he made other figns to let me underftand, that I fhould have meat and drink enough, and very good treatment. Whereupon I once more thought of attempting to break my bonds, but again, when I felt the fmart of their arrows upon my face and hands, which were all in blifters, and many of the darts ftill fticking in them, and obferving likewife that the number of my enemies increafed, I gave tokens to let them know, that they might do with me what they pleafed. Upon this the *hurgo* and his train withdrew with much civility and chearful countenances. Soon after I heard a general fhout, with frequent repetitions of the words, *peplom felan*, and I felt great numbers of people on my left fide relaxing the cords to fuch a degree, that I was able to turn upon my right, and to eafe myfelf with making water; which I very plentifully did, to the great aftonifhment of the people, who conjecturing, by my motion, what I was going to do, immediately opened to the right and left on that fide, to avoid the torrent which fell with fuch noife and violence from me. But before this, they had daubed my face and both my hands with a fort of ointment very pleafant to the fmell, which in a few minutes removed all the fmart of their arrows. Thefe circumftances, added to the refrefhment I had received by their victuals and drink, which were very nourifhing, difpofed me to fleep. I flept about eight hours, as I was afterwards affured; and it was no wonder,

wonder, for the phyſicians, by the emperor's order, had mingled a ſleepy potion in the hogſheads of wine.

It ſeems that, upon the firſt moment I was diſcovered ſleeping on the ground after my landing, the emperor had early notice of it by an expreſs ; and determined in council, that I ſhould be tied in the manner I have related, (which was done in the night while I ſlept) that plenty of meat and drink ſhould be ſent to me, and a machine prepared to carry me to the capital city.

This reſolution perhaps may appear very bold and dangerous, and I am confident would not be imitated by any prince in *Europe* on the like occaſion ; however, in my opinion, it was extremely prudent, as well as generous : for ſuppoſing theſe people had endeavoured to kill me with their ſpears and arrows while I was aſleep, I ſhould certainly have awaked with the firſt ſenſe of ſmart, which might ſo far have rouzed my rage and ſtrength, as to have enabled me to break the ſtrings, wherewith I was tied ; after which, as they were not able to make reſiſtance, ſo they could expect no mercy.

Theſe people are moſt excellent mathematicians, and arrived to a great perfection in mechanicks by the countenance and encouragement of the emperor, who is a renowned patron of learning. This prince hath ſeveral machines fixed on wheels for the carriage of trees and other great weights. He often builds his largeſt men of war, whereof ſome are nine

feet

feet long, in the woods where the timber grows, and has them carried on these engines three or four hundred yards to the sea. Five hundred carpenters and engineers were immediately set at work to prepare the greatest engine they had. It was a frame of wood raised three inches from the ground, about seven feet long and four wide, moving upon twenty-two wheels. The shout I heard was upon the arrival of this engine, which it seems set out in four hours after my landing. It was brought parallel to me, as I lay. But the principal difficulty was to raise and place me in this vehicle. Eighty poles, each of one foot high, were erected for this purpose, and very strong cords of the bigness of packthread were fastened by hooks to many bandages, which the workmen had girt round my neck, my hands, my body, and my legs. Nine hundred of the strongest men were employed to draw up these cords by many pullies fastened on the poles, and thus, in less than three hours, I was raised and flung into the engine, and there tied fast. All this I was told, for, while the whole operation was performing, I lay in a profound sleep by the force of that soporiferous medicine infused into my liquor. Fifteen hundred of the emperor's largest horses, each about four inches and an half high, were employed to draw me towards the metropolis, which, as I said, was half a mile distant.

About four hours after we began our journey, I awaked by a very ridiculous accident; for the carriage

riage being ftopt a while to adjuft fomething, that was out of order, two or three of the young natives had the curiofity to fee how I looked, when I was afleep ; they climbed up into the engine, and advancing very foftly to my face, one of them, an officer in the guards, put the fharp end of his half-pike a good way up into my left noftril, which tickled my nofe like a ftraw, and made me fneeze violently [a] : whereupon they ftole off unperceived, and it was three weeks, before I knew the caufe of my awaking fo fuddenly. We made a long march the remaining part of the day, and refted at night with five hundred guards on each fide of me, half with torches, and half with bows and arrows, ready to fhoot me, if I fhould offer to ftir. The next morning at fun-rife we continued our march, and arrived within two hundred yards of the city-gates about noon. The emperor, and all his court, came out to meet us, but his great officers would by no means fuffer his majefty to endanger his perfon by mounting on my body.

At the place where the carriage ftopt, there ftood an ancient temple, efteemed to be the

---

[a] It has been remarked, that courage in whatever caufe, though it fometimes excites indignation, is never the object of contempt ; but this appears to be true, only becaufe courage is fuppofed to imply fuperiority : for this *officer in the guards* becomes extremely ridiculous and contemptible by an act of the moft daring curiofity, which fets him in comparifon with *Gulliver* ; to whom he was fo much inferior, that a blaft of the *man-mountain*'s noftrils would have endangered his life ; and if heroifm itfelf is not proof againft ridicule, thofe furely are *Lilliputians* in philofophy, who confider ridicule as the teft of truth.

I. S. Müller invi. del. et sc.

largeft in the whole kingdom, which having been polluted fome years before by an unnatural mur-der, was according to the zeal of thofe people looked upon as prophane, and therefore had been applied to common ufe, and all the orna-ments and furniture carried away. In this edi-fice it was determined I fhould lodge. The great gate fronting to the north was about four feet high, and almoft two feet wide, through which I could eafily creep. On each fide of the gate was a fmall window, not above fix inches from the ground : into that on the left fide the king's fmith conveyed fourfcore and eleven chains, like thofe that hang to a lady's watch in *Europe*, and almoft as large, which were locked to my left leg with fix and thirty padlocks. Over-againft this temple, on the other fide of the great highway, at twenty feet diftance, there was a turret at leaft five feet high. Here the emperor afcended with many principal lords of his court to have an oppor-tunity of viewing me, as I was told, for I could not fee them. It was reckoned, that a-bove an hundred thoufand inhabitants came out of the town upon the fame errand ; and in fpite of my guards, I believe, there could not be fewer than ten thoufand at feveral times, who mounted my body by the help of ladders. But a proclamation was foon iffued to forbid it upon pain of death. When the workmen found it was impoffible for me to break loofe, they cut all the ftrings that bound me ; whereupon I rofe up with as melancholy a difpofition, as ever I had

had in my life. But the noife and aftonifhment of the people at feeing me rife and walk are not to be expreffed. The chains, that held my left leg, were about two yards long, and gave me not only the liberty of walking backwards and forwards in a femicircle; but, being fixed within four inches of the gate, allowed me to creep in, and lie at my full length in the temple.

CHAP. II.

The emperor of Lilliput, *attended by feveral of the nobility, comes to fee the author in his confinement. The emperor's perfon and habit defcribed. Learned men appointed to teach the author their language. He gains favour by his mild difpofition. His pockets are fearched, and his fword and piftols taken from him.*

WHEN I found myfelf on my feet, I looked about me, and muft confefs I never beheld a more entertaining profpect. The country around appeared like a continued garden, and the inclofed fields, which were generally forty feet fquare, refembled fo many beds of flowers. Thefe fields were intermingled with woods of half a ftang *, and the talleft trees, as I could judge, appeared to be feven feet high. I viewed the town on my left hand, which looked like the painted fcene of a city in a theatre.

* A *ftang* is a pole or perch; fixteen feet and a half.

I

I had been for some hours extremely preſſed by the neceſſities of nature ; which was no wonder, it being almoſt two days, ſince I had laſt diſburthened myſelf. I was under great difficulties between urgency and ſhame. The beſt expedient I could think on, was to creep into my houſe, which I accordingly did ; and ſhutting the gate after me, I went as far as the length of my chain would ſuffer, and diſcharged my body of that uneaſy load. But this was the only time I was ever guilty of ſo uncleanly an action ; for which I cannot but hope the candid reader will give ſome allowance, after he hath maturely and impartially conſidered my caſe, and the diſtreſs I was in. From this time my conſtant practice was, as ſoon as I roſe, to perform that buſineſs in open air at the full extent of my chain ; and due care was taken every morning before company came, that the offenſive matter ſhould be carried off in wheelbarrows by two ſervants appointed for that purpoſe. I would not have dwelt ſo long upon a circumſtance, that perhaps at firſt ſight may appear not very momentous, if I had not thought it neceſſary to juſtify my character in point of cleanlineſs to the world; which I am told ſome of my maligners have been pleaſed, upon this and other occaſions, to call in queſtion.

When this adventure was at an end, I came back out of my houſe, having occaſion for freſh air. The emperor was already deſcended from the tower, and advancing on horſe-

back towards me, which had like to have coſt
him dear; for the beaſt, though very well
trained, yet wholly unuſed to ſuch a ſight,
which appeared as if a mountain moved before
him, reared up on his hinder feet: but that
prince, who is an excellent horſeman, kept
his ſeat, till his attendants ran in, and held
the bridle, while his majeſty had time to diſ-
mount. When he alighted, he ſurveyed me
round with great admiration; but kept beyond the length of my chain. He ordered
his cooks and butlers, who were already prepared, to give me victuals and drink, which
they puſhed forward in a ſort of vehicles upon
wheels, till I could reach them. I took theſe vehicles, and ſoon emptied them all; twenty of them
were filled with meat, and ten with liquor; each
of the former afforded me two or three good
mouthfuls; and I emptied the liquor of ten
veſſels, which was contained in earthen vials,
into one vehicle, drinking it off at a draught;
and ſo I did with the reſt. The empreſs, and
young princes of the blood of both ſexes, attended by many ladies, ſat at ſome diſtance in
their chairs; but upon the accident that happened to the emperor's horſe, they alighted,
and came near his perſon, which I am now
going to deſcribe. He is taller by almoſt the
breadth of my hail, than any of his court,
which alone is enough to ſtrike an awe into
the beholders. His features are ſtrong and
maſculine, with an *Auſtrian* lip and arched
noſe, his complexion olive, his countenance
erect,

erect, his body and limbs well proportioned, all his motions graceful, and his deportment majeſtic. He was then paſt his prime, being twenty-eight years and three quarters old, of which he had reigned about ſeven in great felicity, and generally victorious. For the better convenience of beholding him, I lay on my ſide, ſo that my face was parallel to his, and he ſtood but three yards off : however, I have had him ſince many times in my hand, and therefore cannot be deceived in the deſcription. His dreſs was very plain and ſimple, and the faſhion of it between the *aſiatick* and the *european :* but he had on his head a light helmet of gold, adorned with jewels, and a plume on the creſt. He held his ſword drawn in his hand to defend himſelf, if I ſhould happen to break looſe*; it was almoſt three inches long; the hilt and ſcabbard were gold enriched with diamonds. His voice was ſhrill, but very clear and articulate, and I could diſtinctly hear it, when I ſtood up. The ladies and courtiers were all moſt magnificently clad, ſo that the ſpot they ſtood upon ſeemed to reſemble a petticoat ſpread on the ground, embroidered with figures of gold and ſilver. His imperial majeſty ſpoke often to me, and I returned anſwers; but nei-

---

* The maſculine ſtrength of features, which *Gulliver* could not ſee, till he laid his face upon the ground; and the awful ſuperiority of ſtature in a being, whom he held in his hand; the helmet, the plume, and the ſword, are a fine reproof of human pride; the objects of which are trifling diſtinctions whether of perſon or rank; the ridiculous parade and oſtentation of a pigmy; which derive not only their origin but their uſe from the folly, weakneſs, and imperfection of ourſelves and others.

ther

ther of us could underftand a fyllable.   There
were feveral of his priefts and lawyers prefent, (as
I conjectured by their habits) who were commanded to addrefs themfelves to me, and I
fpoke to them in as many languages as I had
the leaft fmattering of, which were *high* and
low dutch, latin, french, fpanifh, italian, and
lingua franca; but all to no purpofe.   After
about two hours the court retired, and I was
left with a ftrong guard to prevent the impertinence, and probably the malice of the rabble,
who were very impatient to croud about me
as near as they durft, and fome of them had
the impudence to fhoot their arrows at me, as
I fat on the ground by the door of my houfe,
whereof one very narrowly miffed my left eye.
But the colonel ordered fix of the ring-leaders
to be feized, and thought no punifhment fo
proper as to deliver them bound into my hands;
which fome of his foldiers accordingly did,
pufhing them forwards with the but-ends of
their pikes into my reach : I took them all in
my right hand, put five of them into my coat-
pocket, and as to the fixth, I made a countenance, as if I would eat him alive.   The poor
man fqualled terribly, and the colonel and his
officers were in much pain; efpecially when
they faw me take out my penknife : but I
foon put them out of fear ; for, looking mildly
and immediately cutting the ftrings he was
bound with, I fet him gently on the ground,
and away he ran.   I treated the reft in the
fame manner, taking them one by one out of
                                                    my

my pocket; and I obferved both the foldiers
and people were highly delighted at this mark
of my clemency, which was reprefented very
much to my advantage at court.

Towards night I got with fome difficulty
into my houfe, where I lay on the ground, and
continued to do fo about a fortnight; during
which time the emperor gave orders to have
a bed prepared for me. Six hundred beds * of
the common meafure were brought in carria-
ages, and worked up in my houfe; an hundred
and fifty of their beds, fewn together, made up
the breadth and length; and thefe were four
double, which however kept me but very in-
differently from the hardnefs of the floor, that
was of fmooth ftone. By the fame computation they provided me with fheets, blankets,
and coverlets, tolerable enough for one, who
had been fo long inured to hardfhips.

As the news of my arrival fpread through
the kingdom, it brought prodigious numbers
of rich, idle, and curious people to fee me;
fo that the villages were almoft emptied;
and great neglect of tillage and houfhold affairs muft have enfued, if his imperial majefty had not provided by feveral proclamations
and orders of ftate againft this inconveniency.
He directed, that thofe, who had already beheld me, fhould return home, and not prefume to come within fifty yards of my houfe

* *Gulliver* has obferved great and appearances of the objects
exactnefs in the juft proportion thus leffened. ORRERY.

without

without licence from court; whereby the fecretaries of ftate got confiderable fees.

In the mean time the emperor held frequent
councils to debate, what courfe fhould be
taken with me; and I was afterwards affured
by a particular friend, a perfon of great quality, who was as much in the fecret as any,
that the court was under many difficulties concerning me. They apprehended my breaking
loofe; that my diet would be very expenfive,
and might caufe a famine. Sometimes they
determined to ftarve me, or at leaft to fhoot
me in the face and hands with poifoned arrows, which would foon difpatch me; but a-
gain they confidered, that the ftench of fo
large a carcafe might produce a plague in the
metropolis, and probably fpread through the
whole kingdom. In the midft of thefe conful-
tations feveral officers of the army went to the
door of the great council-chamber, and two
of them being admitted gave an account of
my behaviour to the fix criminals above-mentioned, which made fo favourable an impreffion in the breaft of his majefty, and the whole
board, in my behalf, that an imperial commiffion was iffued out, obliging all the villages
nine hundred yards round the city to deliver
in every morning fix beeves, forty fheep, and
other victuals for my fuftenance; together with
a proportionable quantity of bread, and wine,
and other liquors; for the due payment of
which his majefty gave affignments upon his
treafury. For this prince lives chiefly upon

his

his own demefnes, feldom, except upon great
occafions, raifing any fubfidies upon his fubjects, who are bound to attend him in his
wars at their own expence. An eftablifhment
was alfo made of fix hundred perfons to be my
domefticks, who had board-wages allowed for
their maintenance, and tents built for them very
conveniently on each fide of my door. It was
likewife ordered, that three hundred taylors
fhould make me a fuit of cloaths after the
fafhion of the country: that fix of his majefty's greateft fcholars fhould be employed to
inftruct me in their language: and laftly, that
the emperor's horfes, and thofe of the nobility, and troops of guards, fhould be frequently exercifed in my fight to accuftom themfelves to me. All thefe orders were duly
put in execution, and in about three weeks I
made a great progrefs in learning their language; during which time the emperor frequently honoured me with his vifits, and was
pleafed to affift my mafters in teaching me.
We began already to converfe together in fome
fort; and the firft words I learnt were to exprefs my defire, that he would pleafe to give
me my liberty, which I every day repeated on
my knees. His anfwer, as I could apprehend
it, was, that this muft be a work of time,
not to be thought on without the advice of
his council, and that firft I muft *lumos kelmin
peffo defmar lon empofo;* that is, fwear a peace
with him and his kingdom. However, that I
fhould be ufed with all kindnefs; and he ad-

vifed

vifed me to acquire, by my patience and dif-
creet behaviour, the good opinion of himfelf
and his fubjects. He defired I would not take
it ill, if he gave orders to certain proper officers to fearch me ; for probably I might carry
about me feveral weapons, which muft needs
be dangerous things, if they anfwered the bulk
of fo prodigious a perfon. I faid, his majefty
fhould be fatisfied; for I was ready to ftrip
myfelf, and turn up my pockets before him.
This I delivered part in words, and part in
figns. He replied, that by the laws of the
kingdom I muft be fearched by two of his officers; that he knew this could not be done
without my confent and affiftance ; that he had
fo good an opinion of my generofity and juftice, as to truft their perfons in my hands :
that whatever they took from me, fhould be
returned when I left the country, or paid for
at the rate, which I would fet upon them. I
took up the two officers in my hands, put them
firft into my coat-pockets, and then into every
other pocket about me, except my two fobs,
and another fecret pocket, which I had no
mind fhould be fearched, wherein I had fome
little neceffaries, that were of no confequence
to any but myfelf. In one of my fobs there
was a filver watch, and in the other a fmall
quant:ty of gold in a purfe. Thefe gentlemen,
having pen, ink, and paper about them, made
an exict inventory of every thing they faw ;
and, when they had done, defired I would
let them down, that they might deliver it to
the

the emperor. This inventory I afterwards tranflated into *englifh*, and is word for word as follows.

Imprimis, In the right coat-pocket of the *great man-mountain* (for fo I interpret the words *quinbus fleftrin*) after the ftrictest fearch we found only one great piece of coarfe cloth, large enough to be a foot-cloth for your majefty's chief room of ftate. In the left pocket we faw a huge filver cheft, with a cover of the fame metal, which we the fearchers were not able to lift. We defired it fhould be opened, and one of us ftepping into it, found himfelf up to the mid leg in a fort of duft, fome part whereof flying up to our faces, fet us both a fneezing for feveral times together. In his right waiftcoat-pocket we found a prodigious bundle of white thin fubftances, folded one over another, about the bignefs of three men, tied with a ftrong cable, and marked with black figures; which we humbly conceive to be writings, every letter almoft half as large as the palm of our hands. In the left there was a fort of engine, from the back of which were extended twenty long poles, refembling the palifadoes before your majefty's court; wherewith we conjecture the *man-mountain* combs his head; for we did not always trouble him with queftions, becaufe we found it a great difficulty to make him underftand us. In the large pocket on the right fide of his middle cover (fo I tranflate the word *Ranfu-lo*, by which they meant my breeches) we

we faw a hollow pillar of iron, about
length of a man, faftened to a ftrong piece
timber, larger than the pillar; and upon
fide of the pillar were huge pieces of i
fticking out, cut into ftrange figures, wh
we know not what to make of.   In the
pocket another engine of the fame kind.
the fmaller pocket on the right fide were fe
ral round flat pieces of white and red meta
different bulk; fome of the white, wh
feemed to be filver, were fo large and hea
that my comrade and I could hardly lift th
In the left pocket were two black pillars i
gularly fhaped: we could not without d
culty reach the top of them, as we ftood
the bottom of his pocket.   One of them
covered, and feemed all of a piece: but
the upper end of the other there appeare
white round fubftance, about twice the l
nefs of our heads.   Within each of thefe
inclofed a prodigious plate of fteel; whi
by our orders, we obliged him to fhew
becaufe we apprehended they might be dan
rous engines.   He took them out of tl
cafes, and told us, that in his own country
practice was to fhave his beard with one
thefe, and to cut his meat with the otl
There were two pockets, which we could
enter: thefe he called his fobs; they v
two large flits cut into the top of his mic
cover, but fqueezed clofe by the preffure of
belly.   Out of the right fob hung a great fi
chain, with a wonderful kind of engine at
                                        bott

bottom. We directed him to draw out whatever was at the end of that chain; which appeared to be a globe, half filver, and half of
fome tranfparent metal: for on the tranfparent
fide we faw certain ftrange figures circularly
drawn, and thought we could touch them, till
we found our fingers ftopped by that lucid
fubftance. He put this engine to our ears,
which made an inceffant noife like that of a
water-mill: and we conjecture it is either fome
unknown animal, or the god that he worfhips;
but we are more inclined to the latter opinion,
becaufe he affured us (if we underftood him
right, for he expreffed himfelf very imperfectly) that he feldom did any thing without confulting it. He called it his oracle, and faid, it
pointed out the time for every action of his
life *. From the left fob he took out a net almoft large enough for a fifherman, but contrived to open and fhut like a purfe, and ferved
him for the fame ufe: we found therein feveral
maffy pieces of yellow metal, which, if they
be real gold, muft be of immenfe value.

Having thus, in obedience to your majefty's
commands, diligently fearched all his pockets,
we obferved a girdle about his waift, made of
the hide of fome prodigious animal, from
which on the left fide hung a fword of the
length of five men; and on the right a bag or

* Perhaps the author intended to expofe the probable fallacy of opinions derived from the rela-tions of travellers by fhewing, how little truth need to be mif-underftood to make falfhood fpe-cious.

pouch

pouch divided into two cells, each cell capable of holding three of your majefty's fubjects. In one of thefe cells were feveral globes, or balls, of a moft ponderous metal, about the bignefs of our heads, and required a ftrong hand to lift them : the other cell contained a heap of certain black grains, but of no great bulk or weight, for we could hold above fifty of them in the palms of our hands.

This is an exact inventory of what we found about the body of the *man-mountain*, who ufed us with great civility, and due refpect to your majefty's commiffion. Signed and fealed, on the fourth day of the eighty-ninth moon of your majefty's aufpicious reign.

Clefrin Frelock, Marfi Frelock.

When this inventory was read over to the emperor, he directed me, although in very gentle terms, to deliver up the feveral particulars. He firft called for my fcymiter, which I took out, fcabbard and all. In the mean time he ordered three thoufand of his choiceft troops (who then attended him) to furround me at a diftance, with their bows and arrows juft ready to difcharge : but I did not obferve it, for mine eyes were wholly fixed upon his majefty. He then defired me to draw my fcymiter, which, although it had got fome ruft by the fea-water, was in moft parts exceeding bright. I did fo, and immediately all the troops gave a fhout between terror and furprize ; for the fun fhone clear, and the reflection dazzled their eyes, as I waved the fcymi-

ter

ter to and fro in my hand. His majefty, who is a moft magnanimous prince*, was lefs daunted than I could expect; he ordered me to return it into the fcabbard, and caft it on the ground as gently as I could, about fix feet from the end of my chain. The next thing he demanded, was one of the hollow iron pillars; by which he meant my pocket-piftols. I drew it out, and at his defire, as well as I could, expreffed to him the ufe of it; and charging it only with powder, which by the clofenefs of my pouch happened to efcape wetting in the fea (an inconvenience againft which all prudent mariners take fpecial care to provide) I firft cautioned the emperor not to be afraid, and then I let it off in the air. The aftonifhment here was much greater than at the fight of my fcymiter. Hundreds fell down, as if they had been ftruck dead; and even the emperor, although he ftood his ground, could not recover himfelf in fome time. I delivered up both my piftols in the fame manner, as I had done my fcymiter, and then my pouch of powder and bullets; begging him that the former might be kept from fire, for it would kindle with the fmalleft fpark, and blow up his imperial palace into the air. I likewife delivered up my watch, which the emperor was very curious to fee, and commanded two

---

* He who does not find himfelf difpofed to honour this magnanimity, fhould reflect, that a right to judge of moral and intellectual excellence is with great abfurdity and injuftice arrogated by him who admires, in a being fix feet high, any qualities that he defpifes in one whofe ftature does not exceed fix inches.

of

of his talleft yeomen of the guards to bear it on a pole upon their fhoulders, as dray-men in *England* do a- barrel of ale. He was amazed at the continual noife it made, and the motion of the minute-hand, which he could eafily difcern; for their fight is much more acute than ours: he afked the opinions of his learned men about it, which were various and remote, as the reader may well imagine without my repeating; although indeed I could not very perfectly underftand them. I then gave up my filver and copper money, my purfe with nine large pieces of gold, and fome fmaller ones; my knife and razor, my comb and filver fnuff-box, my handkerchief and journal-book. My fcymiter, piftols, and pouch were conveyed in carriages to his majefty's ftores; but the reft of my goods were returned me.

I had, as I before obferved, one private pocket, which efcaped their fearch, wherein there was a pair of fpectacles (which I fometimes ufe for the weaknefs of mine eyes) a pocket perfpective, and fome other little conveniencies; which being of no confequence to the emperor, I did not think myfelf bound in honour to difcover, and I apprehended they might be loft or fpoiled, if I ventured them out of my poffeffion.

C H A P.

C H A P. III.

The author diverts the emperor and his nobility of both sexes in a very uncommon manner. The diversions of the court of Lilliput *described. The author hath his liberty granted him upon certain conditions.*

MY gentleneſs and good behaviour had gained ſo far on the emperor and his court, and indeed upon the army, and people in general, that I began to conceive hopes of getting my liberty in a ſhort time. I took all poſſible methods to cultivate this favourable diſpoſition. The natives came by degrees to be leſs apprehenſive of any danger from me. I would ſometimes lie down, and let five or ſix of them dance on my hand : and at laſt the boys and girls would venture to come and play at hide and ſeek in my hair. I had now made a good progreſs in underſtanding and ſpeaking their language. The emperor had a mind one day to entertain me with ſeveral of the country ſhows, wherein they exceed all nations I have known both for dexterity and magnificence I was diverted with none ſo much as that of the rope-dancers, performed upon a ſlender white thread, extended about two feet and twelve inches from the ground. Upon which I ſhall deſire liberty, with the reader's patience, to enlarge a little.

This

This diverfion is only practifed by thofe perfons, who are candidates for great employ-ments, and high favour at court. They are trained in this art from their youth, and are not always of noble birth, or liberal education. When a great office is vacant either by death or difgrace (which often happens) five or fix of thofe candidates petition the emperor to en-tertain his majefty and the court with a dance on the rope, and whoever jumps the higheft without falling, fucceeds in the office. Very often the chief minifters themfelves are com-manded to fhew their fkill, and to convince the emperor, that they have not loft their faculty. *Flimnap*, the treafurer, is allowed to cut a ca-per on the ftrait rope at leaft an inch higher, than any other lord in the whole empire. I have feen him do the fummerfet [a] feveral times together upon a trencher, fixed on a rope, which is no thicker than a common packthread in *England*. My friend *Reldrefal*, principal fe-cretary for private affairs, is in my opinion, if I am not partial, the fecond after the treafu-rer; the reft of the great officers are much upon a par.

These diverfions are often attended with fatal accidents, whereof great numbers are on record. I myfelf have feen two or three candi-dates break a limb. But the danger is much greater, when the minifters themfelves are com-

---

[a] Summerfet, or fummerfault, a gambol of a tumbler, in which he fprings up, turns heels over head in the air, and comes down upon his feet.

manded

manded to fhew their dexterity; for, by contending to excel themfelves and their fellows,
they ftrain fo far, that there is hardly one of
them, who hath not received a fall, and fome
of them two or three. I was affured, that a
year or two before my arrival *Flimnap* would
have infallibly broke his neck, if one of the
king's cufhions, that accidentally lay on the
ground, had not weakened the force of his
fall.

There is likewife another diverfion, which
is only fhewn before the emperor and emprefs,
and firft minifter, upon particular occafions.
The emperor lays on the table three fine filken
threads of fix inches long ; one is blue, the
other red, and the third green. Thefe threads
are propofed as prizes for thofe perfons, whom
the emperor hath a mind to diftinguifh by a
peculiar mark of his favour. The ceremony
is performed in his majefty's great chamber of
ftate, where the candidates are to undergo a
trial of dexterity very different from the former, and fuch as I have not obferved the leaft
refemblance of in any other country of the
old or new world. The emperor holds a ftick
in his hands, both ends parallel to the horizon,
while the candidates advancing, one by one,
fometimes leap over the ftick, fometimes creep
under it backwards and forwards feveral times,
according as the ftick is advanced or depreffed.
Sometimes the emperor holds one end of the
ftick, and his firft minifter the other; fometimes the minifter has it entirely to himfelf.

Whoever performs his part with moſt agility, and holds out the longeſt in leaping and creeping, is rewarded with the blue-coloured ſilk; the red is given to the next, and the green to the third, which they all wear girt twice round about the middle; and you ſee few great perſons about this court, who are not adorned with one of theſe girdles.

The horſes of the army, and thoſe of the royal ſtables, having been daily led before me, were no longer ſhy, but would come up to my very feet without ſtarting. The riders would leap them over my hand, as I held it on the ground; and one of the emperor's huntſmen upon a large courſer took my foot, ſhoe and all; which was indeed a prodigious leap. I had the good fortune to divert the emperor one day after a very extraordinary manner. I deſired he would order ſeveral ſticks of two feet high, and the thickneſs of an ordinary cane, to be brought me; whereupon his majeſty commanded the maſter of his woods to give directions accordingly, and the next morning ſix woodmen arrived with as many carriages, drawn by eight horſes to each. I took nine of theſe ſticks, and fixing them firmly in the ground in a quadrangular figure, two feet and a half ſquare, I took four other ſticks, and tied them parallel at each corner about two feet from the ground; then I faſtened my handkerchief to the nine ſticks that ſtood erect; and extended it on all ſides, till it was tight as the top of a drum; and the four pa-

rallel

rallel fticks, rifing about five inches higher than the handkerchief, ferved as ledges on each fide. When I had finifhed my work, I defired the emperor to let a troop of his beft horfe, twenty-four in number, come and exercife upon this plain. His majefty approved of the propofal, and I took them up one by one in my hands, ready mounted and armed, with the proper officers to exercife them. As foon as they got into order, they divided into two parties, performed mock fkirmifhes, difcharged blunt arrows, drew their fwords, fled and purfued, attacked and retired, and in fhort difcovered the beft military difcipline I ever beheld. The parallel fticks fecured them and their horfes from falling over the ftage; and the emperor was fo much delighted, that he ordered this entertainment to be repeated feveral days, and once was pleafed to be lifted up, and give the word of command; and, with great difficulty, perfuaded even the emprefs herfelf to let me hold her in her clofe chair within two yards of the ftage, from whence fhe was able to take a full view of the whole performance. It was my good fortune, that no ill accident happened in thefe entertainments, only once a fiery horfe, that belonged to one of the captains, pawing with his hoof ftruck a hole in my handkerchief, and his foot flipping he overthrew his rider and himfelf; but I immediately relieved them both, and covering the hole with one hand, I fet down the troop with the other, in the fame manner as I took them up. The

horfe

horfe that fell was ftrained in the left fhoulder,
but the rider got no hurt, and I repaired my
handkerchief as well as I could; however, I
would not truft to the ftrength of it any more
in ſuch dangerous enterprizes.

About two or three days before I was ſet at
liberty, as I was entertaining the court with
this kind of feats, there arrived an exprefs to
inform his majefty, that fome of his fubjects,
riding near the place where I was firft taken up,
had feen a great black fubftance lying on the
ground, very oddly fhaped, extending its edges
round as wide as his majefty's bed-chamber,
and rifing up in the middle as high as a man;
that it was no living creature, as they at firft
apprehended, for it lay on the grafs without
motion; and fome of them had walked round
it feveral times; that, by mounting upon each
other's fhoulders, they had got to the top,
which was flat and even, and, ftamping upon
it, they found it was hollow within; that they
humbly conceived it might be fomething belonging to the *man-mountain*; and if his majefty pleafed, they would undertake to bring it
with only five horfes. I prefently knew what
they meant, and was glad at heart to receive
this intelligence. It feems, upon my firft
reaching the fhore after our fhipwreck I was in
fuch confufion, that, before I came to the
place where I went to fleep, my hat, which I
had faftened with a ftring to my head while I
was rowing, and had ftuck on all the time I
was fwimming, fell off after I came to land;
the

the ſtring, as I conjecture, breaking by ſome accident, which I never obſerved, but thought my hat had been loſt at ſea. I intreated his imperial majeſty to give orders, it might be brought to me as ſoon as poſſible, deſcribing to him the uſe and the nature of it: and the next day the waggoners arrived with it, but not in a very good condition ; they had bored two holes in the brim within an inch and half of the edge, and faſtened two hooks in the holes ; theſe hooks were tied by a long cord to the harneſs, and thus my hat was dragged along for above half an *engliſh* mile ; but, the ground in that country being extremely ſmooth and level, it received leſs damage than I expected.

Two days after this adventure the emperor, having ordered that part of his army, which quarters in and about his metropolis, to be in a readineſs, took a fancy of diverting himſelf in a very ſingular manner. He deſired I would ſtand like a *coloſſus*, with my legs as far aſunder as I conveniently could. He then commanded his general (who was an old experienced leader, and a great patron of mine) to draw up the troops in cloſe order, and march them under me ; the foot by twenty-four in a breaſt, and the horſe by ſixteen, with drums beating, colours flying, and pikes advanced. This body conſiſted of three thouſand foot, and a thouſand horſe. His majeſty gave orders, upon pain of death, that every ſoldier in his march ſhould obſerve the ſtricteſt decency with regard to my perſon ; which however could not pre-

vent

vent some of the younger officers from turning up their eyes, as they passed under me : and, to confess the truth, my breeches were at that time in so ill a condition, that they afforded some opportunities for laughter and admiration.

I had sent so many memorials and petitions for my liberty, that his majesty at length mentioned the matter first in the cabinet, and then in a full council; where it was opposed by none, except *Skyresh Bolgolam*, who was pleased, without any provocation, to be my mortal enemy. But it was carried against him by the whole board, and confirmed by the emperor. That minister was *galbet*, or admiral of the realm, very much in his master's confidence, and a person well versed in affairs, but of a morose and sour complexion. However he was at length persuaded to comply; but prevailed that the articles and conditions upon which I should be set free, and to which I must swear, should be drawn up by himself. These articles were brought to me by *Skyresh Bolgolam* in person, attended by two undersecretaries, and several persons of distinction. After they were read, I was demanded to swear to the performance of them; first in the manner of my own country, and afterwards in the method prescribed by their laws, which was to hold my right foot in my left hand, and to place the middle finger of my right hand on the crown of my head, and my thumb on the tip of my right ear. But because the reader may be curious to have some idea of the style and manner
ner

ner of expreſſion peculiar to that people, as well to know the articles upon which I recovered my liberty, I have made a tranſlation of the whole inſtrument word for word, as near as I was able, which I here offer to the public.

Golbaſto Momaren Evlame Gurdilo Shefin Mully Ully Gue, moſt mighty emperor of *Lilliput*, delight and terror of the univerſe, whoſe dominions extend five thouſand *bluſtrugs* (about twelve miles in circumference) to the extremities of the globe; monarch of all monarchs, taller than the ſons of men; whoſe feet preſs down to the center, and whoſe head ſtrikes againſt the ſun; at whoſe nod the princes of the earth ſhake their knees; pleaſant as the ſpring, comfortable as the ſummer, fruitful as autumn, dreadful as winter. His moſt ſublime majeſty propoſeth to the *man-mountain*, lately arrived at our celeſtial dominions, the following articles, which by a ſolemn oath he ſhall be obliged to perform.

1ſt, The *man-mountain* ſhall not depart from our dominions without our licence under our great ſeal.

2d, He ſhall not preſume to come into our metropolis without our expreſs order; at which time the inhabitants ſhall have two hours warning to keep within doors.

3d, The ſaid *man-mountain* ſhall confine his walks to our principal high roads, and not offer to walk or lie down in a meadow or field of corn.

D 4

4th, As he walks the faid roads, he fhall take the utmoft care not to trample upon the bodies of any of our loving fubjects, their horfes, or carriages, nor take any of our fubjects into his hands without their own confent.

5th, If an exprefs requires extraordinary difpatch, the *man-mountain* fhall be obliged to carry in his pocket the meffenger and horfe a a fix days journey once in every moon, and return the faid meffenger back (if fo required) fafe to our imperial prefence.

6th, He fhall be our ally againft our enemies in the ifland of *Blefufcu* [a], and do his utmoft to deftroy their fleet, which is now preparing to invade us.

7th, That the faid *man-mountain* fhall, at his times of leifure, be aiding and affifting to our workmen, in helping to raife certain great ftones, towards covering the wall of the principal park and other our royal buildings.

8th, That the faid *man-mountain* fhall, in two moons time, deliver in an exact furvey of the circumference of our dominions by a computation of his own paces round the coaft.

Laftly, That, upon his folemn oath to obferve all the above articles, the faid *man-mountain* fhall have a daily allowance of meat and drink fufficient for the fupport of 1724 of our fubjects, with free accefs to our royal perfon,

[a] In his defcription of *Lilliput* he feems to have had *England* more immediately in view. In his defcription of *Blefufcu*, he feems to intend the people and kingdom of *France*. ORRERY.

and

and other marks of our favour. Given at our palace at *Belfaborac*, the twelfth day of the ninety-firſt moon of our reign.

I ſwore and ſubſcribed to theſe articles with great chearfulneſs and content, although ſome of them were not ſo honourable as I could have wiſhed; which proceeded wholly from the malice of *Skyreſh Bolgolam*, the high admiral; whereupon my chains were immediately un-locked, and I was at full liberty, The empe-ror himſelf in perſon did me the honour to be by at the whole ceremony. I made my ac-knowledgments by proſtrating myſelf at his majeſty's feet : but he commanded me to riſe; and after many gracious expreſſions, which, to avoid the cenſure of vanity, I ſhall not re-peat, he added, that he hoped I ſhould prove a uſeful ſervant, and well deſerve all the fa-vours he had already conferred upon me, or might do for the future.

The reader may pleaſe to obſerve, that, in the laſt article for the recovery of my liberty, the emperor ſtipulates to allow me a quantity of meat and drink ſufficient for the ſupport of 1724 *Lilliputians*. Some time after aſking a friend at court, how they came to fix on that determinate number; he told me, that his majeſty's mathematicians having taken the heighth of my body by the help of a *quadrant*, and finding it to exceed theirs in the propor-tion of twelve to one, they concluded from the ſimilarity of their bodies, that mine muſt contain at leaſt 1724 of theirs, and conſequent-
ly

ly would require as much food as was neceſſary
to ſupport that number of *Lilliputians.* By
which the reader may conceive an idea of the
ingenuity of that people, as well as the prudent and exact œconomy of ſo great a prince.

C H A P. IV.

Mildendo, *the metropolis of* Lilliput, *deſcribed,*
together with the emperor's palace. A conver-
ſation between the author and a principal ſecre-
tary concerning the affairs of that empire. The
author's offers to ſerve the emperor in his
wars.

THE firſt requeſt I made, after I had obtained my liberty, was, that I might
have licence to ſee *Mildendo,* the metropolis;
which the emperor eaſily granted me, but with
a ſpecial charge to do no hurt either to the inhabitants or their houſes. The people had notice by proclamation of my deſign to viſit the
town. The wall, which encompaſſed it, is
two feet and a half high, and at leaſt eleven
inches broad, ſo that a coach and horſes may
be driven very ſafely round it; and it is flank-
ed with ſtrong towers at ten feet diſtance. I
ſtept over the great weſtern gate, and paſſed
very gently, and ſideling, through the two
principal ſtreets, only in my ſhort waiſt-coat,
for fear of damaging the roofs and eves of the
houſes with the ſkirts of my coat. I walked
with the utmoſt circumſpection to avoid tread-

ing

ing on any ftragglers, who might remain in
the ftreets; although the orders were very
ftrict, that all people fhould keep in their
houfes at their own peril. The garret-win-
dows and tops of houfes were fo crouded with
fpectators, that I thought in all my travels I
had not feen a more populous place. The city
is an exact fquare, each fide of the wall being
five hundred feet long. The two great ftreets,
which run crofs and divide it into four quarters, are five feet wide. The lanes and alleys,
which I could not enter, but only viewed them
as I paffed, are from twelve to eighteen inches.
The town is capable of holding five hundred
thoufand fouls: the houfes are from three to
five ftories: the fhops and markets well provided.

The emperor's palace is in the center of the
city, where the two great ftreets meet. It is
inclofed by a wall of two feet high, and twenty feet diftance from the buildings. I had his
majefty's permiffion to ftep over this wall;
and the fpace being fo wide between that and
the palace, I could eafily view it on every fide.
The outward court is a fquare of forty feet,
and includes two other courts: in the inmoft
are the royal apartments, which I was very defirous to fee, but found it extremely difficult;
for the great gates, from one fquare into another, were but eighteen inches high, and feven inches wide. Now the buildings of the
outer court were at leaft five feet high, and it
was impoffible for me to ftride over them without

out, infinite damage to the pile, though the walls were ftrongly built of hewn ftone, and four inches thick. At the fame time the emperor had a great defire, that I fhould fee the magnificence of his palace; but this I was not able to do till three days after, which I fpent in cutting down with my knife fome of the largeft trees in the royal park, about an hundred yards diftance from the city. Of thefe trees I made two ftools, each about three feet high, and ftrong enough to bear my weight. The people having received notice a fecond time, I went again through the city to the palace with my two ftools in my hands. When I came to the fide of the outer court, I ftood upon one ftool, and took the other in my hand; this I lifted over the roof, and gently fet it down on the fpace between the firft and fecond court, which was eight feet wide. I then ftept over the building very conveniently from one ftool to the other, and drew up the firft after me with a hooked ftick. By this contrivance I got into the inmoft court; and, lying down upon my fide, I applied my face to the windows of the middle ftories, which were left open on purpofe, and difcovered the moft fplendid apartments that can be imagined. There I faw the emprefs and the young princes in their feveral lodgings with their chief attendants about them. Her imperial majefty was pleafed to fmile very gracioufly upon me, and gave me out of the window her hand to kifs.

But

But I shall not anticipate the reader with farther descriptions of this kind, because I reserve them for a greater work, which is now almost ready for the press, containing a general description of this empire, from its first erection, through a long series of princes, with a particular account of their wars and politics, laws, learning, and religion, their plants and animals, their peculiar manners and customs, with other matters very curious and useful; my chief design at present being only to relate such events and transactions, as happened to the public or to myself, during a residence of about nine months in that empire.

One morning, about a fortnight after I had obtained my liberty, *Reldresal*, principal secretary (as they stile him) for private affairs, came to my house attended only by one servant. He ordered his coach to wait at a distance, and desired I would give him an hour's audience; which I readily consented to, on account of his quality and personal merits, as well as of the many good offices he had done me during my sollicitations at court. I offered to lie down, that he might the more conveniently reach my ear; but he chose rather to let me hold him in my hand during our conversation. He began with compliments on my liberty; said, he might pretend to some merit in it: but however added, that, if it had not been for the present situation of things at court, perhaps I might not have obtained it so soon. For, said he, as flourishing a condition as we

may

may appear to be in to foreigners, we labour
under two mighty evils; a violent faction
at home, and the danger of an invasion by a
most potent enemy from abroad. As to the
first, you are to understand, that for above seventy moons past there have been two strug-
gling parties in this empire, under the names
of *Tranecksan* and *Slamecksan* [a], from the high
and low heels of their shoes, by which they
distinguish themselves. It is alledged indeed,
that the high heels are most agreeable to our
ancient constitution; but, however this be,
his majesty hath determined to make use only
of low heels in the administration of the government, and all offices in the gift of the
crown, as you cannot but observe; and particularly, that his majesty's imperial heels are
lower at least by a *drurr* than any of his court
(*drurr* is a measure about the fourteenth part
of an inch.) The animosities between these
two parties run so high, that they will neither eat nor drink, nor talk with each o-
ther. We compute the *Tranecksan*, or high-
heels, to exceed us in number; but the power
is wholly on our side. We apprehend his imperial highness, the heir to the crown, to have
some tendency towards the high-heels; at
least, we can plainly discover, that one of his

[a] High-church and low-church, or whig and tory. As every accidental *difference* between man and man in person and circumstances is by this work rendered extremely contemptible; so *spe-*
culative differences are shewn to be equally ridiculous, when the
zeal with which they are op-
posed and defended too much exceeds their importance.

heels

heels is higher than the other, which gives him a hobble in his gate. Now, in the midſt of theſe inteſtine diſquiets we are threatened with an invaſion from the iſland of *Blefuſcu*, which is the other great empire of the univerſe, almoſt as large and powerful as this of his majeſty. For as to what we have heard you affirm, that there are other kingdoms and ſtates in the world inhabited by human creatures as large as yourſelf, our philoſophers are in much doubt, and would rather conjecture that you dropped from the moon, or one of the ſtars; becauſe it is certain, that an hundred mortals of your bulk would in a ſhort time deſtroy all the fruits and cattle of his majeſty's dominions : beſides, our hiſtories of ſix thouſand moons make no mention of any other regions, than the two great empires of *Lilliput* and *Blefuſcu*. Which two mighty powers have, as I was going to tell you, been engaged in a moſt obſtinate war for ſix and thirty moons paſt. It began upon the following occaſion : it is allowed on all hands, that the primitive way of breaking eggs, before we eat them, was upon the larger end ; but his preſent majeſty's grandfather, while he was a boy, going to eat an egg, and breaking it according to the antient practice, happened to cut one of his fingers. Whereupon, the emperor, his father, publiſhed an edict, commanding all his ſubjects, upon great penalties, to break the ſmaller end of their eggs. The people ſo highly reſented this law, that our hiſtories tell us, there have been fix rebellions raifed on that account; wherein one emperor loft his life, and another his crown. Thefe civil commotions were conftantly fomented by the monarchs of *Blefufcu*; and when they were quelled, the exiles always fled for refuge to that empire. It is computed that eleven thoufand perfons have at feveral times fuffered death, rather than fubmit to break their eggs at the fmaller end. Many hundred large volumes have been publifhed upon this controverfy; but the books of the *Big-endians* have been long forbidden, and the whole party rendered incapable by law of holding employments. During the courfe of thefe troubles, the emperors of *Blefufcu* did frequently expoftulate by their ambaffadors, accufing us of making a fchifm in religion by offending againft a fundamental doctrine of our great prophet *Luftrog*, in the fifty-fourth chapter of the *Blundecral* (which is their *Alcoran.)* This however is thought to be a mere ftrain upon the text; for the words are thefe : *that all true believers break their eggs at the convenient end.* And which is the convenient end, feems in my humble opinion to be left to every man's confcience, or at leaft in the power of the chief magiftrate to determine. Now, the *Big-endian* exiles have found fo much credit in the emperor of *Blefufcu*'s court, and fo much private affiftance and encouragement' from their party here at home, that a bloody war had been carried on between the two empires for fix and

thirty

thirty moons, with various fuccefs; during which time we have loft forty capital fhips, and a much greater number of fmaller veffels, together with thirty thoufand of our beft feamen and foldiers; and the damage received by the enemy is reckoned to be fomewhat greater than ours. However, they have now equipped a numerous fleet, and are juft preparing to make a defcent upon us; and his imperial majefty, placing great confidence in your valour and ftrength, hath commanded me to lay this account of his affairs befoie you.

I defired the fecretary to prefent my humble duty to the emperor, and to let him know, that I thought it would not become me, who was a foreigner, to interfere with parties; but I was ready with the hazard of my life to defend his perfon and ftate againft all invaders *.

* *Gulliver*, without examining the fubject of difpute, readily engaged to defend the emperor againft invafion; becaufe he knew that no fuch monarch had a right to invade the dominions of another, though for the propagation of truth.

C H A P. V.

The author, by an extraordinary stratagem, pre-
vents an invasion. A high title of honour is
conferred upon him. Ambassadors arrive from
the emperor of Blefuscu, *and sue for peace.*
The empress's apartment on fire by an accident;
the author instrumental in saving the rest of the
palace.

THE empire of *Blefuscu* is an island situated to the north-east side of *Lilliput,*
from whence it is parted only by a channel of
eight hundred yards wide. I had not yet seen
it, and upon this notice of an intended invasion I avoided appearing on that side of the
coast, for fear of being discovered by some of
the enemy's ships, who had received no intelligence of me, all intercourse between the two
empires having been strictly forbidden during
the war upon pain of death, and an embargo
laid by our emperor upon all vessels whatso-
ever. I communicated to his majesty a project I had formed of seizing the enemy's whole
fleet: which, as our scouts assured us, lay at
anchor in the harbour ready to sail with the
first fair wind. I consulted the most experienced seamen upon the depth of the channel,
which they had often plumined; who told me,
that in the middle at high-water it was seventy
glumgluffs deep, which is about six feet of eu-
ropean measure; and the rest of it fifty *glum-*
gluffs

gluffs at moft. I walked towards the north-
ealt coaft, overagainft *Blefufcu* ; where, lying
down behind a hillock, I took out my fmall
perfpeative-glafs, and viewed the enemy's fleet
at anchor, confifting of about fifty men of
war, and a great number of tranfports : I then
came back to my houfe, and gave orders (for
which I had a warrant) for a great quantity of
the ftrongeft cable and bars of iron. The cable was about as thick as pack-thread, and the
bars of the length and fize of a knitting-nee-
dle. I trebled the cable to make it ftronger,
and for the fame reafon I twifted three of the
iron bars together, bending the extremities into a hook. Having thus fixed fifty hooks to
as many cables, I went back to the north-eaft
coaft, and putting off my coat, fhoes, and
ftockings, walked into the fea in my leathern
jerkin about half an hour before high-water.
I waded with what hafte I could, and fwam in
the middle about thirty yards, till I felt
ground ; I arrived at the fleet in lefs than half
an hour. The enemy was fo frighted, when
they faw me, that they leaped out of their
fhips, and fwam to fhore, where there could
not be fewer than thirty thoufand fouls :
I then took my tackling, and, faftening a hook
to the hole at the prow of each, I tied all the
cords together at the end. While I was thus
employed, the enemy difcharged feveral thoufand arrows, many of which ftuck in my hands
and face ; and, befides the exceffive fmart,
gave me much difturbance in my work. My

greateſt apprehenſion was for mine eyes, which I ſhould have infallibly loſt, if I had not ſuddenly thought of an expedient. I kept among other little neceſſaries a pair of ſpectacles in a private pocket, which, as I obſerved before, had eſcaped the emperor's ſearchers. Theſe I took out and faſtened as ſtrongly as I could upon my noſe, and thus armed went on boldly with my work in ſpight of the enemy's arrows, many of which ſtruck againſt the glaſſes of my ſpectacles, but without any other effect, farther than a little to diſcompoſe them. I had now faſtened all the hooks, and taking the knot in my hand began to pull ; but not a ſhip would ſtir, for they were all too faſt held by their anchors, ſo that the boldeſt part of my enterprize remained. I therefore let go the cord, and leaving the hooks fixed to the ſhips, I reſolutely cut with my knife the cables that faſtened the anchors, receiving above two hundred ſhots in my face and hands ; then I took up the knotted end of the cables, to which my hooks were tied, and with great eaſe drew fifty of the enemy's largeſt men of war after me.

The *Blefuſcudians,* who had not the leaſt imagination of what I intended, were at firſt confounded with aſtoniſhment. They had ſeen me cut the cables, and thought my deſign was only to let the ſhips run a-drift, or fall foul on each other : but when they perceived the whole fleet moving in order, and ſaw me pulling at the end, they ſet up ſuch a ſcream of grief and deſpair, defpair, as it is almoft impoffible to defcribe or conceive. When I had got out of danger, I ftopt a while to pick out the arrows, that ftuck in my hands and face; and rubbed on fome of the fame ointment, that was given me at my firft arrival, as I have formerly mentioned. I then took off my fpectacles, and waiting about an hour, till the tide was a little fallen, I waded through the middle with my cargo, and arrived fafe at the royal port of *Lilliput*.

The emperor and his whole court ftood on the fhore expecting the iffue of this great adventure. They faw the fhips move forward in a large half-moon, but could not difcern me, who was up to my breaft in water. When I advanced to the middle of the channel, they were yet more in pain, becaufe I was under water to my neck. The emperor concluded me to be drowned, and that the enemy's fleet was approaching in an hoftile manner: but he was foon eafed of his fears, for the channel growing fhallower every ftep I made, I came in a fhort time within hearing, and holding up the end of the cable, by which the fleet was faftened, I cried in a loud voice, *long live the moft puiffant emperor of Lilliput!* This great prince received me at my landing with all poffible encomiums, and created me a *Nardac* upon the fpot, which is the higheft title of honour among them.

His majefty defired, I would take fome other opportunity of bringing all the reft of his enemy's fhips into his ports. And fo unmeafur-

able

able is the ambition of princes, that he feemed to think of nothing lefs than reducing the whole empire of *Blefufcu* into a province, and governing it by a vice-roy; of deftroying the *Big-endian* exiles, and compelling that people to break the fmaller end of their eggs, by which he would remain the fole monarch of the whole world. But I endeavoured to divert him from this defign by many arguments drawn from the topics of policy as well as juftice : and I plainly protefted, that I would never be an inftrument of bringing a free and brave people into flavery. And, when the matter was debated in council, the wifeft part of the miniftry were of my opinion.

This open bold declaration of mine was fo oppofite to the fchemes and politicks of his imperial majefty, that he could never forgive me ; he mentioned it in a very artful manner at council, where I was told that fome of the wifeft appeared at leaft by their filence to be of my opinion ; but others, who were my fecret enemies, could not forbear fome expreffions, which by a fide-wind reflected on me. And from this time began an intrigue between his majefty, and a junto of minifters malicioufly bent againft me, which broke out in lefs than two months, and had like to have ended in my utter deftruction. Of fo little weight are the greateft fervices to princes, when put into the ballance with a refufal to gratify their paffions.

About

About three weeks after this exploit, there arrived a folemn ambaſſy from *Blefuſcu* with humble offers of a peace ; which was foon concluded upon conditions very advantageous to our emperor, wherewith I ſhall not trouble the reader. There were ſix ambaſſadors, with a train of about five hundred perſons ; and their entry was very magnificent, ſuitable to the grandeur of their maſter, and the importance of their búſineſs. When their treaty was finiſhed, wherein I did them ſeveral good offices by the credit I now had, or at leaſt appeared to have at court, their excellencies, who were privately told how much I had been their friend, made me a viſit in form. They began with many compliments upon my valour and generoſity, invited me to that kingdom in ·the emperor their maſter's name, and deſired me to ſhew them ſome proofs of my prodigious ſtrength, of which they had heard ſo many wonders ; wherein I readily obliged them, but ſhall not trouble the reader with the particulars.

When I had for ſome time entertained their excellencies to their infinite ſatisfaction. and ſurprize, I deſired they would do me the honour to preſent my moſt humble reſpects to the emperor their maſter, the renown of whoſe virtues had ſo juſtly filled the whole world with admiration, and whoſe royal perſon I reſolved to attend before I returned to my own country : accordingly, the next time I had the honour to ſee our emperor, I deſired his ge-

neral

neral licence to wait on the *Blefufcudian* monarch, which he was pleafed to grant me, as I
could plainly perceive, in a very cold manner;
but could not guefs the reafon, till I had a
whifper from a certain perfon, that *Flimnap*
and *Bolgolam* had reprefented my intercourfe
with thofe ambaffadors as a mark of difaffec-
tion, from which I am fure my heart was
wholly free. And this was the firft time I
began to conceive fome imperfect idea of courts
and minifters.

It is to be obferved, that thefe ambaffadors
fpoke to me by an interpreter, the languages
of both empires differing as much from each
other as any two in *Europe*, and each nation
priding itfelf upon the antiquity, beauty, and
energy of their own tongues, with an avowed
contempt for that of their neighbour; yet our
emperor, ftanding upon the advantage he had
got by the feizure of their fleet, obliged them
to deliver their credentials, and make their
fpeech in the *Lilliputian* tongue. And it muft
be confeffed, that from the great intercourfe of
trade and commerce between both realms,
from the continual reception of exiles, which
is mutual among them, and from the cuftom
in each empire to fend their young nobility and
richer gentry to the other in order to polifh
themfelves by feeing the world, and underftanding men and manners; there are few perfons of diftinction, or merchants, or feamen,
who dwell in the maritime parts, but what
can hold converfation in both tongues; as I
found

found some weeks after, when I went to pay my respects to the emperor of *Blefuscu*, which in the midst of great misfortunes, through the malice of my enemies, proved a very happy adventure to me, as I shall relate in its proper place.

The reader may remember, that when I signed those articles upon which I recovered my liberty, there were some which I disliked upon account of their being too servile, neither could any thing but an extreme necessity have forced me to submit. But being now a *nardac* of the highest rank in that empire, such offices were looked upon as below my dignity, and the emperor (to do him justice) never once mentioned them to me. However, it was not long before I had an opportunity of doing his majesty, at least, as I then thought, a most signal service. I was alarmed at midnight with the cries of many hundred people at my door; by which being suddenly awaked, I was in some kind of terror. I heard the word *Burglum* repeated incessantly: several of the emperor's court, making their way through the croud, intreated me to come immediately to the palace, where her imperial majesty's apartment was on fire by the carelesness of a maid of honour, who fell asleep while she was reading a romance. I got up in an instant; and orders being given to clear the way before me, and it being likewise a moonshine night, I made a shift to get to the palace without trampling on any of the people I found

I found they had already applied ladders to the walls of the apartment, and were well provided with buckets, but the water was at some distance. These buckets were about the size of a large thimble, and the poor people supplied me with them as fast as they could ; but the flame was so violent, that they did little good. I might easily have stifled it with my coat, which I unfortunately left behind me for haste, and came away only in my leathern jerkin. The case seemed wholly desperate and deplorable, and this magnificent palace would have infallibly been burnt down to the ground, if by a presence of mind unusual to me I had not suddenly thought of an expedient. I had the evening before drank plentifully of a most delicious wine called *Glimigrim* (the *Blefuscadians* call it *Flunec*, but ours is esteemed the better sort) which is very diuretic. By the luckiest chance in the world I had not discharged myself of any part of it. The heat I had contracted by coming very near the flames, and by labouring to quench them, made the wine begin to operate by urine ; which I voided in such a quantity, and applied so well to the proper places, that in three minutes the fire was wholly extinguished, and the rest of that noble pile, which had cost so many ages in erecting, preserved from destruction.

It was now day-light, and I returned to my house without waiting to congratulate with the emperor ; because, although I had done a

very

very eminent piece of fervice, yet I could not tell how his majefty might refent the manner, by which I had performed it : for, by the fundamental laws of the realm, it is capital in any perfon, of what quality foever, to make water within the precincts of the palace. But I was a little comforted by a meffage from his majefty, that he would give orders to the grand jufticiary for paffing my pardon in form; which however I could not obtain. And I was privately affured, that the emprefs, conceiving the greateft abhorrence of what I had done, removed to the moft diftant fide of the court, firmly refolved that thofe buildings fhould never be repaired for her ufe; and, in the prefence of her chief confidents, could not forbear vowing revenge.

C H A P. VI.

Of the inhabitants of Lilliput; *their learning, laws, and cuftoms, the manner of educating their children. The author's way of living in that country. His vindication of a great lady.*

ALTHOUGH I intend to leave the defcription of this empire to a particular treatife, yet in the mean time I am content to gratify the curious reader with fome general ideas. As the common fize of the natives is fomewhat under fix inches high, fo there is an exact proportion in all other animals, as well as plants and trees: for inftance, the
talleft

talleſt horſes and oxen are between four and five inches in heighth, the ſheep an inch and half, more or leſs ; their geeſe about the big-neſs of a ſparrow, and ſo the ſeveral gradations downwards, till you come to the ſmalleſt, which to my ſight were almoſt inviſible ; but nature hath adapted the eyes of the *Lilliputians* to all objects proper for their view : they ſee with great exactneſs, but at no great diſ-tance. And, to ſhew the ſharpneſs of their ſight towards objects that are near, I have been much pleaſed with obſerving a cook pulling a lark, which was not ſo large as a common fly ; and a young girl threading an inviſible needle with inviſible ſilk. Their talleſt trees are about ſeven feet high : I mean ſome of thoſe in the great royal park, the tops whereof I could but juſt reach with my fiſt clinched. The other vegetables are in the ſame proportion : but this I leave to the rea-der's imagination.

I ſhall ſay but little at preſent of their learn-ing, which for many ages hath flouriſhed in all its branches among them : but their man-ner of writing is very peculiar, being neither from the left to the right, like the *europeans* ; nor from the right to the left, like the *arabi-ans* ; nor from up to down, like the *chineſe* ; but aſlant from one corner of the paper to the other, like ladies in *England*.

They bury their dead with their heads di-rectly downwards, becauſe they hold an opi-nion, that in eleven thouſand moons they are

all

all to rife again, in which period the earth (which they conceive to be flat) will turn up-fide down, and by this means they fhall at their refurrection be found ready ftanding on their feet. The learned among them confefs the abfurdity of this doctrine, but the practice ftill continues in compliance to the vulgar.

There are fome laws and cuftoms in this em-pire very peculiar; and, if they were not fo directly contrary to thofe of my own dear country, I fhould be tempted to fay a little in their juftification. It is only to be wifhed they were as well executed. The firft I fhall men-tion, relates to informers. All crimes againft the ftate are punifhed here with the utmoft fe-verity; but, if the perfon accufed maketh his innocence plainly to appear upon his trial, the accufer is immediately put to an ignominious death; and out of his goods or lands the inno-cent perfon is quadruply recompenfed for the lofs of his time, for the danger he underwent, for the hardfhip of his imprifonment, and for all the charges he hath been at in making his defence. Or, if that fund be deficient, it is largely fupplied by the crown. The emperor alfo confers on him fome publick mark of his favour, and proclamation is made of his inno-cence through the whole city.

They look upon fraud as a greater crime than theft, and therefore feldom fail to punifh it with death; for they alledge, that care and vigilance, with a very common underftanding, may preferve a man's goods from thieves, but
honefly

honefty has no fence againft fuperior cunning;
and fince it is neceffary that there fhould be a
perpetual intercourfe of buying and felling,
and dealing upon credit; where fraud is permitted and connived at, or hath no law to punifh it, the honeft dealer is always undone,
and the knave gets the advantage.   I remember when I was once interceding with the king
for a criminal, who had wronged his mafter
of a great fum of money, which he had received by order, and ran away with; and happening to tell his majefty, by way of extenuation, that it was only a breach of truft; the
emperor thought it monftrous in me to offer
as a defence the greateft aggravation of the
crime; and truly I had little to fay in return,
farther than the common anfwer, that different
nations had different cuftoms; for, I confefs, I
was heartily afhamed [a].

Although we ufually call reward and punifhment the two hinges, upon which all government turns, yet I could never obferve this maxim to be put in practice by any nation, except
that of *Lilliput*. Whoever can there bring
fufficient proof, that he hath ftrictly obferved
the laws of his country for feventy-three moons,
hath a claim to certain privileges, according to
his quality and condition of life, with a proportionable fum of money out of a fund appropriated for that ufe: he likewife acquires
the title of *fnilpall*, or *legal*, which is added to

---

[a] An act of parliament hath been fince paffed, by which fome breaches of truft have been made capital.

his

his name, but doth not defcend to his pofterity. And thefe people thought it a prodigious defect of policy among us, when I told them, that our laws were enforced only by penalties, without any mention of reward. It is upon this account, that the image of juftice in their courts of judicature is formed with fix eyes, two before, as many behind, and on each fide one, to fignify circumfpection; with a bag of gold open in her right hand, and a fword fheathed in her left, to fhew fhe is more dif-pofed to reward than to punifh.

In chufing perfons for all employments they have more regard to good morals than to great abilities; for, fince government is neceffary to mankind, they believe that the common fize of human underftanding is fitted to fome ftation or other, and that providence never intended to make the management of public affairs a myftery to be comprehended only by a few perfons of fublime genius, of which there fel-dom are three born in an age: but they fup-pofe truth, juftice, temperance, and the like, to be in every man's power, the practice of which virtues, affifted by experience and a good intention, would qualify any man for the fervice of his country, except where a courfe of ftudy is required. But they thought the want of moral virtues was fo far from being fupplied by fuperior endowments of the mind, that employments could never be put into fuch dangerous hands as thofe of perfons fo quali-fied; and at leaft, that the miftakes committed

by

by ignorance in a virtuous difpofition would
never be of fuch fatal confequence to the public weal, as the practices of a man whofe inclinations led him to be corrupt, and who had
great abilities to manage, to multiply, and defend his corruptions.

In like manner, the difbelief of a divine
providence renders a man uncapable of holding any public ftation; for, fince kings avow
themfelves to be the deputies of providence,
the *Lilliputians* think nothing can be more abfurd than for a prince to employ fuch men as
difown the authority, under which he acteth.

In relating thefe and the following laws, I
would only be underftood to mean the original
inftitutions, and not the moft fcandalous corruptions, into which thefe people are fallen by
the degenerate nature of man. For as to that
infamous practice of acquiring great employments by dancing on the ropes, or badges of
favour and diftinction by leaping over fticks,
and creeping under them, the reader is to obferve, that they were firft introduced by the
grandfather of the emperor now reigning, and
grew to the prefent heighth by the gradual increafe of party and faction.

Ingratitude is among them a capital crime, as
we read it to have been in fome other countries;
for they reafon thus, that whoever makes ill
returns to his benefactor, muft needs be a common enemy to the reft of mankind, from whom
he hath received no obligation, and therefore
fuch a man is not fit to live.

Their

Their notions relating to the duties of parents and children differ extremely from ours. For, since the conjunction of male and female is founded upon the great law of nature in order to propagate and continue the species, the *Lilliputians* will needs have it, that men and women are joined together like other animals by the motives of concupiscence; and that their tenderness towards their young proceeds from the like natural principle: for which reason they will never allow, that a child is under any obligation to his father for begetting him, or to his mother for bringing him into the world, which, considering the miseries of human life, was neither a benefit in itself, nor intended so by his parents, whose thoughts in their love-encounters were otherwise employed. Upon these, and the like reasonings, their opinion is, that parents are the last of all others to be trusted with the education of their own children: and therefore they have in every town public nurseries, where all parents, except cottagers and labourers, are obliged to send their infants of both sexes to be reared and educated when they come to the age of twenty moons, at which time they are supposed to have some rudiments of docility. These schools are of several kinds, suited to different qualities, and to both sexes. They have certain professors well skilled in preparing children for such a condition of life as befits the rank of their parents, and their own capacities as well as

incli-

inclinations. I fhall firft fay fomething of the male nurferies, and then of the female.

The nurferies for males of noble or eminent birth are provided with grave and learned pro-feffors, and their feveral deputies. The clothes and food of the children are plain and fimple. They are bred up in the principles of honour, juftice, courage, modefty, clemency, religion, and love of their country; they are always employed in fome bufinefs, except in the times of eating and fleeping, which are very fhort, and two hours for diverfions confifting of bodily exercifes. They are dreffed by men till four years of age, and then are obliged to drefs themfelves, although their quality be ever fo great ; and the women attendants, who are aged proportionably to ours at fifty, perform only the moft menial offices. They are never fuffered to converfe with fervants, but go together in fmaller or greater numbers to take their diverfions, and always in the pre-fence of a profeffor, or one of his deputies; whereby they avoid thofe early bad impreffions of folly and vice, to which our children are fubject. Their parents are fuffered to fee them only twice a year ; the vifit is to laft but an hour; they are allowed to kifs the child at meeting and parting ; but a profeffor, who al-ways ftands by on thofe occafions, will not fuf-fer them to whifper, or ufe any fondling ex-preffions, or bring any prefents of toys, fweet-meats, and the like.

The penfion from each family for the edu-cation and entertainment of a child, upon fai-
lure

ture of due payment, is levied by the emperor's officers.

The nurseries for children of ordinary gentlemen, merchants, traders, and handicrafts,
are managed 'proportionably after the same
manner; only those designed for trades are put
out apprentices at eleven years old, whereas
those of persons of quality continue in their
exercises till fifteen, which answers to twenty-
one with us: but the confinement is gradually
lessened for the last three years.

In the female nurseries, the young girls of
quality are educated much like the males, only
they are dressed by orderly servants of their own
sex; but always in the presence of a professor
or deputy, till they come to dress themselves,
which is at five years old. And if it be found,
that these nurses ever presume to entertain the
girls with frightful or foolish stories, or the
common follies practised by chamber-maids a-
mong us, they are publickly whipped thrice
about the city, imprisoned for a year, and
banished for life to the most desolate part of
the country. Thus the young ladies there are
as much ashamed of being cowards and fools,
as the men, and despise all personal ornaments
beyond decency and cleanliness: neither did I
perceive any difference in their education,
made by their difference of sex, only that the
exercises of the females were not altogether so
robust; and that some rules were given them
relating to domestick life, and a smaller compass of learning was enjoined them: for their

F 2   maxim

maxim is, that, among people of quality, a
wife fhould be always a reafonable and agreeable companion, becaufe fhe cannot always be
young. When the girls are twelve years old,
which among them is the marriageable age,
their parents or guardians take them home
with great expreffions of gratitude to the pro-
feffors, and feldom without tears of the young
lady and her companions.

In the nurferies of females of the meaner
fort the children are inftructed in all kinds
of works proper for their fex, and their feveral
degrees : thofe intended for apprentices are difmiffed at feven years old, the reft are kept to
eleven.

The meaner families, who have children at
thefe nurferies, are obliged, befides their annual penfion, which is as low as poffible, to
return to the fteward of the nurfery a fmall
monthly fhare of their gettings to be a portion
for the child; and therefore all parents are limited in their expences by the law. For the
Lilliputians think nothing can be more unjuft,
than for people, in fubfervience to their own
appetites, to bring children into the world,
and leave the burthen of fupporting them on
the public. As to perfons of quality, they
give fecurity to appropriate a certain fum for
each child, fuitable to their condition; and
thefe funds are always managed with good huf-
bandry, and the moft exact juftice.

The cottagers and labourers keep their children at home, their bufinefs being only to till

and

and cultivate the earth, and therefore their education is of little confequence to the public : but the old and difeafed among them are fupported by hofpitals : for begging is a trade unknown in this empire.

And here it may perhaps divert the curious reader, to give fome account of my domeftics, and my manner of living in this country during a refidence of nine months and thirteen days. Having a head mechanically turned, and being likewife forced by neceffity, I had made for myfelf a table and chair convenient enough out of the largeft trees in the royal park. Two hundred fempftreffes were employed to make me fhirts, and linnen for my bed and table, all of the ftrongeft and coarfeft kind they could get; which however they were forced to quilt together in feveral folds, for the thickeft was fome degrees finer than lawn. Their linnen is ufually three inches wide, and three feet make a piece. The fempftreffes took my meafure as I lay on the ground, one ftanding at my neck, and another at my mid-leg, with a ftrong cord extended, that each held by the end, while a third meafured the length of the cord with a rule of an inch long. Then they meafured my right thumb, and defired no more ; for by a mathematical computation, that twice round the thumb is once round the wrift, and fo on to the neck and the waift, and by the help of my old fhirt, which I difplayed on the ground before them for a pattern, they fitted me ex-

actly.

actly. Three hundred taylors were employed in the same manner to make me clothes; but they had another contrivance for taking my measure. I kneeled down, and they raised a ladder from the ground to my neck; upon this ladder one of them mounted, and let fall a plum-line from my collar to the floor, which just answered the length of my coat; but my waist and arms I measured myself. When my clothes were finished, which was done in my house (for the largest of theirs would not have been able to hold them) they looked like the patch-work made by the ladies in *England*, only that mine were all of a colour.

I had three hundred cooks to dress my victuals in little convenient huts built about my house, where they and their families lived, and prepared me two dishes a-piece. I took up twenty waiters in my hand, and placed them on the table; an hundred more attended below on the ground, some with dishes of meat, and some with barrels of wine, and other liquors, flung on their shoulders; all which the waiters above drew up, as I wanted, in a very ingenious manner by certain cords, as we draw the bucket up a well in *Europe*. A dish of their meat was a good mouthful, and a barrel of their liquor a reasonable draught. Their mutton yields to ours, but their beef is excellent. I have had a sirloin so large, that I have been forced to make three bits of it; but this is rare. My servants were astonished to see me eat it, bones and all, as in our country

we

we do the leg of a lark. Their geefe and tur-
kies I ufually eat at a mouthful, and I muſt
confeſs, they far exceed ours. Of their ſmaller fowl I could take up twenty or thirty at the
end of my knife.

One day his imperial majeſty, being informed of my way of living, defired that himſelf and
his royal confort, with the young princes of the
blood of both fexes, might have the happineſs
(as he was pleaſed to call it) of dining with
me. They came accordingly, and I placed
them in chairs of ſtate upon my table, juſt over-
againſt me, with their guards about them.
Flimnap, the lord high treaſurer, attended there
likewiſe with his white ſtaff; and I obferved
he often looked on me with a ſcur countenance,
which I would not feem to regard, but eat
more than uſual, in honour to my dear country, as well as to fill the court with admiration.
I have ſome private reaſons to believe, that this
viſit from his majeſty gave *Flimnap* an opportunity of doing me ill offices to his maſter.
That miniſter had always been my fecret enemy, though he outwardly careſſed me more
than was uſual to the moroſeneſs of his nature.
He repreſented to the emperor the low condition
of his treaſury; that he was forced to take up
money at great diſcount; that exchequer bills
would not circulate under nine *per cent.* below
par; that I had coſt his majeſty above a million and a half of *ſprugs* (their greateſt gold
coin, about the bigneſs of a ſpangle) and upon
the whole, that it would be adviſeable in the

emperor

emperor to take the firſt fair occaſion of diſ-
miſſing me.

I am here obliged to vindicate the reputation of an excellent lady, who was an innocent ſufferer upon my account. The treaſurer
took a fancy to be jealous of his wife, from
the malice of ſome evil tongues, who informed him that her grace had taken a violent affection for my perſon ; and the court ſcandal
ran for ſome time, that ſhe once came privately to my lodging. This I ſolemnly declare to
be a moſt infamous falſhood, without any
grounds, farther than that her grace was
pleaſed to treat me with all innocent marks of
freedom and friendſhip. I own ſhe came often
to my houſe, but always publickly, nor ever
without three more in the coach, who were
uſually her ſiſter and young daughter, and ſome
particular acquaintance ; but this was common to many other ladies of the court. And
I ſtill appeal to my ſervants round, whether
they at any time ſaw a coach at my door, without knowing what perſons were in it. On
thoſe occaſions, when a ſervant had given me
notice, my cuſtom was to go immediately to
the door ; and, after paying my reſpects, to
take up the coach and two horſes very carefully in my hands (for, if there were ſix horſes,
the poſtillion always unharneſſed four) and
placed them on a table, where I had fixed a
moveable rim quite round, of five inches high,
to prevent accidents. And I have often had
four coaches and horſes at once on my table
                                              full

full of company, while I fat in my chair, leaning my face towards them; and, when I was
engaged with one fet, the coachmen would
gently drive the others round my table. I
have paffed many an afternoon very agreeably
in thefe converfations. But I defy the treafurer, or his two informers (I will name them,
and let them make their beft of it) *Cluftril* and
Drunlo, to prove that any perfon ever came to
me *incognito*, except the fecretary *Reldrefal*,
who was fent by exprefs command of his imperial majefty, as I have before related. I
fhould not have dwelt fo long upon this particular, if it had not been a point wherein the reputation of a great lady is fo nearly concerned,
to fay nothing of my own, though I then had
the honour to be a *nardac*, which the treafurer himfelf is not; for all the world knows,
that he is only a *glumglum*, a title inferior by
one degree, as that of a marquefs is to a duke
in *England*; yet I allow he preceded me in
right of his poft. Thefe falfe informations,
which I afterwards came to the knowledge of
by an accident not proper to mention, made
the treafurer fhew his lady for fome time an ill
countenance, and me a worfe; and although
he was at laft undeceived and reconciled to her,
yet I loft all credit with him, and found my
intereft decline very faft with the emperor himfelf, who was indeed too much governed by that
favourite.

CHAP.

C H A P. VII.

The author, being informed of a design to accuse him of high-treason, maketh his escape to Blefuscu. *His reception there.*

BEFORE I proceed to give an account o my leaving this kingdom, it may be proper to inform the reader of a private intrigue, which had been for two months forming against me.

I had been hitherto all my life a stranger to courts, for which I was unqualified by th meanness of my condition. I had indeed heard and read enough of the dispositions of great princes and ministers; but never expected to have found such terrible effects of them in so remote a country, governed, as I thought, by very different maxims from those in *Europe*.

When I was just preparing to pay my atten dance on the emperor of *Blefuscu*, a consider able person at court (to whom I had been ve serviceable at a time, when he lay under th highest displeasure of his imperial majesty) cam to my house very privately at night in a clof chair, and, without sending his name, desire admittance: the chairmen were dismissed; put the chair, with his lordship in it, into m coat-pocket; and, giving orders to a tru servant to say I was indisposed and gone sleep, I fastened the door of my house, plac the chair on the table according to my usu

cuftom

custom, and sat down by it. After the common salutations were over, obferving his lordship's countenance full of concern, and enquiring into the reafon, he defired I would hear him with patience in a matter, that highly concerned my honour and my life. His fpeech was to the following effect, for I took notes of it as foon as he left me.

You are to know, faid he, that feveral committees of council have been lately called in the moft private manner on your account; and it is but two days fince his majefty came to a full refolution.

You are very fenfible that *Skyris Bolgolam (galbet,* or high-admiral) hath been your mortal enemy almoft ever fince your arrival : his original reafons I know not; but his hatred is encreafed fince your great fuccefs againft *Blefufcu,* by which his glory, as admiral, is much obfcured. This lord, in conjunction with *Flimnap* the high-treafurer, whofe enmity againft you is notorious on account of his lady, *Limtoc* the general, *Lalcon* the chamberlain, and *Balmuff* the grand jufticiary, have prepared articles of impeachment againft you for treafon and other capital crimes.

This preface made me fo impatient, being confcious of my own merits and innocence, that I was going to interrupt : when he entreated me to be filent, and thus proceeded.

Out of gratitude for the favours you have done me, I procured information of the whole

3   proceedings,

proceedings, and a copy of the articles; wherein I venture my head for your fervice.

Articles of impeachment againſt Quinbus Fleſtrin *the* man-mountain.

ARTICLE I.

Whereas, by a ſtatute made in the reign of his imperial majeſty *Calin Deffar Plune*, it is enacted, that whoever ſhall make water within the precincts of the royal palace, ſhall be liable to the pains and penalties of high treaſon: notwithſtanding the ſaid *Quinbus Fleſtrin* in open breach of the ſaid law, under colour of extinguiſhing the fire kindled in the apartment of his majeſty's moſt dear imperial conſort, did maliciouſly, traiterouſly, and deviliſhly, by diſcharge of his urine put out the ſaid fire kindled in the ſaid apartment, lying and being within the precincts of the ſaid royal palace, againſt the ſtatute in that caſe provided, *etc.* againſt the duty, *etc.*

ARTICLE II.

That the ſaid *Quinbus Fleſtrin* having brought the imperial fleet of *Blefuſcu* into the royal port, and being afterwards commanded by his imperial majeſty to ſeize all the other ſhips of the ſaid empire of *Blefuſcu*, and reduce that empire to a province to be governed by a viceroy from hence, and to deſtroy and put to death not only all the *big-endian exiles*, but likewiſe likewife all the people of that empire, who would not immediately forfake the *big-endian* herefy: he the faid *Fleftrin*, like a falfe traitor againft his moft aufpicious, ferene, imperial majefty, did petition to be excufed from the faid fervice, upon pretence of unwillingnefs to force the confciences, or deftroy the liberties and lives of an innocent people *.

ARTICLE III.

That, whereas certain ambaffadors arrived from the court of *Blefufcu* to fue for peace in his majefty's court: he the faid *Fleftrin* did, like a falfe traitor, aid, abet, comfort, and divert the faid ambaffadors, although he knew them to be fervants to a prince, who was lately an open enemy to his imperial majefty, and in open war againft his faid majefty.

ARTICLE IV.

That the faid *Quinbus Fleftrin*, contrary to the duty of a faithful fubject, is now preparing to make a voyage to the court and empire of *Blefufcu*, for which he hath received only verbal licence from his imperial majefty; and under colour of the faid licence doth falfly and traiteroufly intend to take the faid voyage, and thereby to aid, comfort, and abet the emperor

* A lawyer thinks himfelf honeft if he does the beft he can for his client, and a ftatefman if he promotes the intereft of his country; but the dean here inculcates an higher notion of right and wrong, and obligations to a larger community.

of

of *Blefuscu*, so late an enemy and in open war with his imperial majesty aforesaid.

There are some other articles, but these are the most important, of which I have read you an abstract.

In the several debates upon this impeachment it must be confessed that his majesty gave many marks of his great lenity, often urging the services you had done him, and endeavouring to extenuate your crimes. The treasurer and admiral insisted that you should be put to the most painful and ignominious death by setting fire on your house at night, and the general was to attend with twenty thousand men armed with poisoned arrows to shoot you on the face and hands. Some of your servants were to have private orders to strew a poisonous juice on your shirts and sheets, which would soon make you tear your own flesh, and die in the utmost torture. The general came into the same opinion ; so that for a long time there was a majority against you : but his majesty resolving, if possible, to spare your life, at last brought off the chamberlain.

Upon this incident *Reldresal* principal secretary for private affairs, who always approved himself your true friend, was commanded by the emperor to deliver his opinion, which he accordingly did : and therein justified the good thoughts you have of him. He allowed your crimes to be great, but that still there was room for mercy, the most commendable virtue

in

in a prince, and for which his majesty was so justly celebrated. He said, the friendship between you and him was so well known to the world, that perhaps the most honourable board might think him partial : however, in obedience to the command he had received, he would freely offer his sentiments. That if his majesty, in consideration of your services, and pursuant to his own merciful disposition, would please to spare your life, and only give order to put out both your eyes, he humbly conceived, that by this expedient justice might in some measure be satisfied, and all the world would applaud the lenity of the emperor, as well as the fair and generous proceedings of those who have the honour to be his counsellors. That the loss of your eyes would be no impediment to your bodily strength, by which you might still be useful to his majesty : that blindness is an addition to courage, by concealing dangers from us ; that the fear you had for your eyes, was the greatest difficulty in bringing over the enemies fleet ; and it would be sufficient for you to see by the eyes of the ministers, since the greatest princes do no more.

This proposal was received with the utmost disapprobation by the whole board. *Bolgolam* the admiral could not preserve his temper; but rising up in fury said, he wondered how the secretary durst presume to give his opinion for preserving the life of a traitor : that the services you had performed were, by all true reasons of state, the great aggravation of your crimes ;

crimes; that you, who was able to extinguish
the fire by difcharge of urine in her majefty's
apartment (which he mentioned with horror)
might at another time raife an inundation by
the fame means to drown the whole palace;
and the fame ftrength, which enabled you to
bring over the enemies fleet, might ferve upon
the firft difcontent to carry it back : that he had
good reafons to think you were a *big-endian* in
your heart; and as treafon begins in the heart,
before it appears in overt-acts, fo he accufed
you as a traitor on that account, and therefore
infifted you fhould be put to death.

The treafurer was of the fame opinion : he
fhewed to what ftreights his majefty's revenue
was reduced by the charge of maintaining you,
which would foon grow infupportable : that
the fecretary's expedient of putting out your
eyes was fo far from being a remedy againft
this evil, that it would probably encreafe it;
as is manifeft from the common practice of
blinding fome kind of fowl, after which they
fed the fafter, and grew fooner fat : that his
facred majefty and the council, who are your
judges, were in their own confciences fully
convinced of your guilt, which was a fufficient argument to condemn you to death without the formal proofs required by the ftrict letter of the law [a].

But

---

[a] There is fomething fo odious in whatever is wrong, that
even thofe whom it does not
fubject to punifhment, endeavour to colour it with an appearance of right ; but the attempt
is always unfuccefsful, and only
betrays a confcioufnefs of deformity

But his imperial majesty, fully determined against capital punishment, was graciously pleased to say, that since the council thought the loss of your eyes too easy a censure, some other may be inflicted hereafter: And your friend the secretary, humbly desiring to be heard again, in answer to what the treasurer had objected concerning the great charge his majesty was at in maintaining you, said, that his excellency, who had the sole disposal of the emperor's revenue, might easily provide against that evil by gradually lessening your establishment; by which, for want of sufficient food, you will grow weak and faint, and lose your appetite, and consume in a few months; neither would the stench of your carcase be then so dangerous, when it should become more than half diminished; and immediately upon your death, five or six thousand of his majesty's subjects might in two or three days cut your flesh from your bones; take it away by cart-loads, and bury it in distant parts to prevent infection, leaving the skeleton as a monument of admiration to posterity.

Thus by the great friendship of the secretary the whole affair was compromised. It was strictly enjoined, that the project of starving

---

mity by shewing a desire to hide it. Thus the *Lilliputian* court pretended a right to dispense with the strict letter of the law to put *Gulliver* to death, though by the strict letter of the law only he could be convicted of a crime; the intention of the statute not being to suffer the palace rather to be burnt than piss'd upon.

you by degrees fhould be kept a fecret, but
the fentence of putting out your eyes was entered on the books; none diffenting except
Bolgolam the admiral, who, being a creature
of the emprefs, was perpetually inftigated by
her majefty to infift upon your death, fhe having borne perpetual malice againft you on account of that infamous and illegal method you
took too extinguifh the fire in her apartment.

In three days, your friend the fecretary will
be directed to come to your houfe, and read
before you the articles of impeachment; and
then to fignify the great lenity and favour of
his majefty and council, whereby you are only
condemned to the lofs of your eyes, which his
majefty doth not queftion you will gratefully
and humbly fubmit to; and twenty of his majefty's furgeons will attend in order to fee the
operation well performed by difcharging very
fharp-pointed arrows into the balls of your
eyes, as you lie on the ground.

I leave to your prudence what meafures you
will take; and, to avoid fufpicion, I muft immediately return in as private a manner as I
came.

His lordfhip did fo, and I remained alone
under many doubts and perplexities of mind.

It was a cuftom introduced by this prince
and his miniftry (very different, as I have been
affured, from the practices of former times)
that after the court had decreed any cruel execution either to gratify the monarch's refentment, or the malice of a favourite, the emperor

for always made a speech to his whole council, expressing his great lenity and tenderness, as qualities known and confessed by all the world. This speech was immediately published through the kingdom; nor did any thing terrify the people so much as those encomiums on his majesty's mercy; because it was observed, that, the more these praises were enlarged and insisted on, the more inhuman was the punishment, and the sufferer more innocent. Yet, as to myself, I must confess, having never been designed for a courtier either by my birth or education, I was so ill a judge of things, that I could not discover the lenity and favour of this sentence, but conceived it (perhaps erroneously) rather to be rigorous than gentle. I sometimes thought of standing my trial; for, although I could not deny the facts alledged in the several articles, yet I hoped they would admit of some extenuation. But having in my life perused many state-trials, which I ever observed to terminate as the judges thought fit to direct, I durst not rely on so dangerous a decision, in so critical a juncture, and against such powerful enemies. Once I was strongly bent upon resistance; for, while I had liberty, the whole strength of that empire could hardly subdue me, and I might easily with stones pelt the metropolis to pieces; but I soon rejected that project with horror by remembering the oath I had made to the emperor, the favours I received from him, and the high title of *nardac* he conferred upon me. Neither

had

had I so soon learned the gratitude of courtiers, to persuade myself, that his majesty's present severities acquitted me of all past obligations.

At last I fixed upon a resolution, for which it is probable I may incur some censure, and not unjustly; for I confess I owe the preserving mine eyes, and consequently my liberty, to my own great rashness, and want of experience; because, if I had then known the nature of princes and ministers, which I have since observed in many other courts, and their methods of treating criminals less obnoxious than myself, I should with great alacrity and readiness have submitted to so easy a punishment. But hurried on by the precipitancy of youth, and having his imperial majesty's licence to pay my attendance upon the emperor of *Blefuscu*, I took this opportunity, before the three days were elapsed, to send a letter to my friend the secretary, signifying my resolution of setting out that morning for *Blefuscu*, pursuant to the leave I had got; and, without waiting for an answer, I went to that side of the island where our fleet lay. I seized a large man of war, tied a cable to the prow, and, lifting up the anchors, I stript myself, put my cloaths (together with my coverlet, which I carried under my arm) into the vessel, and drawing it after me, between wading and swimming arrived at the royal port of *Blefuscu*, where the people had long expected me; they lent me two guides to direct me to the capital city, which is of the same name. I held them in my my hands, till I came within two hundred yards of the gate, and defired them to fignify my arrival to one of the fecretaries, and let him know, I there waited his majefty's command. I had an anfwer in about an hour, that his majefty attended by the royal family and great officers of the court was coming out to receive me. I advanced a hundred yards. The emperor and his train alighted from their horfes, the emprefs and ladies from their coaches, and I did not perceive they were in any fright or concern. I lay on the ground to kifs his majefty's and the emprefs's hand. I told his majefty that I was come according to my promife, and with the licence of the emperor my mafter, to have the honour of feeing fo mighty a monarch, and to offer him any fervice in my power confiftent with my duty to my own prince; not mentioning a word of my difgrace, becaufe I had hitherto no regular information of it, and might fuppofe myfelf wholly ignorant of any fuch defign; neither could I reafonably conceive that the emperor would difcover the fecret, while I was out of his power; wherein however it foon appeared I was deceived.

I fhall not trouble the reader with the particular account of my reception at this court, which was fuitable to the generofity of fo great a prince; nor of the difficulties I was in for want of a houfe and bed, being forced to lie on the ground, wrapt up in my coverlet.

G 3

CHAP.

C H A P. VIII.

The author, by a lucky accident, finds means to leave Blefuscu *; and, after some difficulties, returns safe to his native country.*

THREE days after my arrival, walking out of curiosity to the north-east coast of the island, I observed about half a league off, in the sea, somewhat that looked like a boat overturned. I pulled off my shoes and stockings, and, wading two or three hundred yards, I found the object to approach nearer by force of the tide; and then plainly saw it to be a real boat, which I supposed might by some tempest have been driven from a ship: whereupon I returned immediately towards the city, and desired his imperial majesty to lend me twenty of the tallest vessels he had left after the loss of his fleet, and three thousand seamen, under the command of his vice-admiral. This fleet sailed round, while I went back the shortest way to the coast, where I first discovered the boat; I found the tide had driven it still nearer. The seamen were all provided with cordage, which I had beforehand twisted to a sufficient strength. When the ships came up, I stript myself, and waded till I came within an hundred yards of the boat, after which I was forced to swim till I got up to it. The seamen threw me the end of the cord, which
I fastened

I faftened to a hole in the fore-part of the boat, and the other end to a man of war: but I found all my labour to little purpofe; for, being out of my depth, I was not able to work. In this neceffity, I was forced to fwim behind, and pufh the boat forwards as often as I could, with one of my hands; and the tide favouring me I advanced fo far, that I could juft hold up my chin and feel the ground. I refted two or three minutes, and then gave the boat another fhove, and fo on till the fea was no higher than my arm-pits; and now, the moft laborious part being over, I took out my other cables, which were ftowed in one of the fhips, and faftened them firft to the boat, and then to nine of the veffels which attended me; the wind being favourable, the feamen towed, and I fhoved till we arrived within forty yards of the fhore, and, waiting till the tide was out, I got dry to the boat, and by the affiftance of two thoufand men, with ropes and engines, I made a fhift to turn it on its bottom, and found it was but little damaged.

I fhall not trouble the reader with the difficulties I was under by the help of certain paddles, which coft me ten days making, to get my boat to the royal port of *Blefufcu*, where a mighty concourfe of people appeared upon my arrival, full of wonder at the fight of fo prodigious a veffel. I told the emperor, that my good fortune had thrown this boat in

my

my way to carry me to fome place, from whence I might return into my native country, and begged his majefty's orders for getting materials to fit it up, together with his licence to depart, which, after fome kind expoftulations, he was pleafed to grant.

I did very much wonder, in all this time, not to have heard of any exprefs relating to me from our emperor to the court of *Blefufcu*. But I was afterwards given privately to underftand, that his imperial majefty, never imagining I had the leaft notice of his defigns, believed I was only gone to *Blefufcu* in performance of my promife, according to the licence he had given me, which was well known at our court, and would return in a few days when the ceremony was ended. But he was at laft in pain at my long abfence; and, after confulting with the treafurer and the reft of that cabal, a perfon of quality was difpatched with the copy of the articles againft me. This envoy had inftructions to reprefent to the monarch of *Blefufcu* the great lenity of his mafter, who was content to punifh me no farther than with the lofs of mine eyes; that I had fled from juftice, and, if I did not return in two hours, I fhould be deprived of my title of *nardac*, and declared a traitor. The envoy further added, that, in order to maintain the peace and amity between both empires, his mafter expected, that his brother of *Blefufcu* would give orders to have me fent back to *Lilliput,*

liput, bound hand and foot, to be punifhed as a traitor.

The emperor of *Blefufcu,* having taken three days to confult, returned an anfwer confifting of many civilities and excufes. He faid, that, as for fending me bound, his brother knew it was impoffible; that although I had deprived him of his fleet, yet he owed great obligations to me for many good offices I had done him in making the peace. That however both their majefties would fcon be made eafy; for I had found a prodigious veffel on the fhore, able to carry me on the fea, which he had given order to fit up with my own affiftance and direction; and he hoped in a few weeks both empires would be freed from fo infup-portable an incumbrance.

With this anfwer the envoy returned to *Lil-liput,* and the monarch of *Blefufcu* related to me all that had paft; offering me at the fame time (but under the ftricteft confidence) his gracious protection, if I would continue in his fervice; wherein although I believed him fin-cere, yet I refolved never more to put any con-fidence in princes or minifters, where I could poffibly avoid it; and therefore, with all due acknowledgments for his favourable intentions, I humbly begged to be excufed. I told him, that fince fortune, whether good or evil, had thrown a veffel in my way, I was refolved to venture myfelf in the ocean, rather than be an occafion of difference between two fuch migh-ty monarchs. Neither did I find the emperor

at

at all difpleafed; and I difcovered by a certain accident, that he was very glad of my refolution, and fo were moft of his minifters.

Thefe confiderations moved me to haften my departure fomewhat fooner than I intended; to which the court, impatient to have me gone, very readily contributed. Five hundred workmen were imployed to make two fails to my boat, according to my directions, by quilting thirteen fold of their ftrongeft linnen together. I was at the pains of making ropes and cables by twifting ten, twenty, or thirty of the thickeft and ftrongeft of theirs. A great ftone that I happened to find, after a long fearch by the fea-fhore, ferved me for an anchor. I had the tallow of three hundred cows for greafing my boat, and other ufes. I was at incredible pains in cutting down fome of the largeft timber-trees for oars and mafts, wherein I was however much affifted by his majefty's fhip-carpenters, who helped me in fmoothing them after I had done the rough work.

In about a month, when all was prepared, I fent to receive his majefty's commands, and to take my leave. The emperor and royal family came out of the palace; I lay down on my face to kifs his hand, which he very gracioufly gave me; fo did the emprefs, and young princes of the blood. His majefty prefented me with fifty purfes of two hundred *fprugs* a piece, together with his picture at full length, which I put immediately into one of

my

my gloves to keep it from being hurt. The ceremonies at my departure were too many to trouble the reader with at this time.

I ftored the boat with the carcafes of an hundred oxen, and three hundred fheep, with bread and drink proportionable, and as much meat ready dreffed as four hundred cooks could provide. I took with me fix cows and two bulls alive, with as many ewes and rams, intending to carry them into my own country, and propagate the breed. And to feed them on board I had a good bundle of hay, and a bag of corn. I would gladly have taken a dozen of the natives, but this was a thing the emperor would by no means permit; and, befides a diligent fearch into my pockets, his majefty engaged my honour not to carry away any of his fubjects, although with their own confent and defire.

Having thus prepared all things as well as I was able, I fet fail on the twenty-fourth day of *September* 1701, at fix in the morning; and when I had gone about four leagues to the northward, the wind being at fouth-eaft, at fix in the evening I defcried a fmall ifland about half a league to the north-weft. I advanced forward, and caft anchor on the lee-fide of the ifland, which feemed to be uninhabited. I then took fome refrefhment, and went to my reft. I flept well, and as I conjecture at leaft fix hours, for I found the day broke in two hours after I awaked. It was a clear night. I eat my breakfaft before the

sun

ſnn was up ; and heaving anchor, the wind being favourable, I ſteered the ſame courſe, that I had done the day before, wherein I was directed by my pocket-compaſs. My intention was to reach, if poſſible, one of thoſe iſlands which I had reaſon to believe lay to the north-eaſt of *Van Diemen*'s land. I diſcovered nothing all that day ; but upon the next, about three in the afternoon, when I had by my computation made twenty-four leagues from *Blefuſcu*, I deſcried a ſail ſteering to the ſouth-eaſt; my courſe was due eaſt. I hailed her, but could get no anſwer; yet I found I gained upon her, for the wind ſlackened. I made all the ſail I could, and in half an hour ſhe ſpied me, then hung out her antient, and diſcharged a gun. It is not eaſy to expreſs the joy I was in upon the unexpected hope of once more ſeeing my beloved country, and the dear pledges I left in it. The ſhip ſlackened her ſails, and I came up with her between five and ſix in the evening, *September* 26 ; but my heart leapt within me to ſee her *Engliſh* colours. I put my cows and ſheep into my coat-pockets, and got on board with all my little cargo of proviſions. The veſſel was an *Engliſh* merchant-man returning from *Japan* by the *north* and *ſouth-ſeas*; the captain Mr. *John Biddel* of *Deptford*, a very civil man, and an excellent ſailor. We were now in the latitude of 30 degrees ſouth, there were about fifty men in the ſhip ; and here I met an old comrade of mine, one *Peter Williams*,

liams, who gave me a good character to the captain. This gentleman treated me with kindnefs, and defired I would let him know what place I came from laft and whither I was bound; which I did in few words, but he thought I was raving, and that the dangers I had underwent had difturbed my head; whereupon I took my black cattle and fheep out of my pocket, which, after great aftonifhment, clearly convinced him of my veracity. I then fhewed him the gold given me by the emperor of *Befufcu*, together with his majefty's picture at full length, and fome other rarities of that country. I gave him two purfes of two hundred *fprugs* each, and promifed, when we arrived in *England*, to make him a prefent of a cow and a fheep big with young.

. I fhall not trouble the reader with a particular account of this voyage, which was very profperous for the moft part. We arrived in the *Downs* on the 13th of *April* 1702. I had only one misfortune, that the rats on board carried away one of my fheep; I found her bones in a hole, picked clean from the flefh. The reft of my cattle I got fafe a-fhore, and fet them a grazing in a bowling-green at *Greenwich*, where the finenefs of the grafs made them feed very heartily, though I had always feared the contrary: neither could I poffibly have preferved them in fo long a voyage, if the captain had not allowed me fome of his beft bifket, which rubbed to powder, and mingled with water, was their conftant food. The

fhort

short time I continued in *England*, I made a considerable profit by shewing my cattle to many persons of quality, and others: and before I began my second voyage, I sold them for six hundred pounds. Since my last return I find the breed is considerably increased, especially the sheep, which I hope will prove much to the advantage of the woollen manufacture by the fineness of the fleeces,

I stayed but two months with my wife and family; for my insatiable desire of seeing foreign countries would suffer me to continue no longer. I left fifteen hundred pounds with my wife, and fixed her in a good house at *Redriff*. My remaining stock I carried with me, part in money and part in goods, in hopes to improve my fortunes. My eldest uncle *John* had left me an estate in land, near *Epping*, of about thirty pounds a year; and I had a long lease of the *Black Bull* in *Fetter-Lane*, which yielded me as much more: so that I was not in any danger of leaving my family upon the parish. My son *Johnny*, named so after his uncle, was at the grammar school, and a towardly child. My daughter *Betty* (who is now well married, and has children) was then at her needle-work. I took leave of my wife, and boy and girl, with tears on both sides, and went on board the *Adventure*, a merchant-ship of three hundred tons bound for *Surat*, captain *John Nicholas* of *Leverpool* commander. But my account of this voyage must be referred to the second part of my travels.

A VOYAGE

A
VOYAGE
TO
BROBDINGNAG.

CHAP. I.

*A great storm described, the long-boat sent to
fetch water, the author goes with it to discover the country. He is left on shore, is seized
by one of the natives, and carried to a farmer's
house. His reception, with several accidents
that happened there. A description of the inhabitants.*

HAVING been condemned by nature and
fortune to an active and restless life, in
two months after my return I again left my
native country, and took shipping in the
Downs on the 20th day of *June* 1702, in the
Adventure, captain *John Nicholas* a *Cornish* man
commander, bound for *Surat*. We had a very
prosperous gale till we arrived at the *Cape of
Good Hope*, where we landed for fresh water,
but discovering a leak, we unshipped our goods,
and wintered there; for, the captain falling
sick of an ague, we could not leave the *Cape*
till the end of *March*. We then set sail, and
had a good voyage till we passed the *Streights*
of *Madagascar*; but having got northward of
that island, and to about five degrees south latitude,

titude, the winds, which in thofe feas are obferved to blow a conftant equal gale between
the north and weft, from the beginning of
December to the beginning of *May*, on the 19th
of *April* began to blow with much greater violence, and more wefterly than ufual, continuing fo for twenty days together, during which
time, we were driven a little to the eaft of
the *Molucca* iflands, and about three degrees
northward of the line, as our captain found by
an obfervation he took the 2d of *May*, at
which time the wind ceafed, and it was a perfect calm, whereat I was not a little rejoiced.
But he, being a man well experienced in the
navigation of thofe feas, bid us all prepare a-
gainft a ftorm, which accordingly happened the
day following : for the fouthern wind, called
the fouthern *monfoon*, began to fet in.

Finding it was like to overblow, we took in
our fprit-fail, and ftood by to hand the fore-
fail ; but, making foul weather, we looked the
guns were all faft, and handed the miffen.
The fhip lay very broad off, fo we thought it
better fpooning before the fea, than trying or
hulling. We reeft the fore-fail and fet him,
and hawled aft the fore-fheet ; the helm was
hard a weather. The fhip wore bravely. We
belayed the fore-down-hall ; but the fail was
fplit, and we hawled down the yard, and got
the fail into the fhip, and unbound all the
things clear of it. It was a very fierce ftorm ;
the fea broke ftrange and dangerous. We
hawled off upon the lanniard of the whip-

NORTH

AMERICA

BROBDINGNAG

Flanflasnic

Lorbrulgrud

Difcover&A.D.1703

Straits of Annis

C.Blanco

St.Sebaftian

C.Mendocino

Ptogt.Franc.Drak

NEW

ALBION

Mount St.Maria

P.Monterey

ſtaff, and helped the man at the helm. We would not get down our top-maſt, but let all ſtand, becauſe ſhe ſcudded before the ſea very well, and we knew that, the top-maſt being aloft, the ſhip was the wholſomer, and made better way through the ſea, ſeeing we had ſea-room. When the ſtorm was over, we ſet fore-ſail and main-ſail, and brought the ſhip to. Then we ſet the miſſen, main-top-ſail, and the fore-top-ſail. Our courſe was *eaſt-north-eaſt*, the wind was at *ſouth-weſt*. We got the ſtar-board tacks a-board, we caſt off our weather braces and lifts ; we ſet in the lee-braces, and hawled forward by the weather-bowlings, and hawled them tight, and belayed them, and hawled over the miſſen-tack to wind-ward, and kept her full and by as near as ſhe would lie.

During this ſtorm, which was followed by a ſtrong wind *weſt-ſouth-weſt*, we were carried by my computation about five hundred leagues to the *eaſt*, ſo that the oldeſt ſailor on board could not tell in what part of the world we were. Our proviſions held out well, our ſhip was ſtaunch, and our crew all in good health ; but we lay in the utmoſt diſtreſs for water. We thought it beſt to hold on the ſame courſe, rather than turn more northerly, which might have brought us to the *north-weſt* parts of great *Tartary*, and into the frozen ſea.

On the 16th day of *June*, 1703, a boy on the top-maſt diſcovered land. On the 17th, we came in full view of a great iſland or continent (for we knew not whether) on the south-side whereof was a small neck of land jutting out into the sea, and a creek too shallow to hold a ship of above one hundred tons. We cast anchor within a league of this creek, and our captain sent a dozen of his men well armed in the long-boat, with vessels for water, if any could be found. I desired his leave to go with them, that I might see the country, and make what discoveries I could. When we came to land, we saw no river or spring, nor any sign of inhabitants. Our men therefore wandered on the shore to find out some fresh water near the sea, and I walked alone about a mile on the other side, where I observed the country all barren and rocky. I now began to be weary, and seeing nothing to entertain my curiosity, I returned gently down towards the creek; and the sea being full in my view, I saw our men already got into the boat, and rowing for life to the ship. I was going to hollow after them, although it had been to little purpose, when I observed a huge creature walking after them in the sea, as fast as he could: he waded not much deeper than his knees, and took prodigious strides: but our men had the start of him half a league, and, the sea thereabouts being full of sharp-pointed rocks, the monster was not able to overtake the boat. This I was afterwards told, for I durst not stay to see the issue of the adventure; but ran as fast I could the way I first went, and then climbed up a steep hill, which gave

gave me some prospect of the country. I found it fully cultivated; but that which first surprised me was the length of the grass, which, in those grounds that seemed to be kept for hay, was about twenty feet high.

I fell into a high road, for so I took it to be, though it served to the inhabitants only as a foot-path through a field of barley. Here I walked on for some time, but could see little on either side, it being now near harvest, and the corn rising at least forty feet. I was an hour walking to the end of this field, which was fenced in with a hedge of at least one hundred and twenty feet high, and the trees so lofty that I could make no computation of their altitude. There was a stile to pass from this field into the next. It had four steps, and a stone to cross over when you came to the uppermost. It was impossible for me to climb this stile, because every step was six feet high, and the upper stone above twenty. I was endeavouring to find some gap in the hedge, when I discovered one of the inhabitants in the next field advancing towards the stile, of the same size with him whom I saw in the sea pursuing our boat. He appeared as tall as an ordinary spire-steeple, and took about ten yards at every stride, as near I could guess. I was struck with the utmost fear and astonishment, and ran to hide myself in the corn, from whence I saw him at the top of the stile looking back into the next field on the right hand, and heard him call in a voice many degrees louder than a speaking-trumpet; but the noise

H 2   was

was fo high in the air, that at firft I certainly
thought it was thunder. Whereupon feven
monfters, like himfelf, came towards him
with reaping-hooks in their hands, each hook
about the largenefs of fix fcythes. Thefe people were not fo well clad as the firft, whofe
fervants or labourers they feemed to be : for,
upon fome words he fpoke, they went to reap
the corn in the field where I lay.   I kept from
them at as great a diftance as I could, but was
forced to move with extreme difficulty, for the
ftalks of the corn were fometimes not above a
foot diftant, fo that I could hardly fqueefe
my body betwixt them.   However I made a
fhift to go forward, till I came to a part of the
field where the corn had been laid by the rain
and wind.   Here it was impoffible for me to
advance a ftep ; for the ftalks were fo interwoven that I could not creep thorough, and
the beards of the fallen ears fo ftrong and
pointed, that they pierced through my cloaths
into my flefh.   At the fame time I heard the
reapers not above an hundred yards behind
me.   Being quite difpirited with toil, and
wholly overcome by grief and defpair, I lay
down between two ridges, and heartily wifhed
I might there end my days.   I bemoaned my
defolate widow, and fatherlefs children.   I lamented my own folly and wilfulnefs in attempting a fecond voyage againft the advice
of all my friends and relations,   In this terrible agitation of mind I could not forbear
thinking of *Lilliput*, whofe inhabitants looked
upon me as the greateft prodigy that ever appeared

peared in the world : where I was able to draw an imperial fleet in my hand, and perform thofe other actions which will be recorded for ever in the chronicles of that empire, while pofterity fhall hardly believe them, although attefted by millions. I reflected what a mortification it muft prove to me to appear as inconfiderable in this nation, as one fingle *Lilliputian* would be among us. But this I conceived was to be the leaft of my misfortunes : for, as human creatures are obferved to be more favage and cruel in proportion to their bulk, what could I expect but to be a morfel in the mouth of the firft among thefe enormous barbarians, that fhould happen to feize me ? Undoubtedly philofophers are in the right when they tell us, that nothing is great or little otherwife than by comparifon. It might have pleafed fortune to have let the *Lilliputians* find fome nation, where the people were as diminutive with refpect to them, as they were to me. And who knows but that even this prodigious race of mortals might be equally overmatched in fome diftant part of the world, whereof we have yet no difcovery.

Scared and confounded as I was, I could not forbear going on with thefe reflections, when one of the reapers, approaching within ten yards of the ridge where I lay, made me apprehend that with the next ftep I fhould be fquafhed to death under his foot, or cut in two with his reaping-hook. And therefore, when he was again about to move, I fcreamed as

loud

loud as fear could make me. Whereupon the huge creature trod fhort, and, looking round about under him for fome time, at laft efpied me as I lay on the ground. He confidered a while with the caution of one who endeavours to lay hold on a fmall dangerous animal, in fuch a manner that it fhall not be able either to fcratch or to bite him, as I myfelf have fometimes done with a weafel in *England*. At length he ventured to take me up behind by the middle between his fore-finger and thumb, and brought me within three yards of his eyes, that he might behold my fhape more perfectly. I gueffed his meaning, and my good fortune gave me fo much prefence of mind, that I refolved not to ftruggle in the leaft as he held me in the air above fixty feet from the ground, although he grievoufly pinched my fides, for fear I fhould flip through his fingers. All I ventured was to raife mine eyes towards the fun, and place my hands to-gether in a fupplicating pofture, and to fpeak fome words in an humble melancholy tone, fuitable to the condition I then was in. For I apprehended every moment that he would dafh me againft the ground, as we ufually do any little hateful animal, which we have a mind to deftroy *. But my good ftar would have it,

---

* Our inattention to the felicity of fenfitive beings merely becaufe they are fmall is here forcibly reproved : many have wantonly crufhed an infect, who would fhudder at cutting the throat of a dog; but it fhould always be remembered, that the leaft of thefe
" In mortal fufferance feels a
    pang as great
" As when a giant dies."

that

L.L. Müller inv. del. et sc.

that he appeared pleafed with my voice and geftures, and began to look upon me as a curiofity, much wondering to hear me pronounce articulate words, although he could not underftand them. In the mean time I was not able to forbear groaning and fhedding tears, and turning my head towards my fides; letting him know, as well as I could, how cruelly I was hurt by the preffure of his thumb and finger. He feemed to apprehend my meaning; for, lifting up the lappet of his coat, he put me gently into it, and immediately ran along with me to his mafter, who was a fubftantial farmer, and the fame perfon I had firft feen in the field.

The farmer having (as I fuppofe by their talk) received fuch an account of me as his fervant could give him, took a piece of a fmall ftraw, about the fize of a walking-ftaff, and therewith lifted up the lappets of my coat; which it feems he thought to be fome kind of covering that nature had given me. He blew my hairs afide to take a better view of my face. He called his hinds about him, and afked them (as I afterwards learned) whether they had ever feen in the fields any little creature that refembled me: he then placed me foftly on the ground upon all four, but I got immediately up, and walked flowly backwards and forwards to let thofe people fee I had no intent to run away. They all fat down in a circle about me the better to obferve my motions. I pulled off my hat, and made a low bow towards

wards the farmer. I fell on my knees, and lifted up my hands and eyes, and spoke several words as loud as I could : I took a purse of gold out of my pocket, and humbly presented it to him. He received it on the palm of his hand, then applied it close to his eye to see what it was, and afterwards turned it several times with the point of a pin (which he took out of his sleeve) but could make nothing of it. Whereupon I made a sign that he should place his hand on the ground. I then took the purse, and opening it, poured all the gold into his palm. There were six *spanish* pieces of four pistoles each, besides twenty or thirty smaller coins. I saw him wet the tip of his little finger upon his tongue, and take up one of my largest pieces, and then another, but he seemed to be wholly ignorant what they were. He made me a sign to put them again into my purse, and the purse again into my pocket, which, after offering it to him several times, I thought it best to do.

The farmer by this time was convinced I must be a rational creature. He spoke often to me, but the sound of his voice pierced my ears like that of a water-mill, yet his words were articulate enough. I answered as loud as I could in several languages, and he often laid his ear within two yards of me; but all in vain, for we were wholly unintelligible to each other. He then sent his servants to their work, and, taking his handkerchief out of his pocket, he doubled and spread it on

his

his left hand, which he placed flat on the ground with the palm upwards, making me a sign to step into it, as I could easily do, for it was not above a foot in thickness. I thought it my part to obey, and, for fear of falling, laid myself at full length upon the handkerchief, with the remainder of which he lapped me up to the head for farther security, and in this manner carried me home to his house. There he called his wife, and shewed me to her; but she screamed and ran back, as women in *England* do at the sight of a toad or a spider. However, when she had a while seen my behaviour, and how well I observed the signs her husband made, she was soon reconciled, and by degrees grew extremely tender of me.

It was about twelve at noon, and a servant brought in dinner. It was only one substantial dish of meat (fit for the plain condition of an husbandman) in a dish of about four and twenty feet diameter. The company were the farmer and his wife, three children and an old grandmother: when they were sat down, the farmer placed me at some distance from him on the table, which was thirty feet high from the floor. I was in a terrible fright, and kept as far as I could from the edge for fear of falling. The wife minced a bit of meat, then crumbled some bread on a trencher, and placed it before me. I made her a low bow, took out my knife and fork, and fell to eat, which gave them exceeding delight. The mistress sent her maid for a small dram-cup, which held

held about two gallons, and filled it with drink; I took up the veffel with much diffi- culty in both hands, and in a moft refpectful manner drank to her ladyfhip's health, expref- fing the words as loud as I could in *Englifh*, which made the company laugh fo heartily, that I was almoft deafened with the noife. This liquor tafted like a fmall cyder, and was not unpleafant. Then the mafter made me a fign to come to his trencher-fide; but as I walked on the table, being in great furprize all the time, as the indulgent reader will eafily conceive and excufe, I happened to ftumble againft a cruft, and fell flat on my face, but received no hurt. I got up immediately, and obferving the good people to be in much con- cern, I took my hat (which I held under my arm out of good manners) and, waving it over my head, made three huzza's, to fhew I had got no mifchief by my fall. But advancing forwards toward my mafter (as I fhall hence- forth call him) his youngeft fon who fat next him, an arch boy of about ten years old, took me up by the legs, and held me fo high in the air, that I trembled every limb; but his fa- ther fnatched me from him, and at the fame time gave him fuch a box on the left ear, as would have felled an *European* troop of horfe to the earth, ordering him to be taken from the table. But being afraid the boy might owe me a fpight, and well remembering how mifchievous all children among us naturally are to fparrows, rabbits, young kittens, and

puppy-

puppy-dogs, I fell on my knees, and pointing to the boy made my mafter to underftand, as well as I could, that I defired his fon might be pardoned. The father complied, and the lad took his feat again; whereupon I went to him and kiffed his hand, which my mafter took, and made him ftroak me gently with it.

In the midft of dinner, my miftrefs's favourite cat leapt into her lap. I heard a noife behind me like that of a dozen ftocking-weavers at work; and, turning my head, I found it proceeded from the purring of that animal, who feemed to be three times larger than an ox, as I computed by the view of her head, and one of her paws, while her miftrefs was feeding and ftroaking her. The fiercenefs of this creature's countenance altogether difcompofed me; though I ftood at the further end of the table, above fifty feet off; and although my miftrefs held her faft, for fear fhe might give a fpring, and feize me in her talons. But it happened there was no danger; for the cat took not the leaft notice of me, when my mafter placed me within three yards of her. And as I have been always told, and found true by experience in my travels, that flying or difcovering fear before a fierce animal is a certain way to make it purfue or attack you, fo I refolved in this dangerous juncture to fhew no manner of concern. I walked with intrepidity five or fix times before the very head of the cat, and came within half a yard of her; where-

whereupon she drew herself back, as if she were more afraid of me: I had less apprehension concerning the dogs, whereof three or four came into the room, as it is usual in farmers houses; one of which was a mastiff equal in bulk to four elephants, and a greyhound somewhat taller than the mastiff, but not so large.

When dinner was almost done, the nurse came in with a child of a year old in her arms, who immediately spied me, and began a squall, that you might have heard from *London-Bridge* to *Chelsea*, after the usual oratory of infants to get me for a play-thing. The mother out of pure indulgence took me up, and put me towards the child, who presently seized me by the middle, and got my head into his mouth, where I roared so loud that the urchin was frighted, and let me drop, and I should infallibly have broke my neck, if the mother had not held her apron under me. The nurse to quiet her babe made use of a rattle, which was a kind of hollow vessel filled with great stones, and fastened by a cable to the child's waist: but all in vain, so that she was forced to apply the last remedy by giving it suck. I must confess no object ever disgusted me so much as the sight of her monstrous breast, which I cannot tell what to compare with, so as to give the curious reader an idea of its bulk, shape, and colour. It stood prominent six feet, and could not be less than sixteen in circumference. The nipple was about half
the

the bignefs of my head, and the hue both of
that and the dug fo varified with fpots, pim-
ples, and freckles, that nothing could appear
more naufeous : for I had a near fight of her,
fhe fitting down the more conveniently to give
fuck, and I ftanding on the table. This made
me reflect upon the fair fkins of our *Englifh*
ladies, who appear fo beautiful to us, only becaufe they are of our own fize, and their defects not to be feen but through a magnifying-
glafs, where we· find by experiment, that the
fmootheft and whiteft fkins look rough and
coarfe, and ill-coloured.

I remember, when I was at *Lilliput*, the
complexions of thofe diminutive people appeared to me the faireft in the world ; and talking
upon this fubject with a perfon of learning
there, who was an intimate friend of mine,
he faid that my face appeared much fairer and
fmoother when he looked on me from the
ground, than it did upon a nearer view when I
took him up in my hand and brought him clofe,
which he confeffed was at firft a very fhock-
ing fight. He faid he could difcover great
holes in my fkin ; that the ftumps of my beard
were ten times ftronger than the briftles of a
boar, and my complexion made up of feveral
colours altogether difagreeable : although I
muft beg leave to fay for myfelf, that I am as
fair as moft of my fex and country, and very
little fun-burnt by all my travels. On the
other fide, difcourfing of the ladies in that
emperor's court, he ufed to tell me, one had

3   freckles,

freckles, another too wide a mouth, a third too large a nofe, nothing of which I was able to diftinguifh. I confefs this reflection was obvious enough; which however I could not forbear, left the reader might think thofe vaft creatures were actually deformed: for I muft do them juftice to fay, they are a comely race of people; and particularly the features of my mafter's countenance, although he were but a farmer, when I beheld him from the heighth of fixty feet, appeared very well proportioned.

When dinner was done, my mafter went out to his labourers, and, as I could difcover by his voice and gefture, gave his wife a ftrict charge to take care of me. I was very much tired, and difpofed to fleep, which my miftrefs perceiving, fhe put me on her own bed, and covered me with a clean white handkerchief, but larger and coarfer than the main-fail of a man of war.

I flept about two hours, and dreamed I was at home with my wife and children, which aggravated my forrows when I awaked, and found myfelf alone in a vaft room, between two and three hundred feet wide, and above two hundred high, lying in a bed twenty yards wide. My miftrefs was gone about her houfhold affairs, and had locked me in. The bed was eight yards from the floor. Some natural neceffities required me to get down; I durft not prefume to call, and, if I had, it would have been in vain with fuch a voice as mine, at fo great a diftance as from the room
where

where I lay to the kitchen where the family kept. While I was under thefe circumftances, two rats crept up the curtains, and ran fmelling backwards and forwards on the bed. One of them came up almoft to my face, whereupon I rofe in a fright, and drew out my hanger to defend myfelf. Thefe horrible animals had the boldnefs to attack me on both fides, and one of them held his fore-feet at my collar; but I had the good fortune to rip up his belly, before he could do me any mifchief. He fell down at my feet, and the other feeing the fate of his comrade made his efcape, but not without one good wound on the back, which I gave him as he fled, and made the blood run trickling from him. After this exploit, I walked gently to and fro on the bed to recover my breath, and lofs of fpirits. Thefe creatures were of the fize of a large maftiff, but infinitely more nimble and fierce, fo that, if I had taken off my belt before I went to fleep, I muft have infallibly been torn to pieces and devoured. I meafured the tail of the dead rat, and found it to be two yards long, wanting an inch; but it went againft my ftomach to drag the carcafs off the bed, where it lay ftill bleeding; I obferved it had yet fome life, but, with a ftrong flafh crofs the neck, I thoroughly difpatched it.

Soon after my miftrefs came into the room, who feeing me all bloody ran and took me up in her hand. I pointed to the dead rat, fmiling and making other figns to fhew I was not hurt,

hurt, whereat fhe was extremely rejoiced, call-ing the maid to take up the dead rat with a pair of tongs, and throw it out of the win-dow. Then fhe fet me on a table, where I fhewed her my hanger all bloody, and, wip-ing it on the lappet of my coat, returned it to the fcabbard. I was preffed to do more than one thing, which another could not do for me; and therefore endeavoured to make my miftrefs underftand that I defired to be fet down on the floor; which after fhe had done, my bafhful-nefs would not fuffer me to exprefs myfelf far-ther, than by pointing to the door, and bow-ing feveral times. The good woman, with much difficulty, at laft perceived what I would be at, and taking me up again in her hand, walked into the garden, where fhe fet me down. I went on one fide about two hun-dred yards, and beckoning to her not to look or to follow me, I hid myfelf between two leaves of forrel, and there difcharged the ne-ceffities of nature.

I hope the gentle reader will excufe me for dwelling on thefe and the like particulars; which, however infignificant they may appear to grovelling vulgar minds, yet will certainly help a philofopher to enlarge his thoughts and imagination, and apply them to the benefit of public as well as private life, which was my fole defign in prefenting this and other ac-counts of my travels to the world; wherein I have been chiefly ftudious of truth, with-out affecting any ornaments of learning or of
ftyle.

ftyle. But the whole fcene of this voyage made fo ftrong an impreffion on my mind, and is fo deeply fixed in my memory, that in committing it to paper I did not omit one material circumftance: however, upon a ftrict review, I blotted out feveral paffages of lefs moment which were in my firft copy, for fear of being cenfured as tedious and trifling, whereof travellers are often, perhaps not without juftice, accufed.

CHAP. II.

A defcription of the farmer's daughter. The author carried to a market-town, and then to the metropolis. The particulars of his journey.

MY miftrefs had a daughter of nine years old, a child of towardly parts for her age, very dexterous at her needle, and fkilful in dreffing her baby. Her mother and fhe contrived to fit up the baby's cradle for me againft night; the cradle was put into a fmall drawer of a cabinet, 'and the drawer placed upon a hanging fhelf for fear of the rats. This was my bed all the time I ftayed with thofe people, though made more convenient by degrees, as I began to learn their language, and make my wants known. This young girl was fo handy, that, after I had once or twice pulled off my cloaths before her, fhe was able to drefs and undrefs me, though I never gave her

that

that trouble, .when fhe would let me do either
myfelf. She made me feven fhirts, and fome
other linnen, of as fine cloth as could be got,
which indeed was coarfer than fackcloth; and
thefe fhe conftantly wafhed for me with her
own hands. She was likewife my fchool-
miftrefs to teach me the language : when I
pointed to any thing, fhe told me the name of
it in her own tongue, fo that in a few days I
was able to call for whatever I had a mind to.
She was very good-natured, and not above
forty feet high, being little for her age. She
gave me the name of *Grildrig*, which the family took up, and afterwards the whole kingdom. The word imports, what the *Latins* call
nanunculus, the *Italians homunceletino*, and the
Englifh mannikin. To her I chiefly owe my
prefervation in that country : we never parted
while I was there; I called her my *Glumdalclitch*, or little nurfe; and fhould be guilty of
great ingratitude, if I omitted this honourable
mention of her care and affection towards me,
which I heartily wifh it lay in my power to
requite as fhe deferves, inftead of being the
innocent, but unhappy inftrument of her difgrace, as I have too much reafon to fear.

It now began to be known and talked of in
the neighbourhood, that my mafter had found
a ftrange animal in the field, about the bignefs
of a *fplacnuck*, but exactly fhaped in every
part like a human creature; which it likewife
imitated in all its actions; feemed to fpeak in
a little language of its own, had already learned
                                        feveral

several words of theirs, went erect upon two legs, was tame and gentle, would come when it was called, do whatever it was bid, had the finest limbs in the world, and a complexion fairer than a nobleman's daughter of three years old. Another farmer, who lived hard by, and was a particular friend of my master, came on a visit on purpose to enquire into the truth of this story. I was immediately produced, and placed upon a table, where I walked as I was commanded, drew my hanger, put it up again, made my reverence to my master's guest, asked him in his own language how he did, and told him he was welcome, just as my little nurse had instructed me. This man, who was old and dim-sighted, put on his spectacles to behold me better, at which I could not forbear laughing very heartily, for his eyes appeared like the full moon shining into a chamber at two windows. Our people, who discovered the cause of my mirth, bore me company in laughing, at which the old fellow was fool enough to be angry and out of countenance. He had the character of a great miser; and, to my misfortune, he well deserved it by the cursed advice he gave my master to shew me as a sight upon a market-day in the next town, which was half an hour's riding, about two and twenty miles from our house. I guessed there was some mischief contriving, when I observed my master and his friend whispering long together, sometimes pointing at me; and my fears made me fancy

that

that I overheard and underftood fome of their words. But the next morning *Glumdalclitch,* my little nurfe, told me the whole matter, which fhe had cunningly picked out from her mother. The poor girl laid me on her bofom, and fell a weeping with fhame and grief. She apprehended fome mifchief would happen to me from rude vulgar folks, who might fqueefe me to death, or break one of my limbs by taking me in their hands. She had alfo obferved how modeft I was in my nature, how nicely I regarded my honour, and what an indignity I fhould conceive it to be expofed for money as a publick fpectacle to the meaneft of the people. She faid, her *papa* and *mamma* had promifed that *Grildrig* fhould be hers, but now fhe found they meant to ferve her as they did laft year, when they pretended to give her a lamb, and yet, as foon as it was fat, fold it to a butcher. For my own part, I may truly affirm, that I was lefs concerned than my nurfe. I had a ftrong hope, which never left me, that I fhould one day recover my liberty; and as to the ignominy of being carried about for a monfter, I confidered myfelf to be a perfect ftranger in the country, and that fuch a misfortune could never be charged upon me as a reproach, if ever I fhould return to *England*; fince the king of *Great-Britain* himfelf, in my condition, muft have undergone the fame diftrefs.

My mafter, purfuant to the advice of his friend, carried me in a box the next market-day to the neighbouring town, and took along

with

with him his little daughter, my nurfe, upon a pillion behind him. The box was clofe on every fide, with a little door for me to go in and out, and a few gimlet-holes to let in air. The girl had been fo careful as to put the quilt of her baby's bed into it for me to lie down on. However, I was terribly fhaken and dif-compofed in this journey, though it were but of half an hour. For the horfe went a-bout forty feet at every ftep, and trotted fo high, that the agitation was equal to the ri-fing and falling of a fhip in a great ftorm, but much more frequent : our journey was fome-what farther than from *London* to *St. Alban's*. My mafter alighted at an inn which he ufed to frequent ; and after confulting a while with the inn-keeper, and making fome neceffary preparations, he hired the *grultrud* or crier to give notice through the town of a ftrange creature to be feen at the fign of the *Green Eagle*, not fo big as a *fplacnuck* (an animal in that country very finely fhaped, about fix feet long) and in every part of the body refembling an human creature, could fpeak feveral words, and perform an hundred diverting tricks.

I was placed upon a table in the largeft room of the inn, which might be near three hun-dred feet fquare. My little nurfe ftood on a low ftool clofe to the table to take care of me, and direct what I fhould do. My mafter, to avoid a croud, would fuffer only thirty people at a time to fee me. I walked about on the table as the girl commanded : fhe afked me

I 3   queftions,

ter *Glumdalclitch* ride behind him. She carried me on her lap in a box tied about her waift. The girl had lined it on all fides with the fofteft cloth fhe could get, well quilted underneath, furnifhed it with her baby's bed, provided me with linnen and other neceffaries, and made every thing as convenient as fhe could. We had no other company but a boy of the houfe, who rode after us with the luggage.

My mafter's defign was to fhew me in all the towns by the way, and to ftep out of the road for fifty or an hundred miles, to any village, or perfon of quality's houfe, where he might expect cuftom. We made eafy journies of not above feven or eightfcore miles a day: for *Glumdalclitch*, on purpofe to fpare me, complained fhe was tired with the trotting of the horfe. She often took me out of my box at my own defire to give me air, and fhew me the country, but always held me faft by a leading-ftring. We paffed over five or fix rivers many degrees broader and deeper than the *Nile*, or the *Ganges*; and there was hardly a rivulet fo fmall as the *Thames* at *London-Bridge*. We were ten weeks in our journey, and I was fhewn in eighteen large towns, befides many villages and private families.

On the 26th day of *October*, we arrived at the metropolis, called in their language *Lorbrulgrud*, or *Pride of the Univerfe*. My mafter took a lodging in the principal ftreet of the city, not far from the royal palace, and put

out

ut bills in the ufual form, containing an ex-
ɛt defcription of my perfon and parts. He
ired a large room between three and four
undred feet wide. He provided a table fix-
r feet in diameter, upon which I was to act
ıy part, and pallifadoed it round three feet
rom the edge, and as many high, to pre-
ent my falling over. I was fhewn ten times
 day, to the wonder and fatisfaction of all
eople. I could now fpeak the language to-
:rably well, and perfectly underftood every
rord that was fpoken to me. Befides, I had
:arned their alphabet, and could make a fhift
ɔ explain a fentence here and there; for
Humdalclitch had been my inftructor while we
ere at home, and at leifure hours during
ur journey. She carried a little book in her
ocket, not much larger than a *Sanfon's At-*
ıs; it was a common treatife for the ufe of
oung girls, giving a fhort account of their
eligion; out of this fhe taught me my letters,
nd interpreted the words.

CHAP.

C H A P. III.

The author sent for to court. The queen buys him of his master the farmer, and presents him to the king. He disputes with his majesty's great scholars. An apartment at court provided for the author. He is in high favour with the queen. He stands up for the honour of his own country. His quarrels with the queen's dwarf.

THE frequent labours I underwent every day, made in few weeks a very considerable change in my health: the more my master got by me, the more insatiable he grew. I had quite lost my stomach, and was almost reduced to a skeleton. The farmer observed it, and concluding I must soon die, resolved to make as good a hand of me as he could. While he was thus reasoning and resolving with himself, a *sardral*, or gentleman-usher, came from court, commanding my master to carry me immediately thither for the diversion of the queen and her ladies. Some of the latter had already been to see me, and reported strange things of my beauty, behaviour, and good sense. Her majesty, and those who attended her, were beyond measure delighted with my demeanour. I fell on my knees, and begged the honour of kissing her imperial foot; but this gracious princess held out her little finger towards me (after I was set on a table) which I

　　　embraced

embraced in both my arms, and put the tip of it with the utmoſt reſpect to my lip. She made me ſome general queſtions about my country, and my travels, which I anſwered as diſtinctly, and in as few words as I could. She aſked, whether I would be content to live at court. I bowed down to the board of the table, and humbly anſwered that I was my maſter's ſlave; but if I were at my own diſpoſal, I ſhould be proud to devote my life to her majeſty's ſervice. She then aſked my maſter, whether he were willing to ſell me at a good price. He, who apprehended I could not live a month, was ready enough to part with me, and demanded a thouſand pieces of gold, which were ordered him on the ſpot, each piece being about the bigneſs of eight hundred moydores; but, allowing for the proportion of all things between that country and *Europe*, and the high price of gold among them, was hardly ſo great a ſum as a thouſand guineas would be in *England*. I then ſaid to the queen, ſince I was now her majeſty's moſt humble creature and vaſſal, I muſt beg the favour, that *Glumdalclitch*, who had always tended me with ſo much care and kindneſs, and underſtood to do it ſo well, might be admitted into her ſervice, and continue to be my nurſe and inſtructor. Her majeſty agreed to my petition, and eaſily got the farmer's conſent, who was glad enough to have his daughter preferred at court, and the poor girl herſelf was not able to hide her joy: my late maſter withdrew, bidding me

farewel,

farewel, and faying he had left me in a good
fervice; to which I replied not a word, only
making him a flight bow.

The queen obferved my coldnefs, and, when
the farmer was gone out of the apartment,
afked me the reafon. I made bold to tell her
majefty, that I owed no other obligation to my
late mafter, than his not dafhing out the brains
of a poor harmlefs creature found by chance
in his field; which obligation was amply recompenfed by the gain he had made in fhewing
me through half the kingdom, and the price
he had now fold me for. That the life I had
fince led, was laborious enough to kill an animal of ten times my ftrength. That my
health was much impaired by the continual
drudgery of entertaining the rabble every hour
of the day, and that, if my mafter had not
thought my life in danger, her majefty would
not have got fo cheap a bargain. But as I
was out of all fear of being ill treated under
the protection of fo great and good an emprefs, the ornament of nature, the darling of
the world, the delight of her fubjects, the
phœnix of the creation; fo, I hoped my late
mafter's apprehenfions would appear to be
groundlefs, for I already found my fpirits to
revive by the influence of her moft auguft prefence.

This was the fum of my fpeech, delivered
with great improprieties and hefitation; the
latter part was altogether framed in the ftyle
peculiar to that people, whereof I learned fome
phrafes

phrafes from *Glumdalclitch*, while fhe was carrying me to court.

The queen, giving great allowance for my defectivenefs in fpeaking, was however furprifed at fo much wit and good fenfe in fo diminutive an animal. She took me in her own hand, and carried me to the king, who was then retired to his cabinet. His majefty, a prince of much gravity and auftere countenance, not well obferving my fhape at firft view, afked the queen after a cold manner, how long it was fince fhe grew fond of a *fplacnuck*; for fuch it feems he took me to be, as I lay upon my breaft in her majefty's right hand. But this princefs, who hath an infinite deal of wit and humour, fet me gently on my feet upon the fcrutore, and commanded me to give his majefty an account of myfelf, which I did in a very few words; and *Glumdalclitch*, who attended at the cabinet door, and could not endure I fhould be out of her fight, being admitted, confirmed all that had paffed from my arrival at her father's houfe.

The king, although he be as learned a perfon as any in his dominions, had been educated in the ftudy of philofophy, and particularly mathematics; yet when he obferved my fhape exactly, and faw me walk erect, before I began to fpeak, conceived I might be a piece of clock-work (which is in that country arrived to a very great perfection) contrived by fome ingenious artift. But when he heard my voice, and found what I delivered to be regular and rational,

rational, he could not conceal his aftonifhment. He was by no means fatisfied with the rela- tion I gave him of the manner I came into his kingdom, but thought it a ftory concerted be- tween *Glumdalclitch* and her father, who had taught me a fett of words to make me fell at a better price. Upon this imagination he put feveral other queftions to me, and ftill received rational anfwers, no otherwife defective than by a foreign accent, and an imperfect know- ledge in the language, with fome ruftic phra- fes·which I had learned at the farmer's houfe, and did not fuit the polite ftyle of a court.

His majefty fent for three great fcholars, who were then in their weekly waiting accord- ing to the cuftom in that country. Thefe gentlemen, after they had a while examined my fhape with much nicety, were of different opinions concerning me. They all agreed, that I could not be produced according to the regular laws of nature, becaufe I was not framed with a capacity of preferving my life either by fwiftnefs, or climbing of trees, or digging holes in the earth. They obferved by my teeth, which they viewed with great ex- actnefs, that I was a carnivorous animal; yet moft quadrupeds being an overmatch for me, and field-mice with fome others too nimble, they could not imagine how I fhould be able to fupport myfelf, unlefs I fed upon fnails and other infects, which they offered, by many learned arguments, to evince that I

could

)uld not poffibly do ˙. One of thefe virtuofi
emed to think that I might be an embryo,
: abortive birth. But this opinion was re-
ſted by the other two, who obſerved my
mbs to be perfect and finiſhed, and that I had
ved feveral years, as it was manifeſt from my
eard, the ſtumps whereof they plainly dif-
)vered through a magnifying-glaſs. They
/ould not allow me to be a dwarf, becauſe
ıy littleneſs was beyond all degrees of compa-
ſon; for the queen's favourite dwarf, the
nalleſt ever known in that kingdom, was near
hirty feet high. After much debate they
oncluded unanimouſly, that I was only *relplum*
:alcatb, which is interpreted literally *lufus na-*
uræ; a determination exactly agreeable to the
nodern philoſophy of *Europe*, whoſe profeſſors
liſdaining the old evaſion of *occult cauſes*,
vhereby the followers of *Ariſtotle* endeavoured
n vain to diſguiſe their ignorance, have in-
·ented this wonderful ſolution of all difficul-
ies, to the unſpeakable advancement of hu-
nan knowledge.

After this deciſive concluſion I entreated to
)e heard a word or two. I applied myſelf to
he king, and aſſured his majeſty that I came
·rom a country, which abounded with ſeveral
nillions of both ſexes and of my own ſtature;

* By this reaſoning the au-hor probably intended to ridi-ule the pride of thoſe philoſo-)hers, who have thought fit to ırraign the wiſdom of provi-lence in the creation and go-vernment of the world; whoſe cavils are ſpecious, like thoſe of the *Brobdingnagian* ſages, only in proportion to the ignorance of thoſe to whom they are pro-poſed.

where

where the animals, trees, and houfes were all
in proportion, and where by confequence I
might be as able to defend myfelf, and to find
fuftenance, as any of his majefty's fubjects
could do here; which I took for a full anfwer to thofe gentlemens arguments. To this
they only replied with a fmile of contempt,
faying, that the farmer had inftructed me very
well in my leffon[a]. The king, who had a
much better underftanding, difmiffing his learned men, fent for the farmer, who by good fortune was not yet gone out of town : having
therefore firft examined him privately, and
then confronted him with me and the young
girl, his majefty began to think that what we
told him might poffibly be true. He defired
the queen to order that a particular care fhould
be taken of me, and was of opinion, that
Glumdalclitch fhould ftill continue in her office
of tending me, becaufe he obferved we had a
great affection for each other. A convenient
apartment was provided for her at court; fhe
had a fort of governefs appointed to take care
of her education, a maid to drefs her, and
two other fervants for menial offices; but the
care of me was wholly appropriated to herfelf.
The queen commanded her own cabinet-
maker to contrive a box, that might ferve
me for a bed-chamber, after the model that
Glumdalclitch and I fhould agree upon. This

---

[a] This fatire is levelled againft
all, who reject thofe facts for
which they cannot perfectly account, notwithftanding the abfurdity of rejecting the teftimony
by which they are fupported.

man

man was a moft ingenious artift, and according to my directions in three weeks finifhed for me a wooden chamber of fixteen feet fquare, and twelve high, with fafh-windows, a door, and two clofets, like a *London* bed-chamber. The board, that made the cieling, was to be lifted up and down by two hinges to put in a bed ready furnifhed by her majefty's upholfterer, which *Glumdalclitch* took out every day to air, made it with her own hands, and letting it down at night, locked up the roof over me. A nice workman, who was famous for little curiofities, undertook to make me two chairs, with backs and frames, of a fubftance not unlike ivory, and two tables, with a cabinet to put my things in. The room was quilted on all fides, as well as the floor and the cieling, to prevent any accident from the carelefnefs of thofe who carried me, and to break the force of a jolt when I went in a coach. I defired a lock for my door to prevent rats and mice from coming in: the fmith, after feveral attempts, made the fmalleft that ever was feen among them, for I have known a larger at the gate of a gentleman's houfe in *England.* I made a fhift to keep the key in a pocket of my own, fearing *Glumdalclitch* might lofe it. The queen likewife ordered the thinneft filks that could be gotten to make me cloaths, not much thicker than an *Englifh* blanket, very cumberfome, till I was accuftomed to them. They were after the fafhion of the kingdom, partly refembling the *perfian*, and partly the *chinefe*, and are a very grave and decent habit.

The queen became fo fond of my company, that fhe could not dine without me. I had a table placed upon the fame at which her majefty eat, juft at her left elbow, and a chair to fit on. *Glumdalclitch* ftood on a ftool on the floor near my table to affift and take care of me. I had an entire fett of filver difhes and plates and other neceffaries, which in proportion to thofe of the queen, were not much bigger than what I have feen in a *London* toyfhop, for the furniture of a baby-houfe : thefe my little nurfe kept in her pocket in a filver box, and gave me at meals as I wanted them, always cleaning them herfelf. No perfon dined with the queen but the two princeffes royal, the elder fixteen years old, and the younger at that time thirteen and a month. Her majefty ufed to put a bit of meat upon one of my difhes, out of which I carved for myfelf; and her diverfion was to fee me eat in miniature. For the queen (who had indeed but a weak ftomach) took up, at one mouthful, as much as a dozen *Englifh* farmers could eat at a meal, which to me was for fome time a very naufeous fight[a]. She would craunch the wing of a lark,

[a] Among other dreadful and difgufting images which cuftom has render-d familiar are thofe which arife from eating animal food : he who has ever turned with abhorrence from the fkeleton of a beaft which has been picked whole by birds or vermin, muft confefs that habit only could have enabled him to endure the fight of the mangled bones and flefh of a dead carcafs which every day cover his table : and he who reflects on the

ark, bones and all, between her teeth, al-
ough it were nine times as large as that of a
ll grown turkey; and put a bit of bread in
r mouth, as big as two twelve-penny loaves.
ie drank out of a golden cup, above a hog-
ead at a draught. Her knives were twice as
ig as a scythe, set strait upon the handle.
he spoons, forks, and other instruments, were
· in the same proportion. I remember when
umdalclitch carried me out of curiosity to see
me of the tables at court, where ten or a
zen of these enormous knives and forks
ere lifted up together, I thought I had never
l then beheld so terrible a sight.

It is the custom, that every *Wednesday*
rhich, as I have before observed, is their
bbath) the king and queen, with the royal
ue of both sexes, dine together in the a-
irtment of his majesty, to whom I was now
:come a great favourite; and at these times
y little chair and table were placed at his left
ind before one of the salt-cellars. This
ince took a pleasure in conversing with me,
iquiring into the manners, religion, laws,
overnment, and learning of *Europe*; wherein
gave him the best account I was able. His
oprehension was so clear, and his judgment
) exact, that he made very wise reflections

e number of lives that have
en sacrificed to sustain his
vn, should enquire by what
e account has been ballanced,
id whether his life is become
oportionably of more value by
the exercise of virtue and piety,
by the superior happiness which
he has communicated to reasonable beings, and by the glory
which his intellect has ascribed
to God.

and obfervations upon all I faid. But I confefs,
that after I had been a little too copious in
talking of my own beloved country, of our
trade, and wars by fea and land, of our fchifms
in religion, and parties in the ftate; the prejudices of his education prevailed fo far, that
he could not forbear taking me up in his right
hand, and ftroaking me gently with the other,
after an hearty fit of laughing, afked me, whether I was a *whig* or *tory?* Then turning to
his firft minifter, who waited behind him with
a white ftaff near as tall as the main-maft of
the *royal-fovereign*, he obferved how contemptible a thing was human grandeur, which
could be mimicked by fuch diminutive infects
as I: and yet, fays he, I dare engage, thefe
creatures have their titles and diftinction of
honour, they contrive little nefts and burrows,
that they call houfes and cities; they make a
figure in drefs and equipage; they love, they
fight, they difpute, they cheat, they betray.
And thus he continued on, while my colour
came and went feveral times with indignation
to hear our noble country, the miftrefs of arts
and arms, the fcourge of *France*, the arbitrefs
of *Europe*, the feat of virtue, piety, honour
and truth, the pride and envy of the world, fo
contemptuoufly treated.

But as I was not in a condition to refent injuries, fo upon mature thoughts I began to
doubt whether I was injured or no. For, after
having been accuftomed feveral months to the
fight and converfe of this people, and obferved
every

ry object upon which I caſt mine eyes to
of proportionable magnitude, the horror I
. at firſt conceived from their bulk and aſ-
t, was ſo far worn off, that if I had then
eld a company of *Engliſh* lords and ladies
:heir finery, and birth-day cloaths, acting
ir ſeveral parts in the moſt courtly manner
ſtrutting, and bowing, and prating; to ſay
truth, I ſhould have been ſtrongly tempted
.augh as much at them, as the king and
grandees did at me. Neither indeed could
ırbear ſmiling at myſelf, when the queen
l to place me upon her hand towards a
ſing-glaſs, by which both our perſons ap-
red before me in full view together; and
ſe could nothing be more ridiculous than
comparifon: ſo that I really began to ima-
ſ myſelf dwindled many degrees below my
ıl ſize.

Nothing angered and mortified me ſo much
he queen's dwarf, who being of the loweſt
ure that was ever in that country (for I
ly think he was not full thirty feet high)
ame ſo inſolent at ſeeing a creature ſo much
eath him, that he would always affect to
gger and look big as he paſſed by me in the
en's anti-chamber, while I was ſtanding on
ıe table talking with the lords or ladies of
court, and he ſeldom failed of a ſmart
'd or two upon my littleneſs; againſt which
ould only revenge myſelf by calling him
ther, challenging him to wreſtle, and ſuch
ırtees as are uſual in the mouths of *court*

K 3   *pages.*

pages. One day, at dinner, this malicious little cubb was so nettled with something I had said to him, that, raising himself upon the frame of her majesty's chair, he took me up by the middle, as I was sitting down, not thinking any harm, and let me drop into a large silver bowl of cream, and then ran away as fast as he could. I fell over head and ears, and, if I had not been a good swimmer, it might have gone very hard with me; for *Glumdalclitch* in that instant happened to be at the other end of the room, and the queen was in such a fright, that she wanted presence of mind to assist me. But my little nurse ran to my relief, and took me out, after I had swallowed above a quart of cream. I was put to bed; however I received no other damage than the loss of a suit of cloaths, which was utterly spoiled. The dwarf was soundly whipped, and as a farther punishment forced to drink up the bowl of cream, into which he had thrown me; neither was he ever restored to favour: for soon after the queen bestowed him on a lady of high quality, so that I saw him no more, to my very great satisfaction; for I could not tell to what extremity such a malicious urchin might have carried his resentment.

He had before served me a scurvy trick, which set the queen a laughing, although at the same time she was heartily vexed, and would have immediately cashiered him, if I had not been so generous as to intercede. Her majesty had taken a marrow-bone upon her plate,

plate, and, after knocking out the marrow, placed the bone again in the difh erect, as it ftood before; the dwarf watching his opportunity, while *Glumdalclitch* was gone to the fide-board, mounted the ltool that fhe ftood on to take care of me at meals, took me up in both hands, and fqueefing my legs together, wedged them into the marrow-bone above my waift, where I ftuck for fome time, and made a very ridiculous figure. I believe it was near a minute before any one knew what was become of me; for I thought it below, me to cry out. But, as princes feldom get their meat hot, my legs were not fcalded, only my ftockings and breeches in a fad condition. The dwarf, at my entreaty, had no other punifh- ment than a found whipping.

I was frequently rallied by the queen upon account of my fearfulnefs; and fhe ufed to afk me, whether the people of my country were as great cowards as myfelf? The occafion was this: the kingdom is much peftered with flies in fummer; and thefe odious infects, each of them as big as a *Dunftable* lark, hardly gave me any reft while I fat at dinner with their continual humming and buzzing about mine ears. They would fometimes alight upon my victuals, and leave their loathfome excrement or fpawn behind, which to me was very vifible, though not to the natives of that country, whofe large optics were not fo acute as mine in viewing fmaller objects. Sometimes they would fix upon my nofe or forehead,

K 4 where

where they ftung me to the quick, fmelling very offenfively; and I could eafily trace that vifcous matter, which, our naturalifts tell us, enables thofe creatures to walk with their feet upwards upon a cieling. I had much ado to defend myfelf againft thefe deteftable animals, and could not forbear ftarting when they came on my face. It was the common practice of the dwarf to catch a number of thefe infects in his hand, as fchool-boys do among us, and let them out fuddenly under my nofe, on purpofe to frighten me, and divert the queen. My remedy was to cut them in pieces with my knife, as they flew in the air, wherein my dexterity was much admired.

I remember, one morning, when *Glumdal- clitch* had fet me in my box upon a window, as fhe ufually did in fair days to give me air (for I durft not venture to let the box be hung on a nail out of the window, as we do with cages in *England*) after I had lifted up one of my fafhes, and fat down at my table to eat a piece of fweet cake for my breakfaft, a- bove twenty wafps, allured by the fmell, came flying into the room, humming louder than the drones of as many bag-pipes. Some of them feized my cake, and carried it piece- meal away; others flew about my head and face, confounding me with the noife, and put-- ting me in the utmoft terror of their ftings. However, I had the courage to rife and draw my hanger, and attack them in the air. I dif- patched four of them, but the reft got away,
and

and I prefently fhut my window. Thefe infects were as large as partridges; I took out
their ftings, found them an inch and a half
long, and as fharp as needles. I carefully
preferved them all, and having fince fhewn
them with fome other curiofities in feveral
parts of *Europe*, upon my return to *England*,
I gave three of them to *Grefham College*, and
kept the fourth for myfelf.

C H A P. IV.

*The country defcribed. A propofal for correcting
modern maps. The king's palace, and fome account of the metropolis. The author's way of
travelling. The chief temple defcribed.*

I Now intend to give the reader a fhort defcription of this country, as far as I travelled in it, which was not above two thoufand
miles round *Lorbrulgrud*, the metropolis. For
the queen, whom I always attended, never
went farther when fhe accompanied the king
in his progreffes, and there ftaid till his majefty returned from viewing his frontiers. The
whole extent of this prince's dominions reach-
eth about fix thoufand miles in length, and
from three to five in breadth. From whence
I cannot but conclude, that our geographers of
Europe are in a great error, by fuppofing nothing but fea between *Japan* and *California*;
for it was ever my opinion, that there muft be
a balance of earth to counterpoife the great
con-

continent of *Tartary*; and therefore they ought to correct their maps and charts by joining this vaft tract of land to the north-weft parts of *America*, wherein I fhall be ready to lend them my affiftance.

The kingdom is a peninfula, terminated to the north-eaft by a ridge of mountains thirty miles high, which are altogether impaffable by reafon of the volcanoes upon the tops: neither do the moft learned know what fort of mortals inhabit beyond thofe mountains, or whether they be inhabited at all. On the three other fides it is bounded by the ocean. There is not one fea-port in the whole kingdom, and thofe parts of the coafts into which the rivers iffue are fo full of pointed rocks, and the fea generally fo rough, that there is no venturing with the fmalleft of their boats; fo that thefe people are wholly excluded from any commerce with the reft of the world. But the large rivers are full of veffels, and abound with excellent fifh, for they feldom get any from the fea, becaufe the fea-fifh are of the fame fize with thofe in *Europe*, and confequently not worth catching; whereby it is manifeft, that nature in the production of plants and animals of fo extraordinary a bulk is wholly confined to this continent, of which I leave the reafons to be determined by philofophers. However, now and then they take a whale that happens to be dafhed againft the rocks, which the common people feed on heartily. Thefe whales I have known fo large that

that a man could hardly carry one upon his shoulders; and sometimes for curiosity they are brought in hampers to *Lorbrulgrud:* I saw one of them in a dish at the king's table, which passed for a rarity, but I did not observe he was fond of it; for I think indeed the bigness disgusted him, although I have seen one somewhat larger in *Greenland.*

The country is well inhabited, for it contains fifty-one cities, near an hundred walled towns, and a great number of villages. To satisfy my curious reader, it may be sufficient to describe *Lorbrulgrud.* This city stands upon almost two equal parts on each side the river that passes through. It contains above eighty thousand houses, and about six hundred thousand inhabitants. It is in length three *glomglungs* (which make about fifty-four *Eng-lish* miles) and two and a half in breadth, as I measured it myself in the royal map made by the king's order, which was laid on the ground on purpose for me, and extended an hundred feet; I paced the diameter and circumference several times bare foot, and, computing by the scale, measured it pretty exactly.

The king's palace is no regular edifice, but an heap of building about seven miles round: the chief rooms are generally two hundred and forty feet high, and broad and long in proportion. A coach was allowed to *Glumdalclitch* and me, wherein her governess frequently took her out to see the town, or go among the

shops;

fhops; and I was always of the party, carried in my box; although the girl at my own de-fire would often take me out, and hold me in her hand, that I might more conveniently view the houfes and the people, as we paffed along the ftreets. I reckoned our coach to be about a fquare of *Weftminfter-hall*, but not altogether fo high: however, I cannot be very exact. One day the governefs ordered our coachman to ftop at feveral fhops, where the beggars, watching their opportunity, crouded to the fides of the coach, and gave me the moft hor-rible fpectacles that ever an *european* eye be-held. There was a woman with a cancer in her breaft, fwelled to a monftrous fize, full of holes, in two or three of which I could have eafily crept, and covered my whole body. There was a fellow with a wen in his neck larger than five wool-packs, and another with a couple of wooden legs, each about twenty feet high. But the moft hateful fight of all was the lice crawling on their cloaths. I could fee diftinctly the limbs of thefe vermin with my naked eye, much better than thofe of an *european* loufe through a microfcope, and their fnouts with which they rooted like fwine. They were the firft I had ever beheld, and I fhould have been curious enough to diffect one of them, if I had had proper inftruments (which I unluckily left behind me in the fhip) although indeed the fight was fo naufeous, that it perfectly turned my ftomach.

Befide

Beside the large box in which I was usually carried, the queen ordered a smaller one to be made for me of about twelve feet square and ten high for the convenience of travelling, because the other was somewhat too large for *Glumdalclitch*'s lap, and cumbersome in the coach; it was made by the same artist, whom I directed in the whole contrivance. This travelling closet was an exact square with a window in the middle of three of the squares, and each window was latticed with iron wire on the outside to prevent accidents in long journies. On the fourth side, which had no window, two strong staples were fixed, through which the person that carried me, when I had a mind to be on horseback, put a leathern belt, and buckled it about his waist. This was always the office of some grave trusty servant in whom I could confide, whether I attended the king and queen in their progresses, or were disposed to see the gardens, or pay a visit to some great lady or minister of state in the court, when *Glumdalclitch* happened to be out of order: for I soon began to be known and esteemed among the greatest officers, I suppose more upon account of their majesty's favour than any merit of my own. In journies, when I was weary of the coach, a servant on horseback would buckle on my box, and place it upon a cushion before him; and there I had a full prospect of the country on three sides from my three windows. I had in this closet a field-bed and a hammock hung

3   from

from the cieling, two chairs and a table, neatly fcrewed to the floor, to prevent being toffed
about by the agitation of the horfe or the coach.
And having been long ufed to fea-voyages,
thofe motions, although fometimes very violent, did not much difcompofe me.

Whenever I had a mind to fee the town, it
was always in my travelling-clofet, which
Glumdalclitch held in her lap in a kind of open
fedan, after the fafhion of the country, borne
by four men, and attended by two others in
the queen's livery. The people, who had often
heard of me, were very curious to croud about
the fedan, and the girl was complaifant enough
to make the bearers ftop, and to take me in
her hand that I might be more conveniently
feen.

I was very defirous to fee the chief temple,
and particularly the tower belonging to it,
which is reckoned the higheft in the kingdom.
Accordingly one day my nurfe carried me thither, but I may truly fay I came back difappointed; for the heighth is not above three
thoufand feet, reckoning from the ground to
the higheft pinnacle top; which, allowing for
the difference between the fize of thofe people
and us in *Europe*, is no great matter for admiration, nor at all equal in proportion (if I
rightly remember) to *Salifbury* fteeple. But,
not to detract from a nation to which during
my life I fhall acknowledge myfelf extremely
obliged, it muft be allowed that whatever this
famous tower wants in heighth is amply made

up

up in beauty and ftrength. For the walls are near an hundred feet thick, built of hewn ftone, whereof each is about forty feet fquare, and adorned on all fides with ftatues of gods and emperors cut in marble larger than the life, placed in their feveral niches. I meafured a little finger which had fallen down from one of thefe ftatues, and lay unperceived among fome rubbifh, and found it exactly four feet and an inch in length. *Glumdalclitch* wrapped it up in her handkerchief; and carried it home in her pocket to keep among other trinkets, of which the girl was very fond, as children at her age ufually are.

The king's kitchen is indeed a noble build-ing, vaulted at top, and about fix hundred feet high. The great oven is not fo wide by ten paces as the cupola at St. *Paul's*: for I mea-fured the latter on purpofe after my return. But if I fhould defcribe the kitchen-grate, the prodigious pots and kettles, the joints of meat turning on the fpits, with many other particu-lars, perhaps I fhould be hardly believed; at leaft a fevere critic would be apt to think I en-larged a little, as travellers are often fufpected to do. To avoid which cenfure, I fear I have run too much into the other extream; and that if this treatife fhould happen to be tranf-lated into the language of *Brobdingnag*, (which is the general name of that kingdom) and tranfmitted thither, the king and his people would have reafon to complain, that I had

done

done them an injury by a falfe and diminutive reprefentation.

His majefty feldom keeps above fix hundred horfes in his ftables: they are generally from fifty-four to fixty feet high. But, when he goes abroad on folemn days, he is attended for ftate by a militia guard of five hundred horfe, which indeed I thought was the moft fplendid fight that could be ever beheld, till I faw part of his army in battalia, whereof I fhall find another occafion to fpeak.

C H A P. V.

Several adventures that happened to the author. The execution of a criminal. The author fhews his fkill in navigation.

I Should have lived happy enough in that country, if my littlenefs had not expofed me to feveral ridiculous and troublefome acci-dents: fome of which I fhall venture to relate. *Glumdalclitch* often carried me into the gardens of the court in my fmaller box, and would fometimes take me out of it, and hold me in her hand, or fet me down to walk. I remem-ber, before the dwarf left the queen, he fol-lowed us one day into thofe gardens, and my nurfe having fet me down, he and I being clofe together, near fome dwarf apple-trees, I muft need fhew my wit by a filly allufion between him and the trees, which happens to hold in their language as it doth in ours. Whereupon, the

the malicious rogue watching his opportunity, when I was walking under one of them, fhook it directly over my head, by which a dozen apples, each of them near as large as a *Briftol* barrel, came tumbling about my ears; one of them hit me on the back as I chanced to ftoop, and knocked me down flat on my face; but I received no other hurt, and the dwarf was pardoned at my defire, becaufe I had given the provocation.

Another day *Glumdalclitch* left me on a fmooth grafs-plot to divert myfelf, while fhe walked at fome diftance with her governefs. In the mean time there fuddenly fell fuch a violent fhower of hail, that I was immediately by the force of it ftruck to the ground: and when I was down, the hail-ftones gave me fuch cruel bangs all over the body, as if I had been pelted with tennis-balls; however, I made a fhift to creep on all four, and fhelter myfelf by lying flat on my face on the lee-fide of a border of lemon-thyme, but fo bruifed from head to foot, that I could not go abroad in ten days. Neither is this at all to be wondered at, becaufe nature in that country obferving the fame proportion through all her operations, a hail-ftone is near eighteen hundred times as large as one in *Europe*, which I can affert upon experience, having been fo curious to weigh and meafure them.

But a more dangerous accident happened to to me in the fame garden, when my little nurfe believing fhe had put me in a fecure place, which I often entreated her to do, that I might enjoy my own thoughts, and having left my box at home to avoid the trouble of carrying it, went to another part of the garden with her governess, and some ladies of her acquaintance.   While she was absent, and out of hearing, a small white spaniel belonging to one of the chief gardeners, having got by accident into the garden, happened to range near the place where I lay: the dog, following the scent, came directly up, and taking me in his mouth ran strait to his master, wagging his tail, and set me gently on the ground.   By good fortune he had been so well taught, that I was carried between his teeth without the least hurt, or even tearing my cloaths. But the poor gardener who knew me well, and had a great kindness for me, was in a terrible fright: he gently took me up in both his hands, and asked me how I did; but I was so amazed and out of breath, that I could not speak a word.   In a few minutes I came to myself, and he carried me safe to my little nurse, who by this time had returned to the place where she left me, and was in cruel agonies when I did not appear, nor answer when she called: she severely reprimanded the gardener on account of his dog.   But the thing was hushed up, and never known at court; for the girl was afraid of the queen's anger, and truly, as to myself, I thought it would not be for my reputation that such a story should go about.

This

This accident abfolutely determined *Glum-dalclitch* never to truft me abroad for the future out of her fight. I had been long afraid of this refolution, and therefore concealed from her fome little unlucky adventures that happened in thofe times when I was left by myfelf. Once a kite, hovering over the garden, made a ftoop at me, and if I had not refolutely drawn my hanger, and run under a thick efpalier, he would have certainly carried me away in his talons. Another time walking to the top of a frefh mole-hill, I fell to my neck in the hole, through which that animal had caft up the earth, and coined fome lye, not worth remembering, to excufe myfelf for fpoiling my cloaths. I likewife broke my right fhin againft the fhell of a fnail, which I happened to ftumble over, as I was walking alone; and thinking on poor *England*.

I cannot tell, whether I were more pleafed or mortified to obferve in thofe folitary walks, that the fmaller birds did not appear to be at all afraid of me, but would hop about within a yard's diftance, looking for worms and other food with as much indifference and fecurity, as if no creature at all were near them. I remember, a thrufh had the confidence to fnatch out of my hand, with his bill, a piece of cake that *Glumdalclitch* had juft given me for my breakfaft. When I attempted to catch any of thefe birds, they would boldly turn againft me, endeavouring to pick my fingers, which I durft not venture within their reach;

and

and then they would hop back unconcerned to hunt for worms or fnails, as they did before. But one day I took a thick cudgel, and threw it with all my ftrength fo luckily at a linnet, that I knocked him down, and feizing him by the neck with both my hands, ran with him in triumph to my nurfe. However, the bird, who had only been ftunned, recovering himfelf, gave me fo many boxes with his wings on both fides of my head and body, though I held him at arms length, and was out of the reach of his claws, that I was twenty times thinking to let him go. But I was foon relieved by one of our fervants, who wrung off the bird's neck, and I had him next day for dinner by the queen's command. This linnet, as near as I can remember, feemed to be fomewhat larger than an *England* fwan.

The maids of honour often invited *Glumdalclitch* to their apartments, and defired fhe would bring me along with her, on purpofe to have the pleafure of feeing and touching me. They would often ftrip me naked from top to toe, and lay me at full length in their bofoms; wherewith I was much difgufted; becaufe, to fay the truth, a very offenfive fmell came from their fkins; which I do not mention, or intend, to the difadvantage of thofe excellent ladies, for whom I have all manner of refpect; but I conceive that my fenfe was more acute in proportion to my littlenefs, and that thofe illuftrious perfons were no more difagreeable to their lovers, or to each other,

than

than people of the fame quality are with us in *England*. And, after all, I found their natural fmell was much more fupportable, than when they ufed perfumes, under which I immediately' fwooned away. I cannot forget, that an intimate friend of mine in *Lilliput* took the freedom in a warm day, when I had ufed a good deal of exercife, to complain of a ftrong fmell about me, although I am as little faulty that way, as moft of my fex : but I fuppofe his faculty of fmelling was as nice with regard to me, as mine was to that of this people. Upon this point I cannot forbear doing juftice to the queen my miftrefs, and *Glumdalclitch* my nurfe, whofe perfons were as fweet as thofe of any lady in *England*.

That which gave me moft uneafinefs among thefe maids of honour (when my nurfe carried me to vifit them) was to fee them ufe me without any manner of ceremony, like a creature who had no fort of confequence : for they would ftrip themfelves to the fkin, and put put on their fmocks in my prefence, while I was placed on their toylet, directly before their naked bodies, which I am fure to me was very far from being a tempting fight, or from giving me any other emotions, than thofe of horror and difguft. Their fkins appeared fo coarfe and uneven, fo varioufly coloured, when I faw them near, with a mole here and there as broad as a trencher, and hairs hanging from it thicker than packthreads, to fay nothing farther concerning the

L 3   reft

reſt of their perſons. Neither did they at all
ſcruple, while I was by, to diſcharge what they
had drank, to the quantity of at leaſt two hogſheads in a veſſel that held above three tuns.
The handſomeſt amongſt theſe maids of honour,
a pleaſant frolicſome girl of ſixteen, would ſometimes ſet me aſtride upon one of her nipples,
with many other tricks, wherein the reader
will excuſe me for not being over particular.
But I was ſo much diſpleaſed, that I entreated
Glumdalclitch to contrive ſome excuſe for not
ſeeing that young lady any more.

One day a young gentleman, who was ne-
phew to my nurſe's governeſs, came and preſſed them both to ſee an execution. It was of
a man, who had murdered one of that gentleman's intimate acquaintance. *Glumdalclitch*
was prevailed on to be of the company, very
much againſt her inclination, for ſhe was naturally tender-hearted : and as for myſelf, although I abhorred ſuch kind of ſpectacles, yet
my curioſity tempted me to ſee ſomething,
that I thought muſt be extraordinary. The
malefactor was fixed in a chair upon a ſcaffold erected for that purpoſe, and his head cut
off at one blow with a ſword of about forty
feet long. The veins and arteries ſpouted up
ſuch a prodigious quantity of blood, and ſo
high in the air, that the great *Jett d'eau* at
Verſailles was not equal for the time it laſted;
and the head, when it fell on the ſcaffold
floor, gave ſuch a bounce as made me ſtart, although I were at leaſt half an *engliſh* mile diſtant.
The

The queen, who often ufed to hear me talk of my fea-voyages, and took all occafions to divert me when I was melancholy, afked me whether I underftood how to handle a fail or an oar, and whether a little exercife of row-ing might not be convenient for my health? I anfwered, that I underftood both very well: for although my proper employment had been to be furgeon or doctor to the fhip, yet often upon a pinch I was forced to work like a com-mon mariner. But I could not fee how this could be done in their country, where the fmalleft wherry was equal to a firft-rate man of war among us, and fuch a boat as I could manage would never live in any of their ri-vers. Her majefty faid, if I would contrive a boat, her own joiner fhould make it, and fhe would provide a place for me to fail in. The fellow was an ingenious workman, and by my inftructions in ten days finifhed a pleafure-boat, with all its tackling, able conveniently to hold eight *europeans*. When it was finifh-ed, the queen was fo delighted, that fhe ran with it in her lap to the king, who ordered it to be put in a ciftern full of water with me in it by way of trial; where I could not manage my two fculls, or little oars, for want of room. But the queen had before contrived another project. She ordered the joiner to make a wooden trough of three hundred feet long, fifty broad, and eight deep; which be-ing well pitched, to prevent leaking, was placed on the floor along the wall in an outer

room

room of the palace. It had a cock near the bottom to let out the water, when it began to grow ſtale; and two ſervants could eaſily fill it in half an hour. Here I often uſed to row for my own diverſion, as well as that of the queen and her ladies, who thought themſelves well entertained with my ſkill and agility. Sometimes I would put up my ſail, and then my buſineſs was only to ſteer, while the ladies gave me a gale with their fans; and, when they were weary, ſome of their pages would blow my ſail forward with their breath, while I ſhewed my art by ſteering ſtarboard or larboard, as I pleaſed. When I had done, *Glumdalclitch* always carried back my boat into her cloſet, and hung it on a nail to dry.

In this exerciſe I once met an accident, which had like to have coſt me my life: for, one of the pages having put my boat into the trough, the governeſs, who attended *Glumdalclitch*, very officiouſly lifted me up to place me in the boat, but I happened to ſlip through her fingers, and ſhould infallibly have fallen down forty feet upon the floor, if, by the luckieſt chance in the world, I had not been ſtopped by a corking-pin that ſtuck in the good gentlewoman's ſtomacher; the head of the pin paſſed between my ſhirt and the waiſtband of my breeches, and thus I was held by the middle in the air, till *Glumdalclitch* ran to my relief.

Another time, one of the ſervants, whoſe office it was to fill my trough every third day

with

with frefh water, was fo carelefs to let a huge
frog (not perceiving it) flip out of his pail.
The frog lay concealed till I was put into my
boat, but then feeing a refting-place climbed
up, and made it lean fo much on one fide,
that I was forced to balance it with all my
weight on the other to prevent overturning.
When the frog was got in, it hopped at once
half the length of the boat, and then over my
head, backwards and forwards, daubing my
face and clothes with its odious flime. The
largenefs of its features made it appear the
moft deformed animal that can be conceived.
However, I defired *Glumdalclitch* to let me
deal with it alone. I banged it a good while
with one of my fculls, and at laft forced it to
leap out of the boat.

But the greateft danger I ever underwent in
that kingdom, was from a monkey, who belonged to one of the clerks of the kitchen.
Glumdalclitch had locked me up in her clofet,
while fhe went fomewhere upon bufinefs, or
a vifit. The weather being very warm, the
clofet-window was left open, as well as the
windows and the door of my bigger box, in
which I ufually lived, becaufe of its largenefs
and conveniency. As I fat quietly meditating
at my table, I heard fomething bounce in at
the clofet-window, and fkip about from one
fide to the other: whereat although I were
much alarmed, yet I ventured to look out, but
not ftirring from my feat; and then I faw this
frolicfome animal frifking and leaping up and
down,

down, till at laft he came to my box, which
he feemed to view with great pleafure and curiofity, peeping in at the door and every window. I retreated to the farther corner of my
room, or box, but the monkey looking in at
every fide put me into fuch a fright, that I
wanted prefence of mind to conceal myfelf
under the bed, as I might eafily have done.
After fome time fpent in peeping, grinning,
and chattering, he at laft efpied me, and
reaching one of his paws in at the door, as a
cat does when fhe plays with a moufe, although I often fhifted place to avoid him, he
at length feized the lappet of my coat (which,
being made of that country filk, was very
thick and ftrong) and dragged me out. He
took me up in his right fore-foot, and held
me as a nurfe does a child fhe is going to
fuckle, juft as I have feen the fame fort of creature do with a kitten in *Europe*: and when I offered to ftruggle, he fqueefed me fo hard, that
I thought it more prudent to fubmit. I have
good reafon to believe, that he took me for a
young one of his own fpecies, by his often
ftroaking my face very gently with his other
paw. In thefe diverfions he was interrupted
by a noife at the clofet-door, as if fome body
were opening it; whereupon he fuddenly leaped up to the window, at which he had come
in, and thence upon the leads and gutters,
walking upon three legs, and holding me in
the fourth, till he clambered up to a roof that
was next to ours. I heard *Glumdalclitch* give
                                    a fhriek

a fhriek at the moment he was carrying me out. The poor girl was almoft diftracted: that quarter of the palace was all in an uproar; the fervants ran for ladders; the monkey was feen by hundreds in the court, fitting upon the ridge of a building, holding me like a baby in one of his fore-paws, and feeding me with the other, by cramming into my mouth fome victuals he had fqueefed out of the bag on one fide of his chaps, and patting me when I would not eat; whereat many of the rabble below could not forbear laughing; neither do I think they juftly ought to be blamed, for without queftion the fight was ridiculous enough to every body but myfelf. Some of the people threw up ftones, hoping to drive the monkey down; but this was ftrictly forbidden, or elfe very probably my brains had been dafhed out.

The ladders were now applied, and mounted by feveral men, which the monkey obferving, and finding himfelf almoft encompaffed; not being able to make fpeed enough with his three legs, let me drop on a ridge tyle, and made his efcape. Here I fat for fome time, five hundred yards from the ground, expecting every moment to be blown down by the wind, or to fall by my own giddinefs, and come tumbling over and over from the ridge to the eves: but an honeft lad, one of my nurfe's footmen, climbed up, and putting me into his breeches-pocket brought me down fafe.

I was

I was almoſt choaked with the filthy ſtuff the monkey had crammed down my throat; but my dear little nurſe picked it out of my mouth with a ſmall needle, and then I fell a vomiting, which gave me great relief. Yet I was ſo weak, and bruiſed in the ſides with the ſqueezes given me by this odious animal, that I was forced to keep my bed a fortnight. The king, queen, and all the court, ſent every day to enquire after my health, and her majeſty made me ſeveral viſits during my ſickneſs. The monkey was killed, and an order made that no ſuch animal ſhould be kept about the palace.

When I attended the king after my recovery to return him thanks for his favours, he was pleaſed to rally me a good deal upon this adventure. He aſked me, what my thoughts and ſpeculations were while I lay in the monkey's paw; how I liked the victuals he gave me; his manner of feeding; and whether the freſh air on the roof had ſharpened my ſtomach. He deſired to know, what I would have done upon ſuch an occaſion in my own country. I told his majeſty, that in *Europe* we had no monkies, except ſuch as were brought for curioſities from other places, and ſo ſmall, that I could deal with a dozen of them together, if they preſumed to attack me. And as for that monſtrous animal with whom I was ſo lately engaged (it was indeed as large as an elephant) if my fears had ſuffered me to think ſo far as to make uſe of my hanger
(looking

(looking fiercely, and clapping my hand upon the hilt, as I fpoke) when he poked his paw into my chamber, perhaps I fhould have given him fuch a wound, as would have made him glad to withdraw it with more hafte than he put it in. This I delivered in a firm tone, like a perfon who was jealous left his courage fhould be called in queftion. However, my fpeech produced nothing elfe befides a loud laughter, which all the refpect due to his majefty from thofe about him could not make them contain. This made me reflect, how vain an attempt it is for a man to endeavour to do himfelf honour among thofe, who are out of all degree of equality or comparifon with him. And yet I have feen the moral of my own behaviour very frequent in *England* fince my return, where a little contemptible varlet, without the leaft title to birth, perfon, wit, or common fenfe, fhall prefume to look with importance, and put himfelf upon a foot with the greateft perfons of the kingdom.

I was every day furnifhing the court with fome ridiculous ftory ; and *Glumdalclitch*, although fhe loved me to excefs, yet was arch enough to inform the queen, whenever I committed any folly that fhe thought would be diverting to her majefty. The girl, who had been out of order, was carried by her governefs to take the air about an hour's diftance, or thirty miles from town. They alighted out of the coach near a fmall footpath

path in a field, and *Glumdalclitch* setting down
my travelling-box, I went out of it to walk.
There was a cow-dung in the path, and I
must need try my activity by attempting to
leap over it. I took a run, but unfortunately
jumped short, and found myself just in the
middle up to my knees. I waded through
with some difficulty, and one of the footmen
wiped me as clean as he could with his handkerchief; for I was filthily bemired, and my
nurse confined me to my box, till we returned home; where the queen was soon informed
of what had passed, and the footmen spread it
about the court ; so that all the mirth for some
days was at my expence.

C H A P. VI*.

*Several contrivances of the author to please the
king and queen.   He shews his skill in music.
The king enquires into the state of England,
which the author relates to him.   The king's
observations thereon.*

I Used to attend the king's levee once or twice
a week, and had often seen him under the
barber's hand, which indeed was at first very
terrible

---

* In this chapter he gives an
account of the political state of
Europe. ORRERY.

This is a mistake of the noble commentator, for *Gulliver*
has here given a political account of no country but *England*: it is however a mistake
to which any commentator would
have been liable, who had read
little more than the titles or
contents of the chapters, into
which

terrible to behold : for the razor was almoſt twice as long as an ordinary ſcythe. His majeſty, according to the cuſtom of the country, was only ſhaved twice a week. I once prevailed on the barber to give me ſome of the ſuds or lather, out of which I picked forty or fifty of the ſtrongeſt ſtumps of hair. I then took a piece of fine wood, and cut it like the back of a comb, making ſeveral holes in it at equal diſtance with as ſmall a needle as I could get from *Glumdalclitch*. I fixed in the ſtumps ſo artificially, ſcraping and ſloping them with my knife towards the points, that I made a very tolerable comb; which was a ſeaſonable ſupply, my own being ſo much broken in the teeth, that it was almoſt uſeleſs : neither did I know any artiſt in that country ſo nice and exact, as would undertake to make me another.

And this puts me in mind of an amuſement, wherein I ſpent many of my leiſure hours. I deſired the queen's woman to ſave for me the combings of her majeſty's hair, whereof in time I got a good quantity, and conſulting with my friend the cabinet-maker, who had received general orders to do little jobbs for me, I directed him to make two chair-frames, no larger than thoſe I had in my box, and then to bore little holes with a fine awl round thoſe parts where I deſigned the backs and ſeats;

which this work is divided ; for the word *Europe* has in ſome *Engliſh*, and all the *Iriſh*, edi- tions been printed in the title of this chapter inſtead of *England*.

through

through thefe holes I wove the ftrongeft hairs
I could pick out, juft after the manner of
cane-chairs in *England*. When they were
finifhed, I made a present of them to her majefty, who kept them in her cabinet, and ufed
to fhew them for curiofities, as indeed they
were the wonder of every one that beheld
them. The queen would have had me fit
upon one of thefe chairs, but I abfolutely refufed to obey her, protefting I would rather
die a thoufand deaths than place a difhonour-
able part of my body on thofe precious hairs,
that once adorned her majefty's head. Of
thefe hairs (as I had always a mechanical genius) I likewife made a neat little purfe about
five feet long, with her majefty's name decy-
phered in gold letters, which I gave to *Glumdalclitch* by the queen's confent. To fay the
truth, it was more for fhew than ufe, being
not of ftrength to bear the weight of the larger coins, and therefore fhe kept nothing in
it but fome little toys that girls are fond of.

The king, who delighted in mufic, had frequent concerts at court, to which I was fometimes carried, and fet in my box on a table to
hear them : but the noife was fo great, that I
could hardly diftinguifh the tunes. I am confident, that all the drums and trumpets of a
royal army, beating and founding together juft
at your ears, could not equal it. My practice
was to have my box removed from the place
where the performers fat, as far as I could,
then to fhut the doors and windows of it,
                                        and

and draw the window-curtains; after which I found their music not difagreeable.

I had learned in my youth to play a little upon the fpinet. *Glumdalclitch* kept one in her chamber, and a mafter attended twice a week to teach her: I called it a fpinet, becaufe it fomewhat refembled that inftrument, and was played upon in the fame manner. A fancy came into my head, that I would entertain the king and queen with an *Englifh* tune upon this inftrument. But this appeared extremely difficult: for the fpinet was near fixty feet long, each key being almoft a foot wide, fo that with my arms extended I could not reach to above five keys, and to prefs them down required a good fmart ftroak with my fift, which would be too great a labour, and to no purpofe. The method I contrived was this: I prepared two round fticks about the bignefs of common cudgels; they were thicker at one end than the other, and I covered the thicker ends with a piece of a moufe's fkin, that by rapping on them, I might neither damage the tops of the keys, nor interrupt the found. Before the fpinet a bench was placed about four feet below the keys, and I was put upon the bench. I ran fideling upon it that way and this, as faft as I could, banging the proper keys with my two fticks, and made a fhift to play a jigg to the great fatisfaction of both their majefties: but it was the moft violent exercife I ever underwent, and yet I could not ftrike above fixteen

keys,

keys, nor confequently play the bafs and tre-
ble together, as other artifts do ; which was a
great difadvantage to my performance.

The king, who, as I before obferved, was
a prince of excellent underftanding, would frequently order that I fhould be brought in my
box, and fet upon the table in his clofet : he
would then command me to bring one of my
chairs out of the box, and fit down within
three yards diftance upon the top of the cabinet, which brought me almoft to a level with
his face. In this manner I had feveral converfations with him. I one day took the freedom
to tell his majefty, that the contempt he difcovered towards *Europe*, and the reft of the
world, did not feem anfwerable to thofe excellent qualities of mind, that he was mafter
of : that reafon did not extend itfelf with the
bulk of the body; on the contrary, we obferved in our country, that the talleft perfons
were ufually leaft provided with it : that a-
mong other animals, bees and ants had the reputation of more induftry, art, and fagacity,
than many of the larger kinds; and that, as
inconfiderable as he took me to be, I hoped
I might live to do his majefty fome fignal fervice. The king heard me with attention, and
began to conceive a much better opinion of
me than he had ever before. He defired I
would give him as exact an account of the government of *England*, as I poffibly could;
becaufe, as fond as princes commonly are of
their own cuftoms (for fo he conjectured of

other

other monarchs by my former difcourfes) he fhould be glad to hear of any thing that might deferve imitation.

Imagine with thyfelf, courteous reader, how often I then wifhed for the tongue of *Demoftbenes* or *Cicero*, that might have enabled me to celebrate the praife of my own dear native country in a ftyle equal to its merits and felicity.

I began my difcourfe by informing his majefty, that our dominions confifted of two iflands, which compofed three mighty kingdoms under one fovereign, befides our plantations in *America*. I dwelt long upon the fertility of our foil, and the temperature of our climate. I then fpoke at large upon the conftitution of an *Englifh* parliament, partly made up of an illuftrious body called the houfe of peers, perfons of the nobleft blood, and of the moft antient and ample patrimonies. I defcribed that extraordinary care always taken of their education in arts and arms to qualify them for being counfellors both to the king and kingdom; to have a fhare in the legiflature; to be members of the higheft court of judicature, from whence there could be no appeal; and to be champions always ready for the defence of their prince and country, by their valour, conduct, and fidelity. That thefe were the ornament and bulwark of the kingdom, worthy followers of their moft renowned anceftors, whofe honour had been the reward of their virtue, from which their pofte-

rity

rity were never once known to degenerate. To thefe were joined feveral holy perfons as part of that affembly under the title of bifhops, whofe peculiar bufinefs it is to take care of religion, and of thofe who inftruct the people therein. Thefe were fearched and fought out through the whole nation, by the prince and his wifeft counfellors among fuch of the priefthood, as were moft defervedly diftinguifhed by the fanctity of their lives, and the depth of their erudition, who were indeed the fpiritual fathers of the clergy and the people.

That the other part of the parliament confifted of an affembly called the houfe of commons, who were all principal gentlemen, *freely* picked and culled out by the people themfelves, for their great abilities and love of their country, to reprefent the wifdom of the whole nation. And that thefe two bodies made up the moft auguft affembly in *Europe*, to whom in conjunction with the prince the whole legiflature is committed.

I then defcended to the courts of juftice, over which the judges, thofe venerable fages and interpreters of the law, prefided for determining the difputed rights and properties of men, as well as for the punifhment of vice, and protection of innocence. I mentioned the prudent management of our treafury, the valour and atchievements of our forces by fea and land. I computed the number of our people, by reckoning how many millions there

might

might be of each religious fect, or political party among us. I did not omit even our sports and pastimes, or any other particular, which I thought might redound to the honour of my country. And I finished all with a brief historical account of affairs and events in *England* for about an hundred years past.

This conversation was not ended under five audiences, each of several hours; and the king heard the whole with great attention, frequently taking notes of what I spoke, as well as memorandums of what questions he intended to ask me.

When I had put an end to these long discourses, his majesty in a sixth audience consulting his notes proposed many doubts, queries and objections upon every article. He asked what methods were used to cultivate the minds and bodies of our young nobility, and in what kind of business they commonly spent the first and teachable part of their lives. What course was taken to supply that assembly when any noble family became extinct. What qualifications were necessary in those, who are to be created new lords: whether the humour of the prince, a sum of money to a court lady or a prime minister, or a design of strengthening a party opposite to the public interest, ever happened to be motives in those advancements. What share of knowledge these lords had in the laws of their country, and how they came by it, so as to enable them to decide the properties of their fellow-subjects in

the

the laſt reſort. Whether they were always ſo free from avarice, partialities, or want, that a bribe or ſome other ſiniſter view could have no place among them. Whether thoſe holy lords I ſpoke of were always promoted to that rank upon account of their knowledge in religious matters, and the ſanctity of their lives; had never been compliers with the times while they were common prieſts, or ſlaviſh proſtitute chaplains to ſome nobleman, whoſe opinions they continued ſervilely to follow after they were admitted into that aſſembly.

He then deſired to know, what arts were practiſed in electing thoſe whom I called commoners : whether a ſtranger with a ſtrong purſe might not influence the vulgar voters to chuſe him before their own landlord, or the moſt conſiderable gentleman in the neighbourhood. How it came to paſs, that people were ſo violently bent upon getting into this aſſembly, which I allowed to be a great trouble and expence, often to the ruin of their families, without any ſalary or penſion : becauſe this appeared ſuch an exalted ſtrain of virtue and public ſpirit, that his majeſty ſeemed to doubt it might poſſibly not be always ſincere : and he deſired to know, whether ſuch zealous gentlemen could have any views of refunding themſelves for the charges and trouble they were at, by ſacrificing the public good to the deſigns of a weak and vicious prince in conjunction with a corrupted miniſtry. He multiplied his queſtions, and ſifted me thoroughly upon

upon every part of this head, propofing num-
berlefs enquiries and objections, which I think
it not prudent or convenient to repeat.

Upon what I faid in relation to our courts
of juftice, his majefty defired to be fatisfied in
feveral points : and this I was the better able
to do, having been formerly almoft ruined by
a long fuit in chancery, which was decreed for
me with cofts.   He afked what time was ufually fpent in determining between right and
wrong, and what degree of expence.   Whether advocates and orators had liberty to plead
in caufes manifeftly known to be unjuft, vexatious, or oppreffive.   Whether party in religion or politics were obferved to be of any
weight in the fcale of juftice.   Whether thofe
pleading orators were perfons educated in the
general knowledge of equity, or only in pro-
vincial, national, and other local cuftoms.
Whether they or their judges had any part in
penning thofe laws, which they affumed the
liberty of interpreting and gloffing upon at
their pleafure.   Whether they had ever at different times pleaded for and againft the fame
caufe, and cited precedents to prove contrary
opinions.   Whether they were a rich or a poor
corporation. Whether they received any pecuni-
ary reward for pleading or delivering their opinions.   And particularly, whether they were
ever admitted as members in the lower fenate.

He fell next upon the management of our
treafury; and faid, he thought my memory
had failed me, becaufe I computed our taxes

at about five or fix millions a year, and, when I came to mention the iffues, he found they fometimes amounted to more than double; for the notes he had taken were very particular in this point, becaufe he hoped, as he told me, that the knowledge of our conduct might be ufeful to him, and he could not be deceived in his calculations. But, if what I told him were true, he was ftill at a lofs how a kingdom could run out of its eftate like a private perfon. He afked me, who were our creditors; and where we found money to pay them. He wondered to hear me talk of fuch chargeable and expenfive wars; that certainly we muft be a quarrelfome people, or live among very bad neighbours, and that our generals muft needs be richer than our kings. He afked what bufinefs we had out of our own iflands, unlefs upon the fcore of trade or treaty, or to defend the coafts with our fleet. Above all, he was amazed to hear me talk of a mercenary ftanding army in the midft of peace, and among a free people. He faid, if we were governed by our own confent in the perfons of our reprefentatives, he could not imagine of whom we were afraid, or againft whom we were to fight; and would hear my opinion, whether a private man's houfe might not better be defended by himfelf, his children, and family, than by half a dozen rafcals picked up at a venture in the ftreets for fmall wages, who might get an hundred times more by cutting their throats,

He

He laughed at my odd kind of arithmetic (as he was pleafed to call it) in reckoning the numbers of our people by a computation drawn from the feveral fects among us in religion and politics. He faid, he knew no reafon why thofe, who entertain opinions prejudicial to the public, fhould be obliged to change, or fhould not be obliged to conceal them. And as it was tyranny in any government to require the firft, fo it was weaknefs not to enforce the fecond : for a man may be allowed to keep poifons in his clofet, but not to vend them about for cordials.

He obferved, that among the diverfions of our nobility and gentry I had mentioned gaming : he defired to know at what age this entertainment was ufually taken up, and when it was laid down; how much of their time it employed : whether it ever went fo high as to affect their fortunes: whether mean vicious people by their dexterity in that art might not arrive at great riches, and fometimes keep our very nobles in dependance, as well as habituate them to vile companions, wholly take them from the improvement of their minds, and force them by the loffes they received to learn and practife that infamous dexterity upon o-thers.

He was perfectly aftonifhed with the hiftorical account I gave him of our affairs during the laft century, protefting it was only a heap of confpiracies, rebellions, murders, maffacres, revolutions, banifhments, the very worft effects

that

that avarice, faction, hypocrify, perfidioufnefs, cruelty, rage, madnefs, hatred, envy, luft, malice, and ambition could produce.

His majefty in another audience was at the pains to recapitulate the fum of all I had fpoken; compared the queftions he made with the anfwers I had given; then taking me into his hands, and ftroaking me gently, delivered himfelf in thefe words, which I fhall never forget, nor the manner he fpoke them in : My little friend *Grildrig*, you have made a moft admirable panegyric upon your country; you have clearly proved, that ignorance, idlenefs, and vice are the proper ingredients for quali- fying a legiflator; that laws are beft explained, interpreted, and applied by thofe whofe inte- reft and abilities lie in perverting, confound- ing, and eluding them. I obferve among you fome lines of an inftitution, which in its ori- ginal might have been tolerable, but thefe half erafed, and the reft wholly blurred and blotted by corruptions. It doth not appear from all you have faid, how any one perfection is required to- ward the procurement of any one ftation among you; much lefs, that men are ennobled on ac- count of their virtue, that priefts are advanc- ed for their piety or learning, foldiers for their conduct or valour, judges for their integrity, fenators for the love of their country, or coun- fellors for their wifdom. As for yourfelf, con- tinued the king, who have fpent the greateft part of your life in travelling, I am well dif- pofed to hope you may hitherto have efcaped

many

many vices of your country. But by what I have gathered from your own relation, and the anſwers I have with much pains wringed and extorted from you, I cannot but conclude the bulk of your natives to be the moſt pernicious race of little odious vermin, that nature ever ſuffered to crawl upon the ſurface of the earth.

C H A P. VII.

The author's love of his country. He makes a proposal of much advantage to the king, which is rejected. The king's great ignorance in politics. The learning of that country very imperfect and confined. The laws, and military affairs, and parties in the ſtate.

N OTHING but an extreme love of truth could have hindered me from concealing this part of my ſtory. It was in vain to diſcover my reſentments, which were always turned into ridicule ; and I was forced to reſt with patience, while my noble and beloved country was ſo injuriouſly treated. I am as heartily ſorry as any of my readers can poſſibly be, that ſuch an occaſion was given : but this prince happened to be ſo curious and inquiſitive upon every particular, that it could not conſiſt either with gratitude or good manners to refuſe giving him what ſatisfaction I was able. Yet thus much I may be allowed to ſay in my own vindication, That I artfully eluded many of his queſtions, and gave to
every

every point a more favourable turn by many degrees than the ftrictneſs of truth would allow. For I have always borne that laudable partiality to my own country, which *Dionyſius Halicarnaſſenſis* with ſo much juſtice recommends to an hiſtorian : I would hide the frailties and deformities of my political mother, and place her virtues and beauties in the moſt advantageous light. This was my ſincere endeavour in thoſe many diſcourſes I had with that monarch, although it unfortunately failed of ſucceſs.

But great allowances ſhould be given to a king, who lives wholly ſecluded from the reſt of the world, and muſt therefore be altogether unacquainted with the manners and cuſtoms that moſt prevail in other nations : the want of which knowledge will ever produce many *prejudices*, and a certain *narrowneſs of thinking*, from which we and the politer countries of *Europe* are wholly exempted. And it would be hard indeed, if ſo remote a prince's notions of virtue and vice were to be offered as a ſtandard for all mankind.

To confirm what I have now ſaid, and further to ſhew the miſerable effects of a *confined education*, I ſhall here inſert a paſſage which will hardly obtain belief. In hopes to ingratiate myſelf farther into his majeſty's favour, I told him of an invention diſcovered between three and four hundred years ago to make a certain powder, into an heap of which the ſmalleſt ſpark of fire falling would kindle the
whole

whole in a moment, although it were as big as a mountain, and make it all fly up in the air together, with a noife and agitation greater than thunder. That a proper quantity of this powder rammed into an hollow tube of brafs or iron, according to its bignefs, would drive a ball of iron or lead with fuch violence and fpeed, as nothing was able to fuftain its force. That the largeft balls thus difcharged would not only deftroy whole ranks of an army at once, but batter the ftrongeft walls to the ground, fink down fhips, with a thoufand men in each, to the bottom of the fea ; and, when linked together by a chain, would cut through mafts and rigging, divide hundreds of bodies in the middle, and lay all wafte before them. That we often put this powder into large hollow balls of iron, and difcharged them by an engine into fome city we were befieging, which would rip up the pavements, tear the houfes to pieces, burft and throw fplinters on every fide, dafhing out the brains of all who came near. That I knew the ingredients very well, which were cheap and common ; I underftood the manner of compounding them, and could direct his workmen how to make thofe tubes of a fize proportionable to all other things in his majefty's kingdom, and the largeft need not be above an hundred feet long; twenty or thirty of which tubes, charged with the proper quantity of powder and balls, would batter down the walls of the ftrongeft town in his dominions in a few hours, or deftroy the whole
metropolis,

metropolis, if ever it fhould pretend to difpute his abfolute commands. .This I humbly
offered to his majefty,. as a fmall tribute of
acknowledgment in return of fo many marks
that I had received of his royal favour and protection.

The king was ftruck with horror at the defcription I had given of thofe terrible engines,
and the propofal I had made. He was amazed, how fo impotent and groveling an infect
as I (thefe were his expreffions) could entertain fuch inhuman ideas, and in fo familiar a
manner, as to appear wholly unmoved at all
the fcenes of blood and defolation, which I
had painted as the common effects of thofe
deftructive machines, whereof he faid fome
evil genius, enemy to mankind, muft have
been the firft contriver. As for himfelf, he protefted, that although few things delighted him
fo much as new difcoveries in art or in nature, yet he would rather lofe half his kingdom, than be privy to fuch a fecret, which he
commanded me, as I valued my life, never to
mention any more.

A ftrange effect of *narrow principles* and *fhort
views !* that a prince poffeffed of every quality
which procures veneration, love, and efteem;
of ftrong parts, great wifdom, and profound
learning, endowed with admirable talents for
government, and almoft adored by his fubjects,
fhould from a *nice unneceffary fcruple*, whereof
in *Europe* we can have no conception, let flip
an opportunity put into his hands, that would
have

have made him abfolute mafter of the lives,
the liberties, and the fortunes of his people.
Neither do I fay this with the leaft intention
to detract from the many virtues of that excellent king, whofe character I am fenfible will
on this account be very much leffened in the
opinion of an *Englifh* reader: but I take this
defect among them to have rifen from their ignorance, by not having hitherto reduced politics into a fcience, as the more acute wits of
Europe have done. For I remember very well
in a difcourfe one day with the king, when I
happened to fay there were feveral thoufand
books among us written upon the *art of government*, it gave him (directly contrary to my
intention) a very mean opinion of our under-
ftandings. He profeffed both to abominate
and defpife all *myftery, refinement*, and *intrigue*,
either in a prince or a minifter. He could not
tell what I meant by *fecrets of ftate*, where an
enemy, or fome rival nation, were not in the
cafe. He confined the knowledge of governing within very *narrow bounds*, to common
fenfe and reafon, to juftice and lenity, to the
fpeedy determination of civil and criminal
caufes; with fome other obvious topics, which
are not worth confidering. And he gave it for
his opinion, that whoever could make two ears
of corn, or two blades of grafs, to grow upon
a fpot of ground where only one grew before,
would deferve better of mankind, and do more
effential fervice to his country, than the whole
race of politicians put together.

The

The learning of this people is very defective, confisting only in morality, history, poetry, and mathematics, wherein they must be allowed to excel. But the last of these is wholly applied to what may be useful in life, to the improvement of agriculture, and all mechanical arts; so that among us it would be little esteemed. And as to ideas, entities, abstractions, and transcendentals, I could never drive the least conception into their heads.

No law of that country must exceed in words the number of letters in their alphabet, which confists only in two and twenty. But indeed few of them extend even to that length. They are expressed in the most plain and simple terms, wherein those people are not mercurial enough to discover above one interpretation: and to write a comment upon any law is a capital crime. As to the decision of civil causes, or proceedings against criminals, their precedents are so few, that they have little reason to boast of any extraordinary skill in either.

They have had the art of printing, as well as the *chinese*, time out of mind: but their libraries are not very large; for that of the king, which is reckoned the largest, doth not amount to above a thousand volumes placed in a gallery of twelve hundred feet long, from whence I had liberty to borrow what books I pleased. The queen's joiner had contrived in one of *Glumdalclitch*'s rooms a kind of wooden machine five and twenty feet high, formed

like

like a ftanding ladder, the fteps were each fifty
feet long : it was indeed a moveable pair of
ftairs, the loweft end placed at ten feet diftance from the wall of the chamber. The
book I had a mind to read was put up leaning againft the wall : I firft mounted to the
upper ftep of the ladder, and turning my face
towards the book, began at the top of the
page, and fo walking to the right and left a-
bout eight or ten paces, according to the
length of the lines, till I had gotten a little
below the level of mine eyes, and then defcending gradually till I came to the bottom :
after which I mounted again, and began the
other page in the fame manner, and fo turned
over the leaf, which I could eafily do with
both my hands, for it was as thick and ftiff as
a pafte-board, and in the largeft folios not a-
bove eighteen or twenty feet long.

Their ftyle is clear, mafculine, and fmooth,
but not florid ; for they avoid nothing more
than multiplying unneceffary words, or ufing
various expreffions. I have perufed many of
their books, efpecially thofe in hiftory and
morality. Among the reft, I was much diverted with a little old treatife, which always
lay in *Glumdalclitch's* bed-chamber, and belonged to her governefs, a grave elderly gentlewoman, who dealt in writings of morality
and devotion. The book treats of the weaknefs of human kind, and is in little efteem,
except among the women and the vulgar.
However, I was curious to fee what an author

of that country could fay upon fuch a fubject. This writer went through all the ufual topics of *european* moralifts, fhewing how diminutive, contemptible, and helplefs an animal was man in his own nature; how unable to defend himfelf from inclemencies of the air, or the fury of wild beafts : how much he was excelled by one creature in ftrength, by another in fpeed, by a third in forefight, by a fourth in induftry. He added, that nature was degenerated in thefe latter declining ages of the world, and could now produce only fmall abortive births, in comparifon of thofe in antient times. He faid, it was very reafonable to think, not only that the fpecies of men were originally much larger, but alfo that there muft have been giants in former ages; which, as it is afferted by hiftory and tradition, fo it hath been confirmed by huge bones and fkulls cafually dug up in feveral parts of the kingdom, far exceeding the common dwindled race of man in our days. He argued, that the very laws of nature abfolutely required we fhould have been made in the beginning of a fize more large and robuft, not fo liable to deftruction from every little accident of a tile falling from an houfe, or a ftone caft from the hand of a boy, or being drowned in a little brook. From this way of reafoning, the author drew feveral moral applications ufeful in the conduct of life, but needlefs here to repeat. For my own part, I could not avoid reflecting how univerfally this talent was fpread, of drawing

5

lectures in morality, or indeed rather matter of difcontent and repining, from the quarrels we raife with nature. And I believe, upon a ftrict enquiry thofe quarrels might be fhewn as ill-grounded among us, as they are among that people *.

As to their military affairs, they boaft that the king's army confifts of an hundred and feventy-fix thoufand foot, and thirty-two thoufand horfe: if that may be called an army, which is made up of tradefmen in the feveral cities, and farmers in the country, whofe commanders are only the nobility and gentry without pay or reward. They are indeed perfect enough in their exercifes, and under very good difcipline, wherein I faw no great merit; for how fhould it be otherwife, where every farmer is under the command of his own landlord, and every citizen under that of the principal men in his own city, chofen after the manner of *Venice* by *ballot?*

I have often feen the militia of *Lorbrulgrud* drawn out to exercife in a great field near the the city of twenty miles fquare. They were in all not above twenty-five thoufand foot, and fix thoufand horfe; but it was impoffible for me to compute their number, confidering the fpace of ground they took up. A cavalier, mount-

* The author's zeal to juftify providence has before been remarked; and thefe quarrels with nature, or in other words with God, could not have been more forcibly reproved than by fhewing, that the complaints upon which they are founded would be equally fpecious among beings of fuch aftonifhing fuperiority of ftature and ftrength.

ed

ed on a large fteed, might be about ninety feet high. I have feen this whole body of horfe, upon a word of command, draw their fwords at once, and brandifh them in the air. Imagination can figure nothing fo grand, fo furprifing, and fo aftonifhing ! it looked as if ten thoufand flafhes of lightning were darting at the fame time from every quarter of the fky.

I was curious to know how this prince, to whofe dominions there is no acceſs from any other country, came to think of armies, or to teach his people the practice of military difcipline. But I was foon informed both by converfation and reading their hiftories : for in the courfe of many ages they have been troubled with the fame difeafe to which the whole race of mankind is fubject ; the nobility often contending for power, the people for liberty, and the king for abfolute dominion. All which, however happily tempered by the laws of that kingdom, have been fometimes violated by each of the three parties, and have more than once occafioned civil wars, the laft whereof was happily put an end to by this prince's grandfather in a general compofition ; and the militia, then fettled with common confent, hath been ever fince kept in the ftricteft duty.

CHAP.

C H A P. VIII.

The king and queen make a progress to the fron-
tiers. The author attends them. The man-
ner in which he leaves the country very parti-
cularly related. He returns to England.

I Had always a ſtrong impulſe, that I ſhould
ſome time recover my liberty, though it
was impoſſible to conjecture by what means,
or to form any project with the leaſt hope of
ſucceeding. The ſhip in which I ſailed was
the firſt ever known to be driven within ſight
of that coaſt, and the king had given ſtrict
orders, that if at any time another appeared,
it ſhould be taken aſhore, and with all its crew
and paſſengers brought in a tumbril to *Lor-*
brulgrud. He was ſtrongly bent to get me a
woman of my own ſize, by whom I might
propagate the breed : but I think I ſhould rather have died, than undergone the diſgrace of
leaving a poſterity to be kept in cages like tame
canary birds, and perhaps in time ſold about
the kingdom to perſons of quality for curioſities. I was indeed treated with much kindneſs : I was the favourite of a great king and
queen, and the delight of the whole court ;
but it was upon ſuch a foot, as ill became the
dignity of human kind. I could never forget
thoſe domeſtic pledges I had left behind me.
I wanted to be among people with whom I
could converſe upon even terms, and walk a-

bout

bout the ftreets and fields, without being afraid
of being trod to death like a frog, or a young
puppy. But my deliverance came fooner than
I expected, and in a manner not very common: the whole ftory and circumftances of
which I fhall faithfully relate.

I had now been two years in this country;
and about the beginning of the third *Glumdalclitch* and I attended the king and queen in a
progrefs to the *fouth* coaft of the kingdom.
I was carried as ufual in my travelling-box,
which, as I have already defcribed, was a very
convenient clofet of twelve feet wide. And I
had ordered a hammock to be fixed by filken
ropes from the four corners at the top, to break
the jolts, when a fervant carried me before him
on horfeback, as I fometimes defired, and
would often fleep in my hammock while we
were upon the road. On the roof of my clofet, not directly over the middle of the hammock, I ordered the joiner to cut out a hole
of a foot fquare, to give me air in hot weather, as I flept; which hole I fhut at pleafure
with a board, that drew backwards and forwards through a groove.

When we came to our journey's end, the
king thought proper to pafs a few days at a
palace he hath near *Flanflafnic*, a city within
eighteen *Englifh* miles of the fea-fide. *Glumdalclitch* and I were much fatigued: I had gotten a fmall cold, but the poor girl was fo ill
as to be confined to her chamber. I longed
to fee the ocean, which muft be the only
scene

scene of my escape, if ever it should happen.
I pretended to be worse than I really was, and
desired leave to take the fresh air of the sea
with a page, whom I was very fond of, and
who had sometimes been trusted with me. I
shall never forget with what unwillingness *Glum-*
dalclitch consented, nor the strict charge she gave
the page to be careful of me, bursting at the
same time into a flood of tears, as if she had
some foreboding of what was to happen. The
boy took me out in my box about half an
hour's walk from the palace towards the rocks
on the sea-shore. I ordered him to set me
down, and lifting up one of my sashes cast
many a wistful melancholy look towards
the sea. I found myself not very well, and
told the page that I had a mind to take a nap
in my hammock, which I hoped would do
me good. I got in, and the boy shut the
window close down to keep out the cold. I
soon fell asleep, and all I can conjecture is,
that while I slept the page, thinking no danger could happen, went among the rocks to
look for birds eggs, having before observed
him from my window searching about, and
picking up one or two in the clefts. Be that
as it will, I found myself suddenly awaked
with a violent pull upon the ring, which was
fastened at the top of my box for the conveniency of carriage. I felt my box raised very
high in the air, and then borne forward with
prodigious speed. The first jolt had like to
have shaken me out of my hammock, but af-

terwards

terwards the motion was eafy enough. I called out feveral times, as loud as I could raife
my voice, but all to no purpofe. I looked
towards my windows, and could fee nothing
but the clouds and fky. I heard a noife juft
over my head like the clapping of wings, and
then began to perceive the woful condition I
was in, that fome eagle had got the ring of
my box in his beak with an intent to let it
fall on a rock like a tortoife in a fhell, and
then pick out my body, and devour it : for
the fagacity and fmell of this bird enabled him
to difcover his quarry at a great diftance,
though better concealed than I could be within a two-inch board.

In a little time I obferved the noife and flut-
ter of wings to encreafe very faft, and my box
was toffed up and down like a fign in a windy
day. I heard feveral bangs or buffets, as I
thought, given to the eagle (for fuch I am
certain it muft have been that held the ring of
my box in his beak) and then all on a fudden felt myfelf falling perpendicularly down
for above a minute, but with fuch incredible
fwiftnefs that I almoft loft my breath. My
fall was ftopped by a terrible fquafh, that
founded louder to my ears than the cataract of *Niagara* [a] ; after which I was quite

---

[a] *Niagara* is a fettlement of the *French* in *North-America*, and the cataract is produced by the fall of a conflux of water (form- ed of the four vaft lakes of *Ca-* *nada*) from a rocky precipice, the perpendicular height of which is one hundred and thirty-feven feet ; and it is faid to have been heard fifteen leagues.

in

in the dark for another minute, and then my box began to rife fo high that I could fee light from the tops of the windows. I now perceived I was fallen into the fea. My box, by the weight of my body, the goods that were in, and the broad plates of iron fixed for ftrength at the four corners of the top and bottom, floated about five feet deep in water. I did then, and do now fuppofe, that the eagle which flew away with my box was purfued by two or three others, and forced to let me drop while he defended himfelf a-gainft the reft, who hoped to fhare in the prey. The plates of iron faftened at the bottom of the box (for thofe were the ftrongeft) preferved the balance while it fell, and hindered it from being broken on the furface of the water. Every joint of it was well grooved ; and the door did not move on hinges, but up and down like a fafh, which kept my clofet fo tight that very little water came in. I got with much difficulty out of my hammock, having firft ventured to draw back the flip-board on the roof already mentioned, contrived on purpofe to let in air, for want of which I found myfelf almoft ftifled.

How often did I then wifh myfelf with my dear *Glumdalclitch*, from whom one fingle hour had fo far divided me ! And I may fay with truth, that in the midft of my own misfortunes I could not forbear lamenting my poor nurfe, the grief fhe would fuffer for my lofs, the difpleafure of the queen, and the ruin of her fortune.

fortune. Perhaps many travellers have not been under greater difficulties and diftrefs than I was at this juncture, expecting every moment to fee my box dafhed to pieces, or at leaft overfet by the firft violent blaft or rifing wave. A breach in one fingle pane of glafs would have been immediate death : nor could any thing have preferved the windows but the ftrong lattice-wires placed on the outfide againft accidents in travelling. I faw the water ooze in at feveral crannies, although the leaks were not confiderable, and I endeavoured to ftop them as well as I could. I was not able to lift up the roof of my clofet, which otherwife I certainly fhould have done, and fat on the top of it, where I might at leaft preferve myfelf fome hours longer than by being fhut up (as I may call it) in the hold. Or if I efcaped thefe dangers for a day or two, what could I expect but a miferable death of cold and hunger ? I was four hours under thefe circumftances, expecting, and indeed wifhing every moment to be my laft.

I have already told the reader, that there were two ftrong ftaples fixed upon that fide of my box which had no window, and into which the fervant who ufed to carry me on horfeback would put a leathern belt, and buckle it about his waift. Being in this difconfolate ftate, I heard or at leaft thought I heard fome kind of grating noife on that fide of my box where the ftaples were fixed, and foon after I began to fancy, that the box was pulled or
towed

towed along in the fea; for I now and then felt a fort of tugging, which made the waves rife near the tops of my windows, leaving me almoft in the dark. This gave me fome faint hopes of relief; although I was not able to imagine how it could be brought about. I ventured to unfcrew one of my chairs, which were always faftened to the floor; and having made a hard fhift to fcrew it down again directly under the flipping-board that I had lately opened, I mounted on the chair, and putting my mouth as near as I could to the hole, I called for help in a loud voice, and in all the languages I underftood. I then faftened my handkerchief to a ftick I ufually carried, and thrufting it up the hole waved it feveral times in the air, that if any boat or fhip were near, the feamen might conjecture fome unhappy mortal to be fhut up in the box.

I found no effect from all I could do, but plainly perceived my clofet to be moved along; and in the fpace of an hour, or better, that fide of the box where the ftaples were, and had no window, ftruck againft fomething that was hard. I apprehended it to be a rock, and found myfelf toffed more than ever. I plainly heard a noife upon the cover of my clofet like that of a cable, and the grating of it as it paffed through the ring. I then found myfelf hoifted up by degrees at leaft three feet higher than I was before. Whereupon I again thruft up my ftick and handkerchief, calling for help till I was almoft hoarfe. In

return

return to which, I heard a great fhout repeated three times, giving me fuch tranfports
of joy as are not to be conceived but by thofe
who feel them. I now heard a trampling
over my head, and fomebody calling through
the hole with a loud voice in the *Englifh*
tongue, If there be any body below, let them
fpeak. I anfwered, I was an *Englifhman*,
drawn by ill fortune into the greateft calamity
that ever any creature underwent, and begged
by all that was moving to be delivered out of
the dungeon I was in. The voice replied, I
was fafe, for my box was faftened to their
fhip; and the carpenter fhould immediately
come and faw a hole in the cover large enough
to pull me out. I anfwered, that was needlefs, and would take up too much time, for
there was no more to be done, but let one of
the crew put his finger into the ring, and take
the box out of the fea into the fhip, and fo
into the captain's cabbin ᵃ. Some of them
upon hearing me talk fo wildly thought I was
mad; others laughed; for indeed it never
came into my head that I was now got among
people of my own ftature and ftrength. The ᵃ
carpenter came, and in a few minutes fawed a

ᵃ There are feveral little in-
cidents which fhew the author
to have had a deep knowledge
of human nature; and I think
this is one. Although the principal advantages enumerated by
Gulliver in the beginning of
this chapter, of mingling again
among his countrymen, depended on their being of the fame
fize with himfelf, yet this is forgotten in his ardour to be delivered : and he is afterwards be-
trayed into the fame abfurdity
by his zeal to preferve his furniture,

paffage about four feet fquare, then let down a fmall ladder, upon which I mounted, and from thence was taken into the fhip in a very weak condition.

The failors were all in amazement, and afked me a thoufand queftions, which I had no inclination to anfwer. I was equally confounded at the fight of fo many pigmies, for fuch I took them to be, after having fo long accuftomed mine eyes to the monftrous objects I had left. But the captain, Mr. *Thomas Wilcocks*, an honeft worthy *Shropfhire* man, obferving I was ready to faint, took me into his cabbin, gave me a cordial to comfort me, and made me *turn in* upon his own bed, advifing me to take a little reft, of which I had great need. Before I went to fleep, I gave him to underftand that I had fome valuable furniture in my box too good to be loft; a fine hammock; an handfome field-bed, two chairs, a table, and a cabinet. That my clofet was hung on all fides, or rather quilted, with filk and cotton: that if he would let one of the crew bring my clofet into his cabbin, I would open it there before him, and fhew him my goods. The captain hearing me utter thefe abfurdities concluded I was raving: however (I fuppofe to pacify me) he promifed to give order as I defired, and going upon deck fent fome of his men down into my clofet, from whence (as I afterwards found) they drew up all my goods, and ftripped off the quilting; but the chairs, cabinet, and

bedftead,

bedstead, being screwed to the floor, were much damaged by the ignorance of the seamen, who tore them up by force. Then they knocked off some of the boards for the use of the ship, and when they had got all they had a mind for let the hull drop into the sea, which by reason of many breaches made in the bottom and sides sunk to rights. And indeed I was glad not to have been a spectator of the havock they made; because I am confident it would have sensibly touched me by bringing former passages into my mind, which I had rather forget.

I slept some hours, but perpetually disturbed with dreams of the place I had left, and the dangers I had escaped. However, upon waking I found myself much recovered. It was now about eight o'clock at night, and the captain ordered supper immediately, thinking I had already fasted too long. He entertained me with great kindness, observing me not to look wildly, or talk inconsistently; and, when we were left alone, desired I would give him a relation of my travels, and by what accident I came to be set adrift in that monstrous wooden chest. He said, that about twelve o'clock at noon, as he was looking through his glass, he spied it at a distance, and thought it was a sail, which he had a mind to make, being not much out of his course, in hopes of buying some bisket, his own beginning to fall short. That upon coming nearer, and finding his error, he sent out his long-boat to discover difcover what I was; that his men came back in a fright, fwearing they had feen a fwimming houfe.   That he laughed at their folly, and went himfelf in the boat, ordering his men to take a ftrong cable along with them. That the weather being calm he rowed round me feveral times, obferved my windows, and wire-lattices that defended them.   That he difcovered two ftaples upon one fide, which was all of boards without any paffage for light.   He then commanded his men to row up to that fide, and faftening a cable to one of the ftaples, ordered them to tow my cheft (as they called it) towards the fhip.   When it was there, he gave directions to faften another cable to the ring fixed in the cover, and to raife up my cheft with pullies, which all the failors were not able to do above two or three feet.   He faid, they faw my ftick and handkerchief thruft out of the hole, and concluded that fome unhappy man muft be fhut up in the cavity.   I afked, whether he or the crew had feen any prodigious birds in the air about the time he firft difcovered me? to which he anfwered, that, difcourfing this matter with the failors while I was afleep, one of them faid, he had *obferved* three eagles flying towards the *north*, but remarked nothing of their being larger than the ufual fize, which I fuppofe muft be imputed to the great heighth they were at; and he could not guefs the reafon of my queftion.   I then afked the captain, how far he reckoned we might be from land?

he

he said, by the best computation he could
make, we were at least an hundred leagues.
I assured him that he must be mistaken by almost half, for I had not left the country from
whence I came above two hours before I
dropt into the sea. Whereupon he began a-
gain to think that my brain was disturbed, of
which he gave me a hint, and advised me to
go to bed in a cabbin he had provided. I assured him I was well refreshed with his good
entertainment and company, and as much in
my senses as ever I was in my life. He then
grew serious, and desired to ask me freely,
whether I were not troubled in mind by the
consciousness of some enormous crime, for
which I was punished at the command of some
prince by exposing me in that chest, as great
criminals in other countries have been forced
to sea in a leaky vessel without provisions : for
although he should be sorry to have taken so
ill a man into his ship, yet he would engage
his word to set me safe a-shore in the first port
where we arrived. He added, that his suspi-
cions were much increased by some very absurd speeches I had delivered at first to his
sailors, and afterwards to himself, in relation
to my closet or chest, as well as by my odd
looks and behaviour while I was at supper.

I begged his patience to hear me tell my
story, which I faithfully did from the last time
I left *England* to the moment he first discovered me. And as truth always forceth its way
into rational minds, so this honest worthy gentleman,

tleman, who had fome tincture of learning,
and very good fenfe, was immediately convinced of my candour and veracity. But, farther to confirm all I had faid, I entreated him
to give order that my cabinet fhould be
brought, of which I had the key in my pocket, (for he had already informed me how the
feamen difpofed of my clofet). I opened it in
his own prefence, and fhewed him the fmall
collection of rarities I made in the country
from whence I had been fo ftrangely delivered.
There was the comb I had contrived out of
the ftumps of the king's beard, and another of the fame materials, but fixed into a
paring of her majefty's thumb-nail which ferved for the back. There was a collection of
needles and pins from a foot to half a yard
long; four wafp-ftings, like joiners tacks;
fome combings of the queen's hair; a gold
ring which one day fhe made me a prefent of
in a moft obliging manner, taking it from
her little finger, and throwing it over my head
like a collar. I defired the captain would
pleafe to accept this ring in return of his civilities; which he abfolutely refufed. I fhewed
him a corn that I had cut off with my own
hand from a maid of honour's toe; it was a-
bout the bignefs of a *Kentifh* pippin, and
grown fo hard, that, when I returned to *England*, I got it hollowed into a cup, and fet in
filver. Laftly, I defired him to fee the breeches I had then on, which were made of a
moufe's fkin.

I could force nothing on him but a footman's tooth, which I obferved him to examine with great curiofity, and found he had a fancy for it. He received it with abundance of thanks, more than fuch a trifle could deferve. It was drawn by an unfkilful furgeon in a miftake from one of *Glumdalclitch*'s men, who was afflicted with the tooth-ach, but it was as found as any in his head. I got it cleaned, and put it into my cabinet. It was about a foot long, and four inches in diameter.

The captain was very well fatisfied with this plain relation I had given him, and faid, he hoped, when we returned to *England*, I would oblige the world by putting it on paper, and making it public. My anfwer was, that I thought we were already over-ftocked with books of travels: that nothing could now pafs which was not extraordinary; wherein I doubted fome authors lefs confulted truth, than their own vanity, or intereft, or the diverfion of ignorant readers: that my ftory could contain little befides common events, without thofe ornamental defcriptions of ftrange plants, trees, birds, and other animals; or of the barbarous cuftoms and idolatry of favage people, with which moft writers abound. However, I thanked him for his good opinion, and promifed to take the matter into my thoughts.

He faid, he wondered at one thing very much, which was, to hear me fpeak fo loud, afking me whether the king or queen of that

country

)untry were thick of hearing. I told him,
was what I had been ufed to for above two
:ars paft ; and that I admired as much at the
)ices of him and his men, who feemed to me
ily to whifper, and yet I could hear them
ell enough. But, when I fpoke in that coun-
y, it was like a man talking in the ftreet to
1other looking out from the top of a ftee-
le, unlefs when I was placed on a table, or
eld in any perfon's hand. I told him, I had
kewife obferved another thing, that when I
rft got into the fhip, and the failors ftood all
)out me, I thought they were the moft little
)ntemptible creatures I had ever beheld. For
1deed, while I was in that prince's country, I
could never endure to look in a glafs, after
line eyes had been accuftomed to fuch prodi-
ious objects, becaufe the comparifon gave me
) defpicable a conceit of myfelf. The cap-
ain faid, that while we were at fupper, he
bferved me to look at every thing with a fort
f wonder, and that I often feemed hardly a-
lé to contain my laughter, which he knew not
'ell how to take, but imputed it to fome difor-
er in my brain. I anfwered, it was very true; and
wondered how I could forbear, when I faw
is difhes of the fize of a filver three-pence, a
:g of pork hardly a mouthful, a cup not fo
ig as a nut-fhell; and fo I went on, defcrib-
1g the reft of his houfhold-ftuff and provifions
fter the fame manner. For although the
ueen had ordered a little equipage of all things
eceffary for me, while I was in her fervice,

yet my ideas were wholly taken up with what I faw on every fide of me, and I winked at my own littlenefs, as people do at their own faults. The captain underftood my raillery very well, and merrily replied with the old *Englifh* proverb, that he doubted mine eyes were bigger than my belly, for he did not obferve my ftomach fo good although I had .fafted all day; and, continuing in his mirth, protefted he would have gladly given an hundred pounds to have feen my clofet in the eagle's bill, and afterwards in its fall from fo great a heighth into the fea; which would certainly have been a moft aftonifhing object, worthy to have the defcription of it tranfmitted to future ages: and the comparifon of *Phaeton* was fo obvious, that he could not forbear applying it, although I did not much admire the conceit.

The captain, having been at *Tonquin*, was in his return to *England* driven north-eaftward to the latitude of 44 degrees, and of longitude 143. But meeting a trade-wind two days after I came on board him, we failed fouthward a long time, and coafting *New-Holland*, kept our courfe weft-fouth-weft, and then fouth-fouth-weft, till we doubled the *Cape of Good-Hope*. Our voyage was very profperous, but I fhall not trouble the reader with a journal of it. The captain called in at one or two ports, and fent in his long-boat for provifions and frefh water, but I never went out of the fhip till we came into the *Downs*, which was on

the

the third day of *June*, 1706, about nine months after my efcape. I offered to leave my goods in fecurity for payment of my freight; but the captain protefted he would not receive one farthing. We took a kind leave of each o-ther, and I made him promife he would come to fee me at my houfe in *Redriff*. I hired a horfe and guide for five fhillings, which I bor-rowed of the captain.

As I was on the road, obferving the little-nefs of the houfes, the trees, the cattle, and the people, I began to think myfelf in *Lilli-put*. I was afraid of trampling on every tra-veller I met, and often called aloud to have them ftand out of the way, fo that I had like to have gotten one or two broken heads for my impertinence.

When I came to my own houfe, for which I was forced to enquire, one of the fervants opening the door, I bent down to go in (like a goofe under a gate) for fear of ftriking my head. My wife ran out to embrace me, but I ftooped lower than her knees, thinking fhe could otherwife never be able to reach my mouth. My daughter kneeled to afk me blef-fing, but I could not fee her till fhe arofe, hav-ing been fo long ufed to ftand with my head and eyes erect to above fixty feet; and then I went to take her up with one hand by the waift. I looked down upon the fervants, and one or two friends who were in the houfe, as if they had been pigmies, and I a giant. I told my wife fhe had been too thrifty, for I found fhe

O 3 had

had ftarved herfelf and her daughter to nothing. In fhort, I behaved myfelf fo unac-
countably, that they were all of the captain's
opinion when he firft faw me, and concluded I
had loft my wits. This I mention as an inftance of the great power of habit and prejudice.

In a little time, I and my family and friends
came to a right underftanding : but my wife
protefted I fhould never go. to fea any more;
although my evil deftiny fo ordered, that fhe
had not power to hinder me, as the reader may
know hereafter. In the mean time, I here
conclude the fecond part of my unfortunate
voyages [a].

---

[a] From the whole of thefe two voyages to *Lilliput* and *Brob-dingnag* arifes one general remark which, however obvious, has been overlooked by thofe who confider them as little more than the fport of a wanton ima-gination. When human actions are afcribed to pigmies and gi-ants, there are few that do not excite either contempt, difguft, or horror; to afcribe them there-fore to fuch beings was perhaps the moft probable method of en-gaging the mind to examine them with attention, and judge of them with impartiality, by fufpending the fafcination of ha-bit, and exhibiting familiar ob-jects in a new light. The ufe of the fable then is not lefs ap-parent than important and ex-tenfive ; and that this ufe was intended by the author can be doubted only by thofe who are difpofed to affirm, that order and regularity are the effects of chance.

A VOYAGE

Parts Unknown

Straits of

Land
of Jeſso

Company's
Land

Sea
of Corea

Laputa

Balnibarbi

Diſcover'd
A.D.1701

Japon

Luggnag

Glanguenſtald

Glubdubdrib

Urac
Timul

A
VOYAGE
TO
LAPUTA, BALNIBARBI, LUGG-NAGG, GLUBBDUBDRIB, and JAPAN.

CHAP. I.

The author sets out on his third voyage, is taken by pyrates. The malice of a Dutchman. *His arrival at an island. He is received into La-puta.*

I Had not been at home above ten days, when captain *William Robinson*, a *Cornish* man, commander of the *Hope-well*, a stout ship of three hundred tons, came to my house. I had formerly been surgeon of another ship, where he was master and a fourth part owner, in a voyage to the *Levant*; he had always treated me more like a brother, than an inferior officer, and hearing of my arrival. made me a visit, as I apprehended, only out of friendship, for nothing passed more than what is usual after long absences. But repeating his visits often, expressing his joy to find me in good health, asking whether I were now settled for life, adding, that he intended a voyage to the *East-Indies* in two months; at last he plainly invited me, though with some apologies, to be surgeon of the ship; that I should

have

have another furgeon under me, befides our two mates; that my falary fhould be double to the ufual pay; and that having experienced my knowledge in fea-affairs to be at leaft equal to his, he would enter into any engagement to follow my advice, as much as if I had fhared in the command.

He faid fo many other obliging things, and I knew him to be fo honeft a man, that I could not reject his propofal; the thirft I had of feeing the world, notwithftanding my paft misfortunes, continuing as violent as ever. The only difficulty that remained, was to perfuade my wife, whofe confent however I at laft obtained by the profpect of advantage fhe propofed to her children.

We fet out the 5th day of *Auguft*, 1706, and arrived at *Fort St. George* the 11th of *April*, 1707. We ftayed there three weeks to refrefh our crew, many of whom were fick. From thence we went to *Tonquin*, where the captain refolved to continue fome time, becaufe many of the goods he intended to buy were not ready, nor could he expect to be difpatched in feveral months. Therefore, in hopes to defray fome of the charges he muft be at, he bought a floop, loaded it with feveral forts of goods, wherewith the *Tonquinefe* ufually trade to the neighbouring iflands, and putting fourteen men on board, whereof three were of the country, he appointed me mafter of the floop, and gave me power to traffic, while he tranfacted his affairs at *Tonquin*.

We

We had not failed above three days, when, a great ftorm arifing, we were driven five days to the north-north-eaft, and then to the eaft; after which we had fair weather, but ftill with a pretty ftrong gale from the weft. Upon the tenth day we were chaced by two pyrates, who foon overtook us; for my floop was fo deep laden, that fhe failed very flow, neither were we in a condition to defend ourfelves.

We were boarded about the fame time by both the pyrates, who entered furioufly at the head of their men; but finding us all proftrate upon our faces (for fo I gave order) they pinioned us with ftrong ropes, and, fetting a guard upon us, went to fearch the floop.

I obferved among them a *Dutchman*, who feemed to be of fome authority, though he was not commander of either fhip. He knew us by our countenances to be *Englifhmen*, and jabbering to us in his own language, fwore we fhould be tied back to back, and thrown into the fea. I fpoke *Dutch* tolerably well; I told him who we were, and begged him in confideration of our being chriftians and proteftants, of neighbouring countries in ftrict alliance, that he would move the captains to take fome pity on us. This inflamed his rage, he repeated his threatenings, and turning to his companions, fpoke with great vehemence in the *Japanefe* language, as I fuppofe, often ufing the word *chriftianos*.

The

The largeſt of the two pyrate ſhips was commanded by a *Japaneſe* captain, who ſpoke a little *Dutch*, but very imperfectly. He came up to me, and after ſeveral queſtions, which I anſwered in great humility, he ſaid we ſhould not die. I made the captain a very low bow, and then turning to the *Dutchman* ſaid, I was ſorry to find more mercy in an heathen, than in a brother chriſtian. But I had ſoon reaſon to repent thoſe fooliſh words: for that malicious reprobate, having often endeavoured in vain to perſuade both the captains that I might be thrown into the ſea (which they would not yield to after the promiſe made me that I ſhould not die) however prevailed ſo far as to have a puniſhment inflicted on me, worſe, in all human appearance, than death itſelf. My men were ſent by an equal diviſion into both the pyrate ſhips, and my ſloop new manned. As to myſelf, it was determined that I ſhould be ſet a-drift in a ſmall canoe, with paddles and a ſail, and four days proviſions, which laſt the *Japaneſe* captain was ſo kind to double out of his own ſtores, and would permit no man to ſearch me. I got down into the canoe, while the *Dutchman* ſtanding upon the deck loaded me with all the curſes and injurious terms his language could afford.

About an hour before we ſaw the pyrates I had taken an obſervation, and found we were in the latitude of 46 N. and of longitude 183. When I was at ſome diſtance from the pyrates, I diſcovered by my pocket-glaſs ſeveral iſlands

to

to the fouth-eaft. I fet up my fail, the wind being fair, with a defign to reach the neareft of thofe iflands, which I made a fhift to do in about three hours. It was all rocky, how-ever I got many birds eggs, and ftriking fire I kindled fome heath and dry fea-weed, by which I roafted my eggs. I eat no other fup-per, being refolved to fpare my provifions as much as I could. I paffed the night under the fhelter of a rock, ftrewing fome heath un-der me, and flept pretty well.

The next day I failed to another ifland, and thence to a third and fourth, fometimes ufing my fail, and fometimes my paddles. But, not to trouble the reader with a particular account of my diftreffes, let it fuffice, that on the fifth day I arrived at the laft ifland in my fight, which lay fouth-fouth-eaft to the former.

This ifland was at a greater diftance than I expected, and I did not reach it in lefs than five hours. I encompaffed it almoft round, before I could find a convenient place to land in, which was a fmall creek about three times the widenefs of my canoe. I found the ifland to be all rocky, only a little intermingled with tufts of grafs, and fweet-fmelling herbs. I took out my fmall provifions, and after hav-ing refrefhed myfelf, I fecured the remainder in a cave, whereof there were great num-bers. I gathered plenty of eggs upon the rocks, and got a quantity of dry fea-weed, and parched grafs, which I defigned to kindle the next day, and roaft my eggs as well

as

as I could (for I had about me my flint, steel, match, and burning-glafs). I lay all night in the cave where I had lodged my provifions. My bed was the fame dry grafs and fea-weed which I intended for fewel. I flept very little, for the difquiets of my mind prevailed over my wearinefs, and kept me awake. I confidered how impoffible it was to preferve my life in fo defolate a place, and how miferable my end muft be. Yet found myfelf fo liftlefs and defponding, that I had not the heart to rife; and before I could get fpirits enough to creep out of my cave, the day was far advanced. I walked a while among the rocks, the fky was perfectly clear, and the fun fo hot, that I was forced to turn my face from it : when all on a fudden it became obfcure, as I thought, in a manner very different from what happens by the interpofition of a cloud. I turned back, and perceived a vaft opake body between me and the fun, moving forwards towards the ifland : it feemed to be about two miles high, and hid the fun fix or feven minutes, but I did not obferve the air to be much colder, or the fky more darkened, than if I had ftood under the fhade of a mountain. As it approached nearer over the place where I was, it appeared to be a firm fubftance, the bottom flat, fmooth, and fhining very bright from the reflexion of the fea below. I ftood upon a heighth about two hundred yards from the fhore, and faw this vaft body defcending almoft to a parallel with me at lefs than an

Englifh

Englifh mile diftance. I took out my pocket-perfpective, and could plainly difcover numbers of people moving up and down the fides of it, which appeared to be floping ; but, what thofe people were doing, I was not able to diftinguifh.

The natural love of life gave me fome inward motions of joy, and I was ready to entertain a hope, that this adventure might fome way or other help to deliver me from the defolate place and condition I was in. But at the fame time the reader can hardly conceive my aftonifhment, to behold an ifland in the air, inhabited by men, who were able (as it fhould feem) to raife or fink, or put it into a progreffive motion, as they pleafed. But not being at that time in a difpofition to philofophife upon this phænomenon, I rather chofe to obferve what courfe the ifland would take, becaufe it feemed for a while to ftand ftill. Yet foon after it advanced nearer, and I could fee the fides of it encompaffed with feveral gradations of galleries, and ftairs at certain intervals to defcend from one to the other. In the loweft gallery I beheld fome people fifhing with long angling rods, and others looking on. I waved my cap (for my hat was long fince worn out) and my handkerchief towards the ifland; and upon its nearer approach I called and fhouted with the utmoft ftrength of my voice ; and then, looking circumfpectly, I beheld a crowd gathered to that fide which was moft in my view. I

found

found by their pointing towards me and to each other, that they plainly difcovered me, although they made no return to my fhouting. But I could fee four or five men running in great hafte up the ftairs to the top of the ifland, who then difappeared. I happened rightly to conjecture, that thefe were fent for orders to fome perfon in authority upon this occafion.

The number of people encreafed, and in lefs than half an hour the ifland was moved and raifed in fuch a manner, that the loweft galle-ry appeared in a parallel of lefs than an hundred yards diftance from the heighth where I ftood. I then put myfelf into the moft fupplicating poftures, and fpoke in the humbleft accent, but received no anfwer. Thofe, who ftood nearest overagainft me, feemed to be perfons of diftinction, as I fuppofed by their habit. They conferred earneftly with each other, looking often upon me. At length one of them called out in a clear, polite, fmooth dialect, not un-like in found to the *Italian*; and therefore I returned an anfwer in that language, hoping at leaft, that the cadence might be more a-greeable to his ears. Although neither of us underftood the other, yet my meaning was eafily known, for the people faw the diftrefs I was in.

They made figns for me to come down from the rock, and go towards the fhore, which I accordingly did; and the flying ifland being raifed to a convenient heighth, the verge di-rectly

rectly over me, a chain was let down from the loweft gallery with a feat faftened to the bottom, to which I fixed myfelf, and was drawn up by pullies.

C H A P. II.

The humours and difpofitions of the Laputians defcribed. An account of their learning. Of the king, and his court. The author's reception there. The inhabitants fubject to fear and difquietudes. An account of the women.

AT my alighting I was furrounded with a crowd of people, but thofe who ftood neareft feemed to be of better quality. They beheld me with all the marks and circumftances of wonder, neither indeed was I much in their debt; having never till then feen a race of mortals fo fingular in their fhapes, habits, and countenances. Their heads were all reclined either to the right or the left; one of their eyes turned inward, and the other directly up to the zenith *. Their outward garments were adorned with the figures of funs, moons, and ftars, interwoven with thofe of fiddles, flutes, harps, trumpets, guittars, harpficords, and many other inftruments of mufic unknown to us in *Europe*. I obferved here and there many.

---

* By this defcription the author intended to ridicule thofe who wafte life in fpeculative fci- ence, the powers of whofe minds are as abfurdly employed as the eyes of the *Laputians*.

in the habit of fervants with a blown bladder faftened like a flayl to the end of a fhort ftick, which they carried in their hands. In each bladder was a fmall quantity of dried peafe or little pebbles (as I was afterwards informed.) With thefe bladders they now and then flapped the mouths and ears of thofe who ftood near them, of which practice I could not then conceive the meaning. It feems the minds of thefe people are fo taken up with intenfe fpeculations, that they neither can fpeak, nor attend to the difcourfes of others, without being roufed by fome external taction upon the organs of fpeech and hearing ; for which reafon thofe perfons, who are able to afford it, always keep a *flapper* (the original is *climenole*) in their family, as one of their domeftics, nor ever walk abroad or make vifits without him. And the bufinefs of this officer is, when two, three, or more perfons are in company, gently to ftrike with his bladder the mouth of him who is to fpeak, and the right ear of him or them to whom the fpeaker addreffeth himfelf. This *flapper* is likewife employed diligently to attend his mafter in his walks, and upon occafion to give him a foft flap on his eyes, becaufe he is always fo wrapped up in cogitation, that he is in manifeft danger of falling down every precipice, and bouncing his head againft every poft; and in the ftreets of juftling others, or being juftled himfelf into the kennel.

It

J.S.Müller inv. del. et Sc.

It was neceffary to give the reader this information, without which he would be at the fame lofs with me to underftand the proceedings of thefe people, as they conducted me up the ftairs to the top of the ifland, and from thence to the royal palace. While we were afcending, they forgot feveral times what they were about, and left me to myfelf, till their memories were again roufed by their *flappers*; for they appeared altogether unmoved by the fight of my foreign habit and countenance, and by the fhouts of the vulgar, whofe thoughts and minds were more difengaged.

At laft we entered the palace, and proceeded into the chamber of prefence, where I faw the king feated on his throne, attended on each fide by perfons of prime quality. Before the throne was a large table filled with globes and fpheres, and mathematical inftruments of all kinds. His majefty took not the leaft notice of us, although our entrance was not without fufficient noife by the concourfe of all perfons belonging to the court. But he was then deep in a problem, and we attended at leaft an hour, before he could folve it. There ftood by him on each fide a young page with flaps in their hands, and when they faw he was at leifure, one of them gently ftruck his mouth, and the other his right ear; at which he ftarted like one awaked on the fudden, and looking towards me and the compai y I was in, recollected the occafion of our coming, whereof he had been informed before. He

fpoke

spoke some words, whereupon immediately a young man with a flap came up to my side, and flapt me gently on the right ear, but I made signs, as well as I could, that I had no occasion for such an instrument; which, as I afterwards found, gave his majesty and the whole court a very mean opinion of my understanding. The king, as far as I could conjecture, asked me several questions, and I addressed myself to him in all the languages I had. When it was found, that I could neither understand nor be understood, I was conducted by his order to an apartment in his palace, (this prince being distinguished above all his predecessors for his hospitality to strangers) where two servants were appointed to attend me. My dinner was brought, and four persons of quality, whom I remembered to have seen very near the king's person, did me the honour to dine with me. We had two courses of three dishes each. In the first course there was a shoulder of mutton cut into an æquilateral triangle, a piece of beef into a rhomboides, and a pudding into a cycloid. The second course was two ducks trussed up in the form of fiddles; sausages and puddings resembling flutes and haut-boys, and a breast of veal in the shape of a harp. The servants cut our bread into cones, cylinders, parallelograms, and several other mathematical figures.

While we were at dinner, I made bold to ask the names of several things in their language, and those noble persons by the assistance

of

of their *flappers* delighted to give me anfwers; hoping to raife my admiration of their great abilities, if I could be brought to converfe with them. I was foon able to call for bread and drink, or whatever elfe I wanted.

After dinner my company withdrew, and a perfon was fent to me by the king's order attended by a *flapper*. He brought with him pen, ink, and paper, and three or four books, giving me to underftand by figns, that he was fent to teach me the language. We fat together four hours, in which time I wrote down a great number of words in columns with the tranflations over-againft them; I likewife made a fhift to learn feveral fhort fentences. For my tutor would order one of my fervants to fetch fomething, to turn about, to make a bow, to fit, or to ftand, or walk, and the like. Then I took down the fentence in writing. He fhewed me alfo in one of his books the figures of the fun, moon, and ftars, the zodiac; the tropics, and polar circles, together with the denominations of many figures of planes and folids. He gave me the names and defcriptions of all the mufical inftruments, and the general terms of art in playing on each of them. After he had left me, I placed all my words with their interpretations in alphabetical order. And thus in a few days by the help of a very faithful memory I got fome infight into their language.

The word, which I interpret the *flying* or *floating ifland* is in the original *Laputa*, where-

of

of I could never learn the true etymology. *Lap* in the old obsolete language signifieth *high*, and *untuh* a *governor*, from which they say by corruption was derived *Laputa*, from *Lapuntuh*. But I do not approve of this derivation, which seems to be a little strained. I ventured to offer to the learned among them a conjecture of my own, that *Laputa* was *quasi lap outed*; *lap* signifying properly the dancing of the sun-beams in the sea, and *outed* a wing, which however I shall not obtrude, but submit to the judicious reader.

Those to whom the king had entrusted me, observing how ill I was clad, ordered a taylor to come next morning, and take measure for a suit of cloaths. This operator did his office after a different manner from those of his trade in *Europe*. He first took my altitude by a quadrant, and then with rule and compasses described the dimensions and out-lines of my whole body, all which he entered upon paper; and in six days brought my cloaths very ill made, and quite out of shape, by happening to mistake a figure in the calculation. But my comfort was, that I observed such accidents very frequent, and little regarded.

During my confinement for want of cloaths, and by an indisposition that held me some days longer, I much enlarged my dictionary; and when I went next to court was able to understand many things the king spoke, and to return him some kind of answers. His majesty had given orders, that the island should move

north-

north-east and by east to the vertical point over *Lagado*, the metropolis of the whole kingdom below upon the firm earth. It was about ninety leagues diftant, and our voyage lafted four days and an half. I was not in the leaft fenfible of the progreffive motion made in the air by the ifland. On the fecond morning about eleven a clock the king himfelf in perfon attended by his nobility, courtiers, and officers, having prepared all their mufical inftruments, played on them for three hours without intermiffion, fo that I was quite ftunned with the noife; neither could I poffibly guefs the meaning, till my tutor informed me. He faid, that the people of their ifland had their ears adapted to hear the mufic of the fpheres, which always played at certain periods, and the court was now prepared to bear their part, in whatever inftrument they moft excelled.

In our journey towards *Lagado*, the capital city, his majefty ordered that the ifland fhould ftop over certain towns and villages, from whence he might receive the petitions of his fubjects. And to this purpofe feveral packthreads were let down with fmall weights at the bottom. On thefe packthreads the people ftrung their petitions, which mounted up directly, like the fcraps of paper faftened by fchool-boys at the end of the ftring that holds their kite. Sometimes we received wine and victuals from below, which were drawn up by pullies.

The knowledge I had in mathematics gave me great affiftance in acquiring their phrafeo= logy, which depended much upon that fcience and mufic; and in the latter I was not un-fkilled. Their ideas are perpetually conver-fant in lines and figures. If they would for example praife the beauty of a woman, or any other animal, they defcribe it by rhombs, cir-cles, parallelograms, ellipfes, and other geo-metrical terms, or by words of art drawn from mufic, needlefs here to repeat. I obferved in the king's kitchen all forts of mathematical and mufical inftruments, after the figures of which they cut up the joints that were ferved to his majefty's table.

Their houfes are very ill built, the walls be-vil, without one right-angle in any apartment; and this defeɛt arifeth from the contempt they bear to practical geometry, which they defpife as vulgar and mechanic, thofe inftructions they give being too refined for the intellectuals of their workmen, which occafions perpetual mi-ftakes. And although they are dextrous e-nough upon a piece of paper in the manage-ment of the rule, the pencil, and the divider, yet in the common actions and behaviour of life I have not feen a more clumfy, awkward, and unhandy people, nor fo flow and perplex-ed in their conceptions upon all other fubjects, except thofe of mathematics and mufic. They are very bad reafoners, and vehemently given to oppofition, unlefs when they happen to be of the right opinion, which is feldom their cafe.

cafe.   Imagination, fancy, and invention they
are wholly ftrangers to, nor have any words in
their language, by which thofe ideas can be
expreffed; the whole compafs of their thoughts
and mind being fhut up within the two fore-
mentioned fciences.

Moft of them, and efpecially thofe who deal
in the aftronomical part, have great faith in
judicial aftrology, although they are afhamed
to own it publicly.   But what I chiefly admired, and thought altogether unaccountable,
was the ftrong difpofition I obferved in them
towards news and politics, perpetually enquiring into public affairs, .giving their judgments
in matters of ftate, and paffionately difputing
every inch of a party opinion. .I have indeed
obferved the fame difpofition among moft of
the mathematicians I have known in *Europe*,
although I could never difcover the leaft ana-
logy between the two fciences; unlefs thofe
people fuppofe, that becaufe the fmalleft
circle hath as many degrees as the largeft,
therefore the regulation and management of
the world require no more abilities, than the
handling and turning of a globe: but I rather
take this quality to fpring from a very common
infirmity of human nature, inclining us to be
moft curious and conceited in matters where
we have leaft concern, and for which we are
leaft adapted either by ftudy or nature.

Thefe people are under continual difquietudes, never enjoying a minute's peace of
mind; and their difturbances proceed from

caufes,

caufes, which very little affect the reft of mortals. Their apprehenfions arife from feveral
changes they dread in the celeftial bodies. For
inftance, that the earth by the continual approaches of the fun towards it muft in courfe
of time be abforbed, or fwallowed up. That
the face of the fun will by degrees be encruft-
ed with its own effluvia, and give no more
light to the world. That the earth very narrowly efcaped a brufh from the tail of the
laft comet, which would have infallibly reduced it to afhes; and that the next, which
they have calculated for one and thirty years
hence, will probably deftroy us. For, if in
its perihelion it fhould approach within a certain degree of the fun (as by their calculations
they have reafon to dread) it will receive a degree of heat ten thoufand times more intenfe,
than that of red hot glowing iron; and, in
its abfence from the fun, carry a blazing tail
ten hundred thoufand and fourteen miles long;
through which if the earth fhould pafs at the
diftance of one hundred thoufand miles from
the *nucleus*, or main body of the comet, it
muft in its paffage be fet on fire, and reduced
to afhes. That the fun, daily fpending its
rays without any nutriment to fupply them,
will at laft be wholly confumed and annihi-
lated; which muft be attended with the deftruction of this earth and of all the planets
that receive their light from it [a].

[a] All thefe were fuppofitions of perfons eminent in their time for
mathematical knowledge.

They

They are fo perpetually alarmed with the apprehenfions of thefe, and the like impending dangers, that they can neither fleep quietly in their beds, nor have any relifh for the common pleafures or amufements of life. When they meet an acquaintance in the morning, the firft queftion is about the fun's health, how he looked at his fetting and rifing, and what hopes they have to avoid the ftroke of the approaching comet. This converfation they are apt to run into with the fame temper, that boys difcover in delighting to hear terrible ftories of fpirits and hobgoblins, which they greedily liften to, and dare not go to bed for fear.

The women of the ifland have abundance of vivacity; they contemn their hufbands, and are exceedingly fond of ftrangers, whereof there is always a confiderable number from the continent below attending at court, either upon affairs of the feveral towns and corporations, or their own particular occafions, but are much defpifed, becaufe they want the fame endowments. Among thefe the ladies chufe their gallants: but the vexation is, that they act with too much eafe and fecurity, for the hufband is always fo rapt in fpeculation, that the miftrefs and lover may proceed to the greateft familiarities before his face, if he be but provided with paper and implements, and without his *flapper* at his fide.

The wives and daughters lament their confinement to the ifland, although I think it the

moft

moſt delicious ſpot of ground in the world; and although they live here in the greateſt plenty and magnificence, and are allowed to do whatever they pleaſe, they long to ſee the world, and take the diverſions of the metropolis, which they are not allowed to do without a particular licence from the king; and this is not eaſy to be obtained, becauſe the people of quality have found by frequent experience, how hard it is to perſuade their women to return from below. I was told, that a great court lady, who had ſeveral children, is married to the prime miniſter, the richeſt ſubject in the kingdom, a very graceful perſon, extremely fond of her, and lives in the fineſt palace of the iſland, went down to *Lagado* on the pretence of health, there hid herſelf for ſeveral months, till the king ſent a warrant to ſearch for her, and ſhe was found in an obſcure eating-houſe all in rags, having pawned her cloaths to maintain an old deformed foot-man, who beat her every day, and in whoſe company ſhe was taken much againſt her will. And although her huſband received her with all poſſible kindneſs, and without the leaſt reproach, ſhe ſoon after contrived to ſteal down again with all her jewels to the ſame gallant, and hath not been heard of ſince.

This may perhaps paſs with the reader rather for an *European* or *Engliſh* ſtory, than for one of a country ſo remote. But he may pleaſe to conſider, that the caprices of women-kind

are

are not limited by any climate or nation, and
that they are much more uniform than can be
eafily imagined,

In about a month's time, I had made a tolerable proficiency in their language, and was
able to anfwer moft of the king's queftions,
when I had the honour to attend him. His
majefty difcovered not the leaft curiofity to enquire into the laws, government, hiftory, religion, or manners of the countries where I
had been, but confined his queftions to the
ftate of mathematics, and received the account I gave him with great contempt and
indifference, though often roufed by his *flapper*
on each fide.

C H A P. III.

*A phænomenon folved by modern philofophy and
aftronomy. The Laputians great improvements
in the latter. The king's method of fuppreffing
infurrections.*

I Defired leave of this prince to fee the curiofities of the ifland, which he was gracioufly pleafed to grant, and ordered my tutor
to attend me. I chiefly wanted to know, to
what caufe in art or in nature it owed its feveral motions, whereof I will now give a philo-
fophical account to the reader.

The flying or floating ifland is exactly circular, its diameter 7837 yards, or about four
miles and an half, and confequently contains
ten

ten thoufand acres. It is three hundred yards thick. The bottom, or under furface, which appears to thofe who view it from below, is one even regular plate of adamant, fhooting up to the height of about two hundred yards, Above it lie the feveral minerals in their ufual order, and over all is a coat of rich mould, ten or twelve feet deep. The declivity of the upper furface, from the circumference to the center, is the natural caufe why all the dews and rains, which fall upon the ifland, are conveyed in fmall rivulets towards the middle, where they are emptied into four large bafons, each of about half a mile in circuit, and two hundred yards diftant from the center. From thefe bafons the water is continually exhaled by the fun in the day-time, which effectually prevents their overflowing. Befides, as it is in the power of the monarch to raife the ifland above the region of clouds and vapours, he can prevent the falling of dews and rains whenever he pleafes. For the higheft clouds cannot rife above two miles, as naturalifts agree, at leaft they were never known to do fo in that country.

At the center of the ifland there is a chafm about fifty yards in diameter, from whence the aftronomers defcend into a large dome, which is therefore called *flandona gagnole*, or the *aftronomer's cave*, fituated at the depth of a hundred yards beneath the upper furface of the adamant. In this cave are twenty lamps continually burning, which from the reflection of

the

the adamant, caſt a ſtrong light into every part. The place is ſtored with great variety of ſextants, quadrants, teleſcopes, aſtrolabes, and other aſtronomical inſtruments. But the greateſt curioſity, upon which the fate of the iſland depends, is a loadſtone of a prodigious ſize, in ſhape reſembling a weaver's ſhuttle. It is in length ſix yards, and in the thickeſt part at leaſt three yards over. This magnet is ſuſtained by a very ſtrong axle of adamant paſſing through its middle, upon which it plays, and is poiſed ſo exactly, that the weakeſt hand can turn it. It is hooped round with an hollow cylinder of adamant, four feet deep, as many thick, and twelve yards in diameter, placed horizontally, and ſupported by eight adamantine feet, each ſix yards high. In the middle of the concave ſide there is a groove twelve inches. deep, in which the extremities of the axle are lodged, and turned round as there is occaſion.

The ſtone cannot be moved from its place by any force, becauſe the hoop and its feet are one continued piece with that body of a-damant, which conſtitutes the bottom of the iſland.

By means of this load-ſtone the iſland is made to riſe and fall, and move from one place to another. For, with reſpect to that part of the earth over which the monarch pre-ſides, the ſtone is endued at one of its ſides with an attractive power, and at the other with a repulſive. Upon placing the magnet erect, with its attracting end towards the earth,
the

the ifland defcends ; but when the repelling extremity points downwards, the ifland mounts directly upwards. When the pofition of the ftone, is oblique, the motion of the ifland is fo too : for in this magnet the forces always act in lines parallel to its direction.

By this oblique motion the ifland is conveyed to different parts of the monarch's dominions. To explain the manner of its progrefs, let *A B* reprefent a line drawn crofs the dominions of *Balnibarbi*, let the line *c d* reprefent the load-ftone, of which let *d* be the repelling end, and *c* the attracting end, the ifland being over *C*; let the ftone be placed in the pofition *c d*, with its repelling end downwards ; then the ifland will be driven upwards obliquely towards *D*. When it is arrived at *D*, let the ftone be turned upon its axle till its attracting end points towards *E*, and then the ifland will be carried obliquely towards *E*; where if the ftone be again turned upon its axle till it ftands in the pofition *E F*, with its repelling point downward, the ifland will rife obliquely towards *F*, where, by directing the attracting end towards *G*, the ifland may be carried to *G*, and from *G* to *H* by turning the ftone, fo as to make its repelling extremity point directly downward. And thus, by changing the fituation of the ftone as often as there is occafion, the ifland is made to rife and fall by turns in an oblique direction, and by thofe alternate rifings and fallings (the obliquity being not confiderable) is conveyed
from

from one part of the dominions to the o-
ther.

But it muft be obferved, that this ifland
cannot move beyond the extent of the dominions below, nor can it rife above the heighth
of four miles. For which the aftronomers
(who have written large fyftems concerning
the ftone) affign the following reafon : that the
magnetic virtue does not extend beyond the
diftance of four miles, and that the mineral,
which acts upon the ftone in the bowels of the
earth, and in the fea about fix leagues diftant
from the fhore, is not diffufed through the
whole globe, but terminated with the limits
of the king's dominions; and it was eafy, from
the great advantage of fuch a fuperior fituation,
for a prince to bring under his obedience
whatever country lay within the attraction of
that magnet.

When the ftone is put parallel to the plane
of the horizon, the ifland ftandeth ftill ; for in
that cafe the extremities of it, being at equal
diftance from the earth, act with equal force,
the one in drawing downwards, the other in
pufhing upwards, and confequently no motion
can enfue.

This load-ftone is under the care of certain
aftronomers, who from time to time give it
fuch pofitions as the monarch directs. They
fpend the greateft part of their lives in obferving the celeftial bodies, which they do by the
affiftance of glaffes far excelling ours in good-
nefs. For, although their largeft telefcopes
do

do not exceed three feet, they magnify much more than thofe of an hundred with us, and fhew the ftars with greater clearnefs. This advantage hath enabled them to extend their difcoveries much farther than our aftronomers in *Europe*; for they have made a catalogue of ten thoufand fixed ftars, whereas the largeft of ours do not contain above one third part of that number. They have likewife difcovered two leffer ftars, or *fatellites*, which revolve a-bout *Mars*, whereof the innermoft is diftant from the center of the primary planet exactly three of his diameters, and the outermoft, five; the former revolves in the fpace of ten hours, and the latter in twenty-one and a half; fo that the fquares of their periodical times are very near in the fame proportion with the cubes of their diftance from the center of *Mars*, which evidently fhews them to be go-verned by the fame law of gravitation, that influences the other heavenly bodies.

They have obferved ninety-three different comets, and fettled their periods with great exactnefs. If this be true (and they affirm it with great confidence) it is much to be wifh-ed, that their obfervations were made public, whereby the theory of comets, which at pre-fent is very lame and defective, might be brought to the fame perfection with other parts of aftronomy.

The king would be the moft abfolute prince in the univerfe, if he could but prevail on a miniftry to join with him ; but thefe having
their

their eftates below on the continent, and confidering that the office of a favourite hath a very uncertain tenure; would never confent to the enflaving their country.

If any town fhould engage in rebellion or mutiny, fall into violent factions, or refufe to pay the ufual tribute, the king hath two methods of reducing them to obedience. The firft and the mildeft courfe is by keeping the ifland hovering over fuch a town, and the lands about it, whereby he can deprive them of the benefit of the fun and the rain, and confequently afflict the inhabitants with dearth and difeafes And if the crime deferve it, they are at the fame time pelted from above with great ftones, againft which they have no defence but by creeping into cellars or caves, while the roofs of their houfes are beaten to pieces. But if they ftill continue obftinate, or offer to raife infurrections, he proceeds to the laft remedy by letting the ifland drop directly upon their heads, which makes an univerfal deftruction both of houfes and men. However, this is an extremity to which the prince is feldom driven, neither indeed is he willing to put it in execution, nor dare his minifters advife him to an action, which as it would render them odious to the people, fo it would be a great damage to their own eftates, which lie all below, for the ifland is the king's demefn.

But there is ftill indeed a more weighty reafon, why the kings of this country have

been always averfe from executing fo terrible
an action, unlefs upon the utmoft neceffity.
For if the town intended to be deftroyed
fhould have in it any tall rocks, as it generally falls out in the larger cities, a fituation
probably chofen at firft with a view to prevent
fuch a cataftrophe; or if it abound in high
fpires, or pillars of ftone, a fudden fall might
endanger the bottom or under furface of
the ifland, which, although it confift, as I
have faid, of one intire adamant two hundred
yards thick, might happen to crack by too
great a fhock, or burft by approaching too
near the fires from the houfes below, as the
backs both of iron and ftone will often do in our
chimnies. Of all this the people are well ap-
prifed, and underftand how far to carry their
obftinacy, where their liberty or property is
concerned. And the king, when he is higheft provoked, and moft determined to prefs a
city to rubbifh, orders the ifland to defcend
with great gentlenefs out of a pretence of tendernefs to his people; but indeed for fear of
breaking the adamantine bottom; in which
cafe, it is the opinion of all their philofophers,
that the load-ftone could no longer hold it
up, and the whole mafs would fall to the
ground.

By a fundamental law of this realm neither
the king, nor either of his two elder fons, are
permitted to leave the ifland, nor the queen,
till fhe is paft child-bearing.

CHAP.

CHAP. IV.

The author leaves Laputa, *is conveyed to* Balnibarbi, *arrives at the metropolis. A description of the metropolis, and the country
adjoining. The author hospitably received by
a great lord. His conversation with that
lord.*

ALthough I cannot say that I was ill treated
in this island, yet I must confess I thought
myself too much neglected, not without some
degree of contempt. For neither prince nor
people appeared to be curious in any part of
knowledge, except mathematics and music,
wherein I was far their inferior, and upon
that account very little regarded.

On the other side, after having seen all the
curiosities of the island, I was very desirous
to leave it, being heartily weary of those people. They were indeed excellent in two
sciences, for which I have great esteem,
and wherein I am not unversed, but at the
same time so abstracted and involved in spe-
culation, that I never met with such disagreeable companions. I conversed only with women, tradesmen, *flappers*, and court-pages,
during two months of my abode there; by
which at last I rendered myself extremely contemptible; yet these were the only people,
from whom I could ever receive a reasonable
answer.

I had

I had obtained by hard ftudy a good degree of knowledge in their language: I was weary of being confined to an ifland, where I received fo little countenance, and refolved to leave it with the firft opportunity.

There was a great lord at court, nearly related to the king, and for that reafon alone, ufed with refpect. He was univerfally reckoned the moft ignorant and ftupid perfon among them. He had performed many eminent fervices for the crown, had great natural and acquired parts, adorned with integrity and honour, but fo ill an ear for mufic, that his detractors reported he had been often known to beat time in the wrong place; neither could his tutors, without extreme difficulty teach him to demonftrate the moft eafy propofition in the mathematics. He was pleafed to fhew me many marks of favour, often did me the honour of a vifit, defired to be informed in the affairs of *Europe*, the laws and cuftoms, the manners and learning of the feveral countries where I had travelled. He liftened to me with great attention, and made very wife obfervations on all I fpoke. He had two *flappers* attending him for ftate, but never made ufe of them, except at court and in vifits of ceremony, and would always command them to withdraw, when we were alone together.

I entreated this illuftrious perfon to intercede in my behalf with his majefty for leave to depart, which he accordingly did, as he was pleafed to tell me with regret: for indeed

he

he had made me several offers very advantageous, which however I refused with expres-
sions of the highest acknowledgment.

On the 16th of *February* I took leave of
his majesty and the court. The king made
me a present to the value of about two hundred pounds *English*, and my protector, his
kinsman, as much more, together with a letter
of recommendation to a friend of his in *Lagado*, the metropolis : the island being then
hovering over a mountain about two miles
from it, I was let down from the lowest gallery, in the same manner as I had been taken
up.

The continent, as far as it is subject to the
monarch of the *flying island*, passes under the
general name of *Balnibarbi* ; and the metropolis, as I said before, is called *Lagado*. I felt
some little satisfaction in finding myself on
firm ground. I walked to the city without
any concern, being clad like one of the natives, and sufficiently instructed to converse
with them. I soon found out the person's
house, to whom I was recommended, presented my letter from his friend the grandee in
the island, and was received with much kindness. This great lord, whose name was *Munodi*, ordered me an apartment in his own
house, where I continued during my stay,
and was entertained in a most hospitable manner.

The next morning after my arrival he took
me in his chariot to see the town, which is

about half the bignefs of *London*, but the
houfes very ftrangely built, and moft of them
out of repair. The people in the ftreets walked faft, looked wild, their eyes fixed, and
were generally in rags. We paffed through
one of the town gates, and went about three
miles into the country, where I faw many labourers working with feveral forts of tools in
the ground, but was not able to conjecture
what they were about; neither did I obferve
any expectation either of corn or grafs, although the foil appeared to be excellent. I
could not forbear admiring at thefe odd appearances both in town and country; and I made
bold to defire my conductor, that he would be
pleafed to explain to me, what could be meant
by fo many bufy heads, hands, and faces both
in the ftreets and the fields, becaufe I did not
difcover any good effects they produced; but,
on the contrary, I never knew a foil fo unhap-
pily cultivated, houfes fo ill contrived and fo
ruinous, or a people whofe countenances and
habit expreffed fo much mifery and want.

This lord *Munodi* was a perfon of the firft
rank, and had been fome years governor of
Lagado; but by a cabal of minifters was difcharged for infufficiency. However, the king
treated him with tendernefs, as a well-mean-
ing man, but of a low contemptible underftanding.

When I gave that free cenfure of the country and its inhabitants, he made no further
anfwer, than by telling me, that I had not
                                                     been

been long enough among them to form a judgment; and that the different nations of the world had different cuſtoms; with other common topics to the ſame purpoſe. But, when we returned to his palace, he aſked me how I liked the building, what abſurdities I obſerved, and what quarrel I had with the dreſs or looks of his domeſtics. This he might ſafely do; becauſe every thing about him was magnificent, regular, and polite. I anſwered, that his excellency's prudence, quality, and fortune, had exempted him from thoſe de- fects, which folly and beggary had produced in others. He ſaid, if I would go with him to his country-houſe about twenty miles di- ſtant, where his eſtate lay, there would be more leiſure for this kind of converſation. I told his excellency, that I was entirely at his diſpoſal; and accordingly we ſet out next morning.

During our journey he made me obſerve the ſeveral methods uſed by farmers in managing their lands; which to me were wholly unac- countable; for except in ſome very few places I could not diſcover one ear of corn, or blade of graſs. But in three hours travelling the ſcene was wholly altered; we came into a moſt beautiful country; farmers houſes at ſmall diſtances neatly built, the fields en- cloſed, containing vineyards, corn-grounds, and meadows. Neither do I remember to have ſeen a more delightful proſpect. His excel- lency obſerved my countenance to clear up;

he

he told me with a figh, that there his eftate began, and would continue the fame, till we fhould come to his houfe. That his country-men ridiculed and defpifed him for managing his affairs no better, and for fetting fo ill an example to the kingdom, which however was followed by very few, fuch as were old, and wilful, and weak like himfelf.

We came at length to the houfe, which was indeed a noble ftructure, built according to the beft rules of ancient architecture. The foun-tains, gardens, walks, avenues, and groves, were all difpofed with exact judgment and tafte. I gave due praifes to every thing I faw, whereof his excellency took not the leaft no-tice till after fupper; when, there being no third companion, he told me with a very me-lancholy air, that he doubted he muft throw down his houfes in town and country to re-build them after the prefent mode, deftroy all his plantations, and caft others into fuch a form as modern ufage required, and give the fame directions to all his tenants, unlefs he would fubmit to incur the cenfure of pride, fingularity, affectation, ignorance, caprice, and perhaps encreafe his majefty's difpleafure.

That the admiration I appeared to be under, would ceafe or diminifh, when he had inform-ed me of fome particulars, which probably I never heard of at court, the people there be-ing too much taken up in their own fpecula-tions to have regard to what paffed here be-low.

The

The fum of his difcourfe was to this effect: that about forty years ago certain perfons went up to *Laputa*, either upon bufinefs or diverfion, and after five months' continuance came back with a very little fmattering in mathematics, but full of volatile fpirits acquired in that airy region.   That thefe perfons upon their return began to diflike the management of every thing below, and fell into fchemes of putting all arts, fciences, languages, and mechanics upon a new foot.   To this end they procured a royal patent for erecting an academy of projectors in *Lagado*; and the humour prevailed fo ftrongly among the people, that there is not a town of any confequence in the kingdom without fuch an academy.   In thefe colleges the profeffors contrive new rules and methods of agriculture and building, and new inftruments and tools for all trades and manufactures, whereby, as they undertake, one man fhall do the work of ten, a palace may be built in a week of materials fo durable, as to laft for ever without repairing.   All the fruits of the earth fhall come to maturity at whatever feafon we think fit to chufe, and increafe an hundred fold more than they do at prefent ; with innumerable other happy propofals.   The only inconvenience is, that none of thefe projects are yet brought to perfection; and in the mean time the whole country lies miferably wafte, the houfes in ruins, and the people without food or cloaths.   By all which, inftead of being difcouraged, they are fifty times more violent-

3   ly

ly bent upon profecuting their fchemes, driven e-
qually on by hope and defpair : that as for himfelf,
being not of an enterprifing fpirit, he was content to go on in the old forms, to live in the
houfes his anceftors had built, and act as they
did in. every part of life without innovation.
That fome few other perfons of quality and
gentry had done the fame, but were looked
on with an eye of contempt and ill-will, as
enemies to art, ignorant, and ill common-
wealths-men, preferring their own eafe and
floth before the general improvement of their
country.

His lordfhip added, that he would not by
any further particulars prevent the pleafure I
fhould certainly take in viewing the grand
academy, whither he was refolved I fhould
go. He only defired me to obferve a ruined building upon the fide of a mountain
about three miles diftant, of which he gave
me this account : that he had a very convenient mill within half a mile of his houfe,
turned by a current from a large river, and
fufficient for his own family as well as a
great number of his tenants. That about feven years ago, a club of thofe projectors
came to him with propofals to deftroy this
mill, and build another on the fide of that
mountain, on the long ridge whereof a long
canal muft be cut for a repofitory of water
to be conveyed up by pipes and engines to
fupply the mill : becaufe the wind and air
upon a heighth agitated the water, and thereby

by made it fitter for motion : and becaufe the water defcending down a declivity would turn the mill with half the current of a ri-ver, whofe courfe is more upon a level. He faid, that being then not very well with the court, and preffed by many of his friends, he complied with the propofal; and after em-ploying an hundred men for two years the work mifcarried, the projectors went off, lay-ing the blame intirely upon him, railing at him ever fince, and putting others upon the fame experiment with equal affurance of fuc-cefs, as well as equal difappointment.

In a few days we came back to town, and his excellency confidering the bad cha-racter he had in the academy would not go with me himfelf, but recommended me to a friend of his to bear me company thither. My lord was pleafed to reprefent me as a great ad-mirer of projects, and a perfon of much cu-riofity, and eafy belief; which indeed was not without truth; for I had myfelf been a fort of projector in my younger days.

C H A P.

C H A P. V.

The author permitted to see the grand academy of
Lagado. *The academy largely described. The*
arts wherein the professors employ them-
selves [a].

THIS academy is not an entire single
building, but a continuation of several
houses on both sides of a street, which growing waste was purchased, and applied to that
use.

I was received very kindly by the warden,
and went for many days to the academy. Every
room hath in it one or more projectors; and
I believe I could not be in fewer than five
hundred rooms.

The first man I saw was of a meagre as-
pect, with sooty hands and face, his hair and
beard long, ragged and singed in several places. His cloaths, shirt, and skin, were all of
the same colour. He had been eight years
upon a project for extracting sun-beams out
of cucumbers, which were to be put in vials

[a] However wild the description of the flying island and
the manners and various projects of the philosophers of *La-*
gado may appear, yet it is a
real picture embellished with
much *latent* wit and humour.
ORRERY.
This note in general seems
o be a testimony of his lordship's approbation, but it is not
easy to discover what in particular is meant by the word *real*,
since every picture is a real picture, whether it be copied from
nature or fancy; and indeed it
is equally difficult to conceive
how a *picture* of any kind can
be embellished with that which
is *hidden*.

hermetically

hermetically fealed, and let out to warm the air in raw inclement fummers. He told me, he did not doubt, that in eight years more he fhould be able to fupply the governor's gardens with fun-fhine at a reafonable rate; but he complained that his ftock was low, and entreated me to give him fomething as an encouragement to ingenuity, efpecially fince this had been a very dear feafon for cucumbers. I made him a fmall prefent, for my lord had furnifhed me with money on purpofe, becaufe he knew their practice of begging from all who go to fee them.

I went into another chamber, but was ready to haften back, being almoft overcome with a horrible ftink. My conductor preffed me forward, conjuring me in a whifper to give no offence, which would be highly refented, and therefore I durft not fo much as ftop my nofe. The projector of this cell was the moft ancient ftudent of the academy; his face and beard were of a pale yellow; his hands and cloaths dawbed over with filth. When I was prefented to him he gave me a clofe embrace (a compliment I could well have excufed.) His employment from his firft coming into the academy was an operation to reduce human excrement to its original food by feparating the feveral parts, removing the tincture which it receives from the gall, making the odour exhale, and fcumming off the faliva. He had a weekly allowance from the fociety of

a veffel

a veffel filled with human ordure about the bignefs of a *Briftol* barrel.

I faw another at work to calcine ice into
gunpowder, who likewife fhewed me a treatife he had written concerning the malleabili-
ty of fire, which he intended to publifh.

There was a moft ingenious architect, who
had contrived a new method for building
houfes by beginning at the roof, and working downwards to the foundation, which he
juftified to me by the like practice of thofe
two prudent infects the bee and the fpider.

There was a man born blind, who had feveral apprentices in his own condition : their
employment was to mix colours for painters,
which their mafter taught them to diftinguifh
by feeling and fmelling. It was indeed my
misfortune to find them at that time not very
perfect in their leffons, and the profeffor himfelf happened to be generally miftaken. This
artift is much encouraged and efteemed by the
whole fraternity.

In another apartment I was highly pleafed
with a projector, who had found a device of
plowing the ground with hogs to fave the
charges of ploughs, cattle, and labour. The
method is this : in an acre of ground you bury
at fix inches diftance and eight deep a quantity of acorns, dates, chefnuts, and other mafte
or vegetables, whereof thefe animals are fond-
eft : then you drive fix hundred or more of
them into the field, where in a few days they
will root up the whole ground in fearch of
their

their food, and make it fit for fowing, at the fame time manuring it with their dung; it is true, upon experiment they found the charge and trouble very great, and they had little or no crop. However, it is not doubted that this invention may be capable of great improvement.

I went into another room, where the walls and cieling were all hung round with cobwebs, except a narrow paffage for the artift to go in and out. At my entrance he called aloud to me not to difturb his webs. He lamented the fatal miftake the world had been fo long in of ufing filk-worms, while we had fuch plenty of domeftic infects who infinitely excelled the former, becaufe they underftood how to weave as well as fpin. And he propofed farther, that by employing fpiders the charge of dying filks fhould be wholly faved; whereof I was fully convinced, when he fhewed me a vaft number of flies moft beautifully coloured, wherewith he fed his fpiders, affuring us that the webs would take a tincture from them; and as he had them of all hues, he hoped to fit every body's fancy, as foon as he could find proper food for the flies, of certain gums, oils, and other glutinous matter to give a ftrength and confiftence to the threads.

There was an aftronomer, who had under-taken to place a fun-dial upon the great wea-ther-cock on the town-houfe, by adjufting the annual and diurnal motions of the earth and fun,

fun, fo as to anfwer and coincide with all accidental turnings of the wind.

I was complaining of a fmall fit of the cho-
lic, upon which my conductor led me into a
room where a great phyfician refided, who
was famous for curing that difeafe by contrary
operations from the fame inftrument. He had
a large pair of bellows with a long flender
muzzle of ivory : this he conveyed eight inches up the *anus*, and drawing in the wind he
affirmed he could make the guts as lank as a
dried bladder. But when the difeafe was
more ftubborn and violent, he let in the muzzle while the bellows were full of wind,
which he difcharged into the body of the patient ; then withdrew the inftrument to re-
plenifh it, clapping his thumb ftrongly againft
the orifice of the fundament ; and this being
repeated three or four times, the adventitious
wind would rufh out, bringing the noxious a-
long with it (like water put into a pump) and
the patient recover. I faw him try both ex-
periments upon a dog, but could not difcern
any effect from the former. After the latter
the animal was ready to burft, and made fo
violent a difcharge, as was very offenfive to
me and my companions. The dog died on the
fpot, and we left the doctor endeavouring to
recover him by the fame operation.

I vifited many other apartments, but fhall
not trouble my reader with all the curiofities I
obferved, being ftudious of brevity.

I had

I had hitherto feen only one fide of the academy, the other being appropriated to the ad-
vancers of fpeculative learning, of whom I
fhall fay fomething when I have mentioned
one illuftrious perfon more, who is called a-
mong them *the univerfal artift*. He told us,
he had been thirty years employing his thoughts
for the improvement of human life. He had
two large rooms full of wonderful curiofities,
and fifty men at work. Some were condenf-
ing air into a dry tangible fubftance by extracting the nitre, and letting the aqueous or
fluid particles percolate; others foftening marble for pillows and pincufhions; others petri-
fying the hoofs of a living horfe to preferve
them from foundering. The artift himfelf
was at that time bufy upon two great defigns;
the firft to fow land with chaff, wherein he
affirmed the true feminal virtue to be contained, as he demonftrated by feveral experi-
ments, which I was not fkilful enough to
comprehend. The other was by a certain compofition of gums, minerals, and vegetables,
outwardly applied to prevent the growth of
wool upon two young lambs; and he hoped in
a reafonable time to propagate the breed of
naked fheep all over the kingdom.

We croffed a walk to the other part of the
academy, where as I have already faid the projectors in fpeculative learning refided.

The firft profeffor I faw was in a very large
room with forty pupils about him. After fa-
lutation obferving me to look earneftly upon a

frame, which took up the greateſt part of
both the length and breadth of the room, he
ſaid perhaps I might wonder to ſee him employed in a projeƈt for improving ſpeculative
knowledge by praƈtical and mechanical operations. But the world would ſoon be ſenſible
of its uſefulneſs; and he flattered himſelf,
that a more noble exalted thought never ſprang
in any other man's head. Every one knew,
how laborious the uſual method is of attain-
ing to arts and ſciences; whereas by his contrivance the moſt ignorant perſon at a reaſonable charge and with a little bodily labour might
write books in philoſophy, poetry, politics,
law, mathematics, and theology, without the
leaſt aſſiſtance from genius or ſtudy. He then
led me to the frame, about the ſides whereof
all his pupils ſtood in ranks. It was twenty
feet ſquare, placed in the middle of the room.
The ſuperficies was compoſed of ſeveral bits
of wood about the bigneſs of a dye, but ſome
larger than others. They were all linked together by ſlender wires. Theſe bits of wood
were covered on every ſquare with paper paſt-
ed on them; and on theſe papers were written all the words of their language in their
ſeveral moods, tenſes, and declenſions; but
without any order. The profeſſor then deſired me to obſerve; for he was going to ſet
his engine at work. The pupils at his command took each of them hold of an iron handle, whereof there were forty fixed round the
edges of the frame; and giving them a ſudden
turn

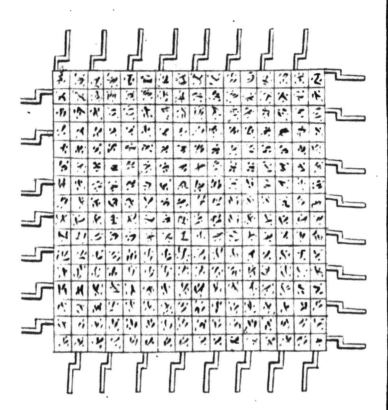

turn the whole difpofition of the words was intirely changed: He then commanded fix and thirty of the lads to read the feveral lines foftly, as they appeared upon the frame; and where they found three or four words toge-ther, that might make part of a fentence, they dictated to the four remaining boys, who were fcribes. This work was repeated three or four times, and at every turn the engine was fo contrived, that the words fhifted into new places, as the fquare bits of wood moved upfide down.

Six hours a day the young ftudents were em-ployed in this labour, and the profeffor fhewed me feveral volumes in large folio already col-lected of broken fentences, which he intended to piece together, and out of thofe rich mate-rials to give the world a compleat body of all arts and fciences; which however might be ftill improved and much expedited, if the pub-lic would raife a fund for making and employ-ing five hundred fuch frames in *Lagado*, and oblige the managers to contribute in common their feveral collections.

He affured me, that this invention had em-ployed all his thoughts from his youth; that he had emptied the whole vocabulary into his frame, and made the ftricteft computation of the general proportion there is in books be-tween the numbers of particles, nouns, and verbs, and other parts of fpeech.

I made my humbleft acknowledgment to this illuftrious perfon for his great communi-

R 2   cativenefs;

cativeneſs; and promiſed, if ever I had the
good fortune to return to my native country,
that I would do him juſtice, as the ſole inventor
of this wonderful machine; the form and
contrivance of which I deſired leave to deli-
neate upon paper, as in the figure here an-
nexed. I told him, although it were the cuſtom of our learned in *Europe* to ſteal inventions from each other, who had thereby at
leaſt this advantage, that it became a contro-
verſy which was the right owner; yet I would
take ſuch caution, that he ſhould have the
honour intire without a rival.

We next went to the ſchool of languages,
where three profeſſors ſat in conſultation upon
improving that of their own country.

The firſt project was to ſhorten diſcourſe by
cutting polyſyllables into one, and leaving out
verbs and participles; becauſe in reality all
things imaginable are but nouns.

The other project was a ſcheme for intirely
aboliſhing all words whatſoever; and this was
urged as a great advantage in point of health,
as well as brevity. For it is plain, that every
word we ſpeak, is in ſome degree a diminu-
tion of our lungs by corroſion; and conſe-
quently contributes to the ſhortening of our
lives. An expedient was therefore offered,
that ſince words are only names for *things*, it
would be more convenient for all men to carry about them ſuch *things* as were neceſſary
to expreſs the particular buſineſs they are to
diſcourſe on. And this invention would certainly

tainly have taken place, to the great eafe as well as health of the fubject, if the women in conjunction with the vulgar and illiterate had not threatened to raife a rebellion, unlefs they might be allowed the liberty to fpeak with their tongues after the manner of their fore-fathers, fuch conftant irreconcileable enemies to fcience are the common people. How-ever, many of the moft learned and wife ad-here to the new fcheme of exprefling them-felves by *things*; which hath only this incon-venience attending it, that if a man's bufinefs be very great and of various kinds, he muft be obliged in proportion to carry a greater bundle of *things* upon his back, unlefs he can afford one or two ftrong fervants to attend him. I have often beheld two of thofe fages almoft finking under the weight of their packs, like pedlars among us; who, when they met in the ftreets, would lay down their loads, open their facks, and hold converfation for an hour together; then put up their implements, help each other to refume their burthens, and take their leave.

But for fhort converfations a man may carry implements in his pockets and under his arms enough to fupply him; and in his houfe he cannot be at a lofs. Therefore the room, where company meet who practife this art, is full of all *things* ready at hand requifite to furnifh matter for this kind of artificial con-verfe.

R 3   Another

Another great advantage propofed by this invention was, that it would ferve as an univerfal language to be underftood in all civilized nations, whofe goods and utenfils are generally of the fame kind, or nearly refembling, fo that their ufes might eafily be comprehended. And thus ambaffadors would be qualified to treat with foreign princes, or minifters of ftate, to whofe tongues they were utter ftrangers.

I was at the mathematical fchool, where the mafter taught his pupils after a method fcarce imaginable to us in *Europe*. The propofition and demonftration were fairly written on a thin wafer with ink compofed of a cephalic tincture. This the ftudent was to fwallow upon a fafting ftomach, and for three days following eat nothing but bread and water. As the wafer digefted, the tincture mounted to his brain, bearing the propofition along with it. But the fuccefs hath not hitherto been anfwerable, partly by fome error in the *quantum* or compofition, and partly by the perverfenefs of lads ; to whom this bolus is fo naufeous, that they generally fteal afide and difcharge it upwards, before it can operate ; neither have they been yet perfuaded to ufe fo long an abftinence as the prefcription requires.

CHAP.

C H A P. VI.

A further account of the academy. The author proposes some improvements, which are honourably received.

IN the school of political projectors I was but ill entertained ; the professors appearing in my judgment wholly out of their senses ; which is a scene, that never fails to make me melancholy. These unhappy people were proposing schemes for perfuading monarchs to chufe favourites upon the fcore of their wifdom, capacity, and virtue ; of teaching minifters to confult the public good ; of rewarding merit, great abilities, and eminent fervices ; of inftructing princes to know their true intereft, by placing it on the fame foundation with that of their people ; of chufing for employments perfons qualified to exercife them ; with many other wild impoffible chimæras, that never entered before into the heart of man to conceive ; and confirmed in me the old obfervation, that there is nothing fo extravagant and irational, which fome philofophers have not, maintained for truth.

But however, I fhall fo far do juftice to this part of the academy, as to acknowledge that all of them were not fo vifionary. There was a moft ingenious doctor, who feemed to be perfectly verfed in the whole nature and fyftem of government. This illuftrious perfon

R 4   had

had very ufefully employed his ftudies in finding out effectual remedies for all difeafes and
corruptions, to which the feveral kinds of
public adminiftration are fubject by the vices
or infirmities of thofe who govern, as well as
by the licentioufnefs of thofe who are to obey.
For inftance; whereas all writers and reafoners have agreed, that there is a ftrict univerfal
refemblance between the natural and the political body; can there be any thing more evi-
dent, than that the health of both muft be
preferved and the difeafes cured by the fame
prefcriptions? It is allowed, that fenates and
great counfels are often troubled with redun-
dant, ebullient, and other peccant humours;
with many difeafes of the head, and more of
the heart; with ftrong convulfions, with grievous contractions of the nerves and finews in
both hands, but efpecially the right; with
fpleen, flatus, vertigos and deliriums; with
fcrophulous tumours full of foetid purulent
matter; with four frothy ructations; with ca-
nine appetites, and crudenefs of digeftion, befides many others needlefs to mention. This
doctor therefore propofed, that upon the meeting of a fenate certain phyficians fhould attend at the three firft days of their fitting, and
at the clofe of each day's debate feel the pulfes
of every fenator; after which, having maturely confidered and confulted upon the nature of
the feveral maladies and the methods of cure,
they fhould on the fourth day return to the
fenate-houfe attended by their apothecaries
                                                              ftored

ftored with proper medicines; and before the members fat, adminifter to each of them lenitives, aperitives, abfterfives, corrofives, reftringents, palliatives, laxatives, cephalalgics, icterics, apophlegmatics, acouftics, as their feveral cafes required; and according as thefe medicines fhould operate, repeat, alter, or omit them at the next meeting.

This project could not be of any great expence to the public; and might in my poor opinion be of much ufe for the difpatch of bufinefs in thofe countries, where fenates have any fhare in the legiflative power; beget unanimity, fhorten debates, open a few mouths which are now clofed, and clofe many more which are now open; curb the petulancy of the young, and correct the pofitivenefs of the old; rouze the ftupid, and damp the pert.

Again; becaufe it is a general complaint, that the favourites of princes are troubled with fhort and weak memories; the fame doctor propofed, that whoever attended a firft minifter, after having told his bufinefs with the utmoft brevity and in the plaineft words, fhould at his departure give the faid minifter a tweak by the nofe, or a kick on the belly, or tread on his corns, or lug him thrice by both ears, or run a pin into his breech, or pinch his arm black and blue, to prevent forgetfulnefs: and at every levee day repeat the fame operation, till the bufinefs were done or abfolutely refufed.

He

He likewife directed, that every fenator in
the great council of a nation, after he had delivered his opinion, and argued in the defence
of it, fhould be obliged to give his vote directly contrary; becaufe if that were done, the
refult would infallibly terminate in the good of
the public.

When parties in a ftate are violent, he offered a wonderful contrivance to reconcile
them. The method is this : you take an hundred leaders of each party; you difpofe them
into couples of fuch, whofe heads are nearest
of a fize; then let two nice operators faw off
the *occiput* of each couple at the fame time in
fuch a manner, that the brain may be equally
divided. Let the *occiputs* thus cut off be in-
terchanged, applying each to the head of his
oppofite party-man. It feems indeed to be a
work that requireth fome exactnefs, but the
profeffor affured us, that if it were dextroufly
performed the cure would be infallible. For
he argued thus; that the two half brains being left to debate the matter between themfelves within the fpace of one fcull would foon
come to a good underftanding, and produce
that moderation, as well as regularity of thinking, fo much to be wifhed for in the heads of
thofe, who imagine they come into the world
only to watch and govern its motion : and as
to the difference of brains in quantity or quality, among thofe who are directors in faction;
the doctor affured us from his own knowledge,
that it was a perfect trifle.

3

I heard

I heard a very warm debate between two profeffors about the moft commodious and effeftual ways and means of raifing money without grieving the fubject. The firft affirmed, the jufteft method would be to lay a certain tax upon vices and folly; and the fum fixed upon every man to be rated after the faireft manner by a jury of his neighbours. The fecond was of an opinion directly contrary; to tax thofe qualities of body and mind, for which men chiefly value themfelves; the rate to be more or lefs according to the degrees of excelling; the decifion whereof fhould be left intirely to their own breaft. The higheft tax was upon men, who are the greateft favourites of the other fex, and the affeffments according to the number and natures of the favours they have received; for which they are allowed to be their own vouchers. Wit, valour, and politenefs were likewife propofed to be largely taxed, and collected in the fame manner, by every perfon's giving his own word for the quantum of what he poffeffed. But as to honour, juftice, wifdom, and learning, they fhould not be taxed at all; becaufe they are qualifications of fo fingular a kind, that no man will either allow them in his neighbour, or value them in himfelf.

The women were propofed to be taxed according to their beauty and fkill in dreffing; wherein they had the fame privilege with the men, to be determined by their own judgment. But conftancy, chaftity, good fenfe, and good

good nature were not rated, becaufe they would not bear the charge of collecting.

To keep fenators in the intereft of the crown it was propofed, that the members fhould raffle for employments; every man firft taking an oath, and giving fecurity, that he would vote for the court, whether he won or no; after which the lofers had in their turn the liberty of raffling upon the next vacancy. Thus hope and expectation would be kept a-live; none would complain of broken promi-fes, but impute their difappointments whol-ly to fortune, whofe fhoulders are broader and ftronger than thofe of a miniftry.

Another profeffor fhewed me a large paper of inftructions for difcovering plots and con-fpiracies againft the government. He advifed great ftatefmen to examine into the dyet of all fufpected perfons; their times of eating; upon which fide they lay in bed; with which hand they wiped their pofteriors; to take a ftrict view of their excrements, and from the colour, the odour, the tafte, the confiftence, the crudenefs, or maturity of digeftion, form a judgment of their thoughts and defigns. Be-caufe men are never fo ferious, thoughtful, and intent, as when they are at ftool, which he found by frequent experiment: for in fuch conjunctures, when he ufed meerly as a trial to confider which was the beft way of mur-dering the king, his ordure would have a tinc-ture of green; but quite different, when he
thought

thought only of raiſing an inſurrection, or burning the metropolis.

The whole diſcourſe was written with great acuteneſs, containing many obſervations both curious and uſeful for politicians; but as I conceived not altogether compleat. This I ventured to tell the author, and offered if he pleaſed to ſupply him with ſome additions. He received my propoſition with more compliance, than is uſual among writers, eſpecially thoſe of the projecting ſpecies; profeſſing he would be glad to receive farther information.

I told him, that in the kingdom of *Tribnia,* by the natives called *Langdon,* where I had ſojourned ſome time in my travels, the bulk of the people conſiſt in a manner wholly of diſcoverers, witneſſes, informers, accuſers, proſecutors, evidences, ſwearers, together with their ſeveral ſubſervient and ſubaltern inſtruments, all under the colours, the conduct, and pay of miniſters of ſtate and their deputies. The plots in that kingdom are uſually the workmanſhip of thoſe perſons who deſire to raiſe their own characters of profound politicians; to reſtore new vigour to a crazy adminiſtration; to ſtifle or divert general diſcontents; to fill their coffers with forfeitures; and raiſe or ſink the opinion of public credit, as either ſhall beſt anſwer their private advantage. It is firſt agreed, and ſettled among them, what ſuſpected perſons ſhall be accuſed of a plot: then, effectual care is taken to ſecure

cure all their letters and papers, and put the owners in chains. Thefe papers are delivered to a fett of artifts, very dexterous in finding out the myfterious meanings of words, fyllables, and letters : for inftance, they can difcover a clofeftool to fignify a privy-council; a flock of geefe, a fenate; a lame dog *, an invader; the plague, a ftanding army; a buzzard, a prime minifter; the gout, an high prieft; a gibbet, a fecretary of ftate; a chamber-pot, a committee of grandees; a fieve, a court-lady; a broom, a revolution; a moufetrap, an employment; a bottomlefs pit, a treafury; a fink, a court; a cap and bells, a favourite; a broken reed, a court of juftice; an empty tun, a general; a running fore, the adminiftration.

When this method fails, they have two others more effectual, which the learned among them call *acroftics* and *anagrams*. *Firft*, they can decypher all initial letters into political meanings. Thus, N fhall fignify a plot, B, a regiment of horfe, L, a fleet at fea : or, *fecondly*, by tranfpofing the letters of the alphabet in any fufpected paper, they can lay open the deepeft defigns of a difcontented party. So for example, if I fhould fay in a letter to a friend, *Our brother* Tom *has juft got the piles,* a fkilful decypherer would difcover, that the fame letters, which compofe that fentence, may be analyfed into the following words,

* See the proceedings againft Dr. *Atterbury*, bifhop of *Rocheftcr* State Trials, Vol. VI.

Refift,

Refift, —— *a plot is brought home*——*The tour.*
And this is the anagrammatic method.

The profeffor made me great acknowledgments for communicating thefe obfervations, and promifed to make honourable mention of me in his treatife.

I faw nothing in this country, that could invite me to a longer continuance, and began to think of returning home to *England.*

CHAP. VII.

The author leaves Lagado, *arrives at* Maldonada. *No fhip ready. He takes a fhort voyage to* Glubbdubdrib. *His reception by the governor.*

THE continent, of which this kingdom is a part, extends itfelf, as I have reafon to believe, eaftward to that unknown tract of *America* weftward of *California,* and north to the *Pacific* ocean, which is not above a hundred and fifty miles from *Lagado*; where there is a good port, and much commerce with the great ifland of *Luggnagg,* fituated to the northweft about 29 degrees north latitude, and 140 longitude. This ifland of *Luggnagg* ftands fouth-eaftward of *Japan,* about an hundred leagues diftant. There is a ftrict alliance between the *Japanefe* emperor and the king of *Luggnagg,* which affords frequent opportunities of failing from one ifland to the other. I determined therefore to direct my courfe this way

way in order to my return to *Europe.* I hired
two mules, with a guide, to shew me the way,
and carry my small baggage. I took leave of
my noble protector; who had shewn me so
much favour, and made me a generous present at my departure.

My journey was without any accident or adventure worth relating. When I arrived at
the port of *Maldonada* (for so it is called) there
was no ship in the harbour bound for *Luggnagg*, nor like to be in some time. The town
is about as large as *Portsmouth.* I soon fell into some acquaintance, and was very hospitably received. A gentleman of distinction said
to me, that since the ships bound for *Luggnagg* could not be ready in less than a month,
it might be no disagreeable amusement for me
to take a trip to the little island of *Glubbdubdrib*, about five leagues off to the south-west.
He offered himself and a friend to accompany
me, and that I should be provided with a small
convenient barque for the voyage.

Glubbdubdrib, as nearly as I can interpret
the word, signifies the island of *sorcerers* or *magicians.* It is about one third as large as the
Isle of Wight, and extremely fruitful: it is governed by the head of a certain tribe, who
are all magicians. This tribe marries only a-
mong each other, and the eldest in succession
is prince or governor. He hath a noble palace, and a park of about three thousand a-
cres, surrounded by a wall of hewn stone
twenty feet high. In this park are several
small

ſmall incloſures for cattle, corn, and gardening.

The governor and his family are ſerved and attended by domeſtics of a kind ſomewhat unuſual. By his ſkill in necromancy he hath a power of calling whom he pleaſeth from the dead, and commanding their ſervice for twenfour hours, but no longer; nor can he call the ſame perſons up again in leſs than three months, except upon very extraordinary occaſions.

When we arrived at the iſland, which was about eleven in the morning, one of the gentlemen, who accompanied me, went to the governor, and deſired admittance for a ſtranger, who came on purpoſe to have the honour of attending on his highneſs. This was immediately granted, and we all three entered the gate of the palace, between two rows of guards armed and dreſſed after a very antic manner, and ſomething in their countenances that made my fleſh creep with a horror I cannot expreſs. We paſſed through ſeveral apartments between ſervants of the ſame ſort ranked on each ſide, as before, till we came to the chamber of preſence, where, after three profound obeyſances and a few general 'queſtions, we were permitted to ſit on three ſtools near the loweſt ſtep of his highneſs's throne. He underſtood the language of *Balnibarbi*, although it were different from that of this iſland. He deſired me to give him ſome account of my travels; and, to let me ſee that I ſhould be treated without ceremony, he diſ-miffed all his attendants with a turn of his finger, at which to my great aftonifhment they vanifhed in an inftant, like vifions in a dream, when we awake on a fudden. I could not recover myfelf in fome time, till the governor affured me, that I fhould receive no hurt; and obferving my two companions to be under no concern, who had been often entertained in the fame manner, I began to take courage, and related to his highnefs a fhort hiftory of my feveral adventures; yet not without fome hefitation, and frequently looking behind me to the place, where I had feen thofe domeftic fpectres. I had the honour to dine with the governor, where a new fett of ghofts ferved up the meat, and waited at table. I now obferved myfelf to be lefs terrified, than I had been in the morning. I ftayed till fun-fet, but humbly defired his highnefs to excufe me for not accepting his invitation of lodging in the palace. My two friends and I lay at a private houfe in the town adjoining, which is the capital of this little ifland; and the next morning we returned to pay our duty to the governor, as he was pleafed to command us.

After this manner we continued in the ifland for ten days, moft part of every day with the governor, and at night in our lodging. I foon grew fo familiarized to the fight of fpirits, that after the third or fourth time they gave me no emotion at all; or if I had any apprehenfions left, my curiofity prevailed over them. For his highnefs the governor ordered me to

call

call up whatever perfons I would chufe to
name, and in whatever numbers, among all
the dead from the beginning of the world to
the prefent time, and command them to anfwer any queftions I fhould think fit to afk;
with this condition, that my queftions muft
be confined within the compafs of the times
they lived in. And one thing I might depend
upon, that they would certainly tell me truth,
for lying was a talent of no ufe in the lower
world. I made my humble acknowledgments
to his highnefs for fo great a favour. We
were in a chamber, from whence there was a
fair profpect into the park. And, becaufe my
firft inclination was to be entertained with
fcenes of pomp and magnificence, I defired
to fee *Alexander the Great* at the head of his
army juft after the battle of *Arbela*, which,
upon a motion of the governor's finger, immediately appeared in a large field under the
window, where we ftood. *Alexander* was called up into the room : it was with great difficulty that I underftood his *Greek*[a], and had
but little of my own. He affured me upon his
honour, that he was not poifoned, but died of
a fever by exceffive drinking[b].

S 2   Next

[a] An hint from *Gulliver*, that we have loft the true *Greek* idiom. ORRERY.

[b] In this paffage there is a peculiar beauty, though it is not difcovered at an hafty view. The appearance of *Alexander* with a victorious army immediately af-ter the battle of *Arbela* produced only a declaration that he died by drunkennefs; thus inadequate and ridiculous in the eye of reafon is the ultimate purpofe for which *Alexander* with his army marched into a remote country, fubverted a mighty empire, and

Next I faw *Hannibal* paffing the *Alps*, who told me, he had not a drop of vinegar in his camp [a].

I faw *Cæfar* and *Pompey* at the head of their troops juft ready to engage. I faw the former in his laft great triumph. I defired, that the fenate of *Rome* might appear before me in one large chamber, and a modern reprefentative in counterview in another. The firft feemed to be an affembly of heroes and demy-gods, the other a knot of pedlars, pick-pockets, high-waymen, and bullies.

The governor at my requeft gave the fign for *Cæfar* and *Brutus* to advance towards us. I was ftruck with a profound veneration at the fight of *Brutus*, and could eafily difcover the moft confummate virtue, the greateft intrepi-dity and firmnefs of mind, the trueft love of his country, and general benevolence for man-kind, in every lineament of his countenance. I obferved with much pleafure, that thefe two perfons were in good intelligence with each o-ther; and *Cæfar* freely confeffed to me, that the greateft actions of his own life were not equal by many degrees to the glory of taking

and deluged a nation with blood; he gained no more than an epi-thet to his name, which after a few repetitions was no longer re-garded even by himfelf: thus the purpofe of his refurrection appears to be at leaft equally im-portant with that of his life, upon which it is a fatire not more bitter than juft.

[a] *Livy* the *Roman* hiftorian has related, that *Hannibal* burnt a great pile of wood upon a rock that ftopped his paffage, and when it was thus heated poured *vinegar* upon it, by which it was made fo foft as to be eafily cut through.

it

it away. I had the honour to have much converſation with *Brutus*; and was told, that his
anceſtor *Junius, Socrates, Epaminondas, Cato*
the younger *, Sir *Thomas More*, and himſelf
were perpetually together : a *ſextumvirate*, to
which all the ages of the world cannot add a
ſeventh.

It would be tedious to trouble the reader
with relating, what vaſt numbers of illuſtri-
ous perſons were called up to gratify that in-
ſatiable deſire I had to ſee the world in every
period of antiquity placed before me. I chiefly fed mine eyes with beholding the deſtroyers
of tyrants and uſurpers, and the reſtorers of
liberty to oppreſſed and injured nations. But
it is impoſſible to expreſs the ſatisfaction I received in my own mind, after ſuch a manner
as to make it a ſuitable entertainment to the
reader.

---

* I am in ſome doubt whether *Cato* the *cenſor* can fairly claim a rank among ſo choice a group of ghoſts. ORRERY.

This note of his lordſhip is an encomium on the judgment of our author, who knew that *Cato* the *cenſor* and *Cato* the *younger* were very different perſons, and for good reaſons pre-ferred the *latter*.

S 3   CHAP.

CHAP. VIII.

A further account of Glubbdubdrib. *Ancient and modern history corrected.*

HAving a desire to see those ancients, who were most renowned for wit and learning, I set apart one day on purpose. I proposed that *Homer* and *Aristotle* might appear at the head of all their commentators; but these were so numerous, that some hundreds were forced to attend in the court and outward rooms of the palace. I knew and could distinguish those two heroes at first sight, not only from the croud, but from each other. *Homer* was the taller and comlier person of the two, walked very erect for one of his age, and his eyes were the most quick and piercing I ever beheld. *Aristotle* stooped much, and made use of a staff. His visage was meagre, his hair lank and thin, and his voice hollow [a]. I soon discovered that both of them were perfect strangers to the rest of the company, and had never seen or heard of them before. And

---

[a] This description of *Aristotle* is fine, and in a few words represents the true nature of his works. By not having the immortal spirit of *Homer*, he was unable to keep his body erect; and his staff which feebly supported him, like his commentators, made this defect more conspicuous. He wanted not some useful qualities, but these *real ornaments* like his hair were thin and *ungraceful*. ORRERY.

In this the noble commentator seems to be mistaken, for it cannot be believed that *Aristotle's real ornaments* however few were *ungraceful*.

I had

I had a whisper from a ghost, who shall be nameless, that these commentators always kept in the most distant quarters from their principals in the lower world, through a consciousness of shame and guilt, because they had so horribly misrepresented the meaning of those authors to posterity. I introduced *Didymus* and *Eustathius* to *Homer*, and prevailed on him to treat them better than perhaps they deserved, for he soon found they wanted a genius to enter into the spirit of a poet. But *Aristotle* was out of all patience with the account I gave him of *Scotus* and *Ramus*, as I presented them to him, and he asked them whether the rest of the tribe were as great dunces as themselves.

I then desired the governor to call up *Descartes* and *Gassendi* [a], with whom I prevailed to explain their systems to *Aristotle*. This great philosopher freely acknowledged his own mistakes in natural philosophy, because he proceeded in many things upon conjecture, as all men must do; and he found, that *Gassendi*, who had made the doctrine of *Epicurus* as palatable as he could, and the *vortices* of *Descartes* were equally to be exploded. He predicted the same fate to *attraction*, whereof the present learned are such zealous asserters. He said,

[a] *Gassendi* was esteemed one of the greatest ornaments of *France*; he was a doctor of divinity and royal professor of mathematics; he was born in *Provence* in 1592, and died in 1655. With great industry he collected whatever related to the person and to the philosophy of *Epicurus*, the latter of which he has reduced into a compleat System. ORRERY.

that

e. I was

was not

d myself

which

to their

r, from

, why a

for two

: why a

d, and a

me what

at house,

cruelty,

character-

re distin-

of arms;

ble house,

crophulous

er could I

h an inter-

ys, valets,

, captains,

ern history.

persons of

ces for an

the world

to ascribe

that new fyftems of nature were but new fafhions, which would vary in every age; and
even thofe, who pretend to demonftrate them
from mathematical principles, would flourifh
but a fhort period of time, and be out of vogue
when that was determined.

I fpent five days in converfing with many o-
thers of the ancient learned. I faw moft of
the firft *Roman* emperors. I prevailed on the
governor to call up *Eliogabalus*'s cooks to drefs
us a dinner, but they could not fhew us much
of their fkill for want of materials. A *belot*
of *Agefilaus* made us a difh of *Spartan* broth,
but I was not able to get down a fecond fpoon-
ful.

The two gentlemen, who conducted me to
the ifland, were preffed by their private affairs
to return in three days, which I employed in
feeing fome of the modern dead, who had
made the greateft figure for two or three hundred years paft in our own and other countries
of *Europe*; and having been always a great ad-
mirer of old illuftrious families, I defired the
governor would call up a dozen or two of
kings, with their anceftors in order for eight
or nine generations. But my difappointment
was grievous and unexpected. For, inftead of
a long train with royal diadems, I faw in one
family two fidlers, three fpruce courtiers, and
an *Italian* prelate. In another, a barber, an
abbot, and two cardinals. I have too great a
veneration for crowned heads to dwell any
longer on fo nice a fubject. But as to counts,

mar-

marqueffes, dukes, earls, and the like, I was not fo fcrupulous. And, I confefs, it was not without fome pleafure, that I found myfelf able trace the particular features, by which certain families are diftinguifhed up, to their originals. I could plainly difcover, from whence one family derives a long chin, why a fecond hath abounded with knaves for two generations, and fools for two more; why a third happened to be crack-brained, and a fourth to be fharpers; whence it came what *Polydore Virgil* fays of a certain great houfe, *Nec vir fortis, nec fœmina cafta;* how cruelty, falfhood, and cowardice grew to be character-iftics, by which certain families are diftin-guifhed as much as by their coats of arms; who firft brought the pox into a noble houfe, which hath lineally defcended in fcrophulous tumours to their pofterity. Neither could I wonder at all this, when I faw fuch an inter-ruption of lineages by pages, lacqueys, valets, coachmen, gamefters, fidlers, players, captains, and pick-pockets.

I was chiefly difgufted with modern hiftory. For having ftrictly examined all the perfons of greateft name in the courts of princes for an hundred years paft, I found how the world had been mifled by proftitute writers to afcribe the greateft exploits in war to cowards, the wifeft counfel to fools, fincerity to flatterers, *roman* virtue to betrayers of their country, pi-ety to atheifts, chaftity to fodomites, truth to informers: how many innocent and excellent

perfons

perfons had been condemned to death or banifhment by the practifing of great minifters upon the corruption of judges, and the malice of factions : how many villains had been exalted to the higheft places of truft, power, dignity, and profit : how great a fhare in the motions and events of courts, councils, and fenates, might be challenged by bawds, whores, pimps, parafites, and buffoons : how low an opinion I had of human wifdom and integrity, when I was truly informed of the fprings and motives of great enterprizes and revolutions in the world, and of the contemptible accidents to which they owed their fuccefs.

Here I difcovered the roguery and ignorance of thofe, who pretend to write *anecdotes,* or fecret hiftory ; who fend fo many kings' to their graves with a cup of poifon ; will repeat the difcourfe between a prince and chief minifter, where no witnefs was by ; unlock the thoughts and cabinets of ambaffadors and fecretaries of ftate ; and have the perpetal misfortune to be miftaken. Here I difcovered the true caufes of many great events that have furprifed the world ; how a whore can govern the back-ftairs, the back-ftairs a council, and the council a fenate. A general confeffed in my prefence, that he got a victory purely by the force of cowardice and ill conduct : and an admiral, that for want of proper intelligence he beat the enemy, to whom he intended to betray the fleet. Three kings protefted to me, that in their whole reigns they never did

did once prefer any perfon of merit, unlefs by miftake, or treachery of fome minifter in whom they confided: neither would they do it if they were to live again; and they fhewed with great ftrength of reafon, that the royal throne could not be fupported without corruption, becaufe that pofitive, confident, reftive temper, which virtue infufed into a man, was a perpetual clog to public bufinefs.

I had the curiofity to enquire in a particular manner, by what method great numbers had procured to themfelves high titles of honour and prodigious eftates; and I confined my enquiry to a very modern period, however without grating upon prefent times, becaufe I would be fure to give no offence even to foreigners; for I hope the reader need not to be told, that I do not in the leaft intend my own country in what I fay upon this occafion. A great number of perfons concerned were called up, and upon a very flight examination difcovered fuch a fcene of infamy, that I cannot reflect upon it without fome ferioufnefs. Perjury, oppreffion, fubornation, fraud, pandarifm, and the like *infirmities* were amongft the moft excufable arts they had to mention; and for thefe I gave, as it was reafonable, great allowance. But when fome confeffed they owed their greatnefs and wealth to fodomy, or inceft; others to the proftituting of their own wives and daughters; others to the betraying their country or their prince; fome to poifoning, more to the perverting of

juftice

juftice in order to deftroy the innocent : I
hope I may be pardoned, if thefe difcoveries
inclined me a little to abate of that profound
veneration, which I am naturally apt to pay to
perfons of high rank, who ought to be treated
with the utmoft refpect due to their fublime
dignity by us their inferiors.

I had often read of fome great fervices done
to princes and ftates, and defired to fee the
perfons, by whom thofe fervices were performed. Upon enquiry I was told, that their
names were to be found on no record, except
a few of them, whom hiftory hath reprefented as the vileft rogues and traitors. As to the
reft, I had never once heard of them. They
all appeared with dejected looks, and in the
meaneft habit, moft of them telling me they
died in poverty and difgrace, and the reft on a
fcaffold or a gibbet.

Among others there was one perfon, whofe
cafe appeared a little fingular. He had a
youth about eighteen years old ftanding by his
fide. He told me he had for many years been
commander of a fhip ; and in the fea fight at
Actium, had the good fortune to break through
the enemies great line of battle, fink three of
their capital fhips, and take a fourth, which
was the fole caufe of *Anthony*'s flight, and of
the victory that enfued ; that the youth ftanding by him, his only fon, was killed in the
action. He added, that upon the confidence
of fome merit, the war being at an end, he
went to *Rome*, and follicited at the court of
Auguftus

Auguſtus to be preferred to a greater ſhip, whoſe commander had been killed; but without any regard to his pretenſions it was given to a boy, who had never ſeen the ſea, the ſon of *Libertina*, who waited on one of the emperor's miſtreſſes. Returning back to his own veſſel he was charged with neglect of duty, and the ſhip given to a favourite page of *Publicola*, the vice-admiral; whereupon he retired to a poor farm at a great diſtance from *Rome*, and there ended his life. I was ſo curious to know the truth of this ſtory, that I deſired *Agrippa* might be called, who was admiral in that fight. He appeared, and confirmed the whole account, but with much more advantage to the captain, whoſe modeſty had extenuated or concealed a great part of his merit.

I was ſurpriſed to find corruption grown ſo high and ſo quick in that empire, by the force of luxury ſo lately introduced, which made me leſs wonder at many parallel caſes in other countries, where vices of all kinds have reigned ſo much longer, and where the whole praiſe, as well as pillage, hath been engroſſed by the chief commander, who perhaps had the leaſt title to either.

As every perſon called up made exactly the ſame appearance he had done in the world, it gave me melancholy reflections to obſerve, how much the race of human kind was degenerated among us within theſe hundred years paſt. How the pox under all its conſequen-

ces

ces and denominations had altered every lineament of an *english* countenance : fhortened the
fize of bodies, unbraced the nerves, relaxed the
firews and mufcles, introduced a fallow complexion, and rendered the flefh loofe and *rancid*.

I defcended fo low as to defire, that fome
english yeomen of the old ftamp, might be
fummoned to appear; once fo famous for the
fimplicity of their manners, diet, and drefs;
for juftice in their dealings; for their true
fpirit of liberty; for their valour and love of
their country. Neither could I be wholly
unmoved, after comparing the living with the
dead, when I confidered how all thefe pure
native virtues were proftituted for a piece of
money by their grand-children, who in felling
their votes, and managing at elections, have
acquired every vice and corruption that can
poffibly be learned in a court.

C H A P. IX.

The author returns to Maldonada. *Sails to the
kingdom of* Luggnagg. *The author confined. He
is fent for to court. The manner of his admittance. The king's great lenity to his fubjects.*

THE day of our departure being come, I
took leave of his highnefs, the governor
of *Glubbdubdribb*, and returned with my two
companions to *Maldanada*, where after a fortnight's waiting, a fhip was ready to fail for
Luggnagg. The two gentlemen, and fome o-
thers,

thers, were so generous and kind as to furnish me with provisions, and see me on board. I was a month in this voyage. We had one violent storm, and were under a necessity of steering westward to get into the trade-wind, which holds for above sixty leagues. On the 21st of *April*, 1708, we sailed into the river of *Clumegnig*, which is a sea-port town, at the south-east point of *Luggnagg*. We cast anchor within a league of the town, and made a signal for a pilot. Two of them came on board in less than half an hour, by whom we were guided between certain shoals and rocks, which are very dangerous in the passage, to a large basin, where a fleet may ride in safety within a cable's length of the town wall.

Some of our sailors, whether out of treachery or inadvertence, had informed the pilots that I was a stranger and a great traveller; whereof these gave notice to a custom-house officer, by whom I was examined very strictly upon my landing. This officer spoke to me in the language of *Balnibarbi*, which by the force of much commerce is generally understood in that town, especially by sea-men, and those employed in the customs. I gave him a short account of some particulars, and made my story as plausible and consistent as I could; but I thought it necessary to disguise my country, and call myself an *Hollander*, because my intentions were for *Japan*, and I knew the *Dutch* were the only *Europeans* permitted to enter into that kingdom. I therefore

fore told the officer, that having been shipwrecked on the coaft of *Balnibarbi*, and caft on
a rock, I was received up into *Laputa*, or the
flying ifland (of which he had often heard)
and was now endeavouring to get to *Japan*,
from whence I might find a convenience of
returning to my own country. The officer
faid, I muft be confined till he could receive
orders from court, for which he would write
immediately, and hoped to receive an anfwer
in a fortnight. I was carried to a convenient
lodging with a centry placed at the door ; however, I had the liberty of a large garden, and
was treated with humanity enough, being
maintained all the time at the king's charge.
I was invited by feveral perfons, chiefly out of
curiofity, becaufe it was reported that I came
from countries very remote, of which they
had never heard.

I hired a young man, who came in the
fame fhip, to be an interpreter; he was a native of *Luggnagg*, but had lived fome years at
Maldonada, and was a perfect mafter of both
languages. By his affiftance I was able to hold
a converfation with thofe who came to vifit
me ; but this confifted only of their queftions
and my anfwers.

The difpatch came from court about the
time we expected. It contained a warrant for
conducting me and my retinue to *Traldrag-
dubb*, or *Trildrogdrib*, for it is pronounced both
ways, as near as I can remember, by a party
of ten horfe. All my retinue was that poor
lad

had for an interpreter, whom I perſuaded into my ſervice, and at my humble requeſt we had each of us a mule to ride on. A meſſenger was diſpatched half a day's journey before us to give the king notice of my approach, and to deſire that his majeſty would pleaſe to appoint a day and hour, when it would be his gracious pleaſure, that I might have the honour to *lick the duſt before his foot-ſtool.* This is the court ſtyle, and I found it to be more than matter of form. For, upon my admittance two days after my arrival, I was commanded to crawl upon my belly, and lick the floor as I advanced; but on account of my being a ſtranger care was taken to have it made ſo clean, that the duſt was not offenſive. However, this was a peculiar grace, not allowed to any but perſons of the higheſt rank, when they deſire an admittance. Nay, ſometimes the floor is ſtrewed with duſt on purpoſe, when the perſon to be admittted happens to have powerful enemies at court. And I have ſeen a great lord with his mouth ſo crammed, that, when he had crept to the proper diſtance from the throne, he was not able to ſpeak a word. Neither is there any remedy; becauſe it is capital for thoſe, who receive an audience, to ſpit or wipe their mouths in his majeſty's preſence. There is indeed another cuſtom which I cannot altogether approve of: when the king hath a mind to put any of his nobles to death in a gentle, indulgent manner, he commands the floor to be ſtrewed with a certain brown powder of a deadly compofition, which being licked up infallibly kills him in twenty-four hours. But in juftice to this prince's great clemency, and the care he hath of his fubjects lives (wherein it were much to be wifhed, that the monarchs of *Europe* would imitate him) it muft be mentioned for his honour, that ftrict orders are given to have the infected parts of the floor well wafhed after every fuch execution; which if his domeftics neglect, they are in danger of incurring his royal difpleafure. I myfelf heard him give directions, that one of his pages fhould be whipt, whofe turn it was to give notice about wafhing the floor after an execution, but malicioufly had omitted it, by which neglect a young lord of great hopes coming to an audience was unfortunately poifoned, although the king at that time had no defign againft his life. But this good prince was fo gracious, as to forgive the poor page his whipping upon promife, that he would do fo no more without fpecial orders.

To return from this digreffion; when I had crept within four yards of the throne, I raifed myfelf gently upon my knees, and then, ftriking my forehead feven times againft the ground, I pronounced the following words, as they had been taught me the night before, *Ickpling gloff-throbb fquut ferumm blhiop mlafhnalt zwin tnod-balkuffbflbiophad gurdlubh afht.* This is the compliment eftablifhed by the laws of the land for all perfons admitted to the king's prefence. It may be rendered into *Englifh* thus: *May your*

your cœleſtial majeſty out-live the ſun, eleven moons and a half. To this the king returned ſome anſwer, which although I could not under-ſtand, yet I replied as I had been directed : *Flute drin yalerick dwuldom praſtrad mirpuſh,* which properly ſignifies, *My tongue is in the mouth of my friend;* and by this expreſſion was meant, that I deſired leave to bring my inter-preter ; whereupon the young man already mentioned was accordingly introduced, by whoſe intervention I anſwered as many queſ-tions, as his majeſty could put in above an hour. I ſpoke in the *Balnibarbian* tongue, and my interpreter delivered my meaning in that of *Luggnagg.*

The king was much delighted with my company, and ordered his *Bliffmarklub,* or high chamberlain, to appoint a lodging in the court for me and my interpreter, with a daily allowance for my table, and a large purſe of gold for my common expences.

I ſtayed three months in this country out of perfect obedience to his majeſty, who was pleaſed highly to favour me, and made me very honourable offers. But I thought it more conſiſtent with prudence and juſtice to paſs the remainder of my days with my wife and fa-mily.

C H A P.

C H A P. X.

The Luggnuggians *commended. A particular description of the* Struldbrugs, *with many conversations between the author and some eminent persons upon that subject.*

THE *Luggnuggians* are a polite and generous people; and although they are not without some share of that pride, which is peculiar to all *eastern* countries, yet they shew themselves courteous to strangers, especially such who are countenanced by the court. I had many acquaintance among persons of the best fashion, and being always attended by my interpreter, the conversation we had was not disagreeable.

One day, in much good company, I was asked by a person of quality, whether I had seen any of their *struldbrugs* or *immortals*. I said, I had not; and desired he would explain to me, what he meant by such an appellation applied to a mortal creature. He told me, that sometimes, though very rarely, a child happened to be born in a family with a red circular spot in the forehead directly over the left eyebrow, which was an infallible mark, that it should never die. The spot, as he described it, was about the compass of a silver threepence, but in the course of time grew larger, and changed its colour; for at twelve years old it became green, so continued till five and twenty, then turned to a deep blue; at five and

and forty it grew coal black, and as large as
an *englifh* fhilling ; but never admitted any farther alteration. He faid, thefe births were fo rare,
that he did not believe there could be above e-
leven hundred *firuldbrugs* of both fexes in the
whole kingdom, of which he computed about
fifty in the metropolis, and among the reft a
young girl born about three years ago : that
thefe productions were not peculiar to any family, but a meer effect of chance ; and the
children of the *firuldbrugs* themfelves were e-
qually mortal with the reft of the people.

I freely own myfelf to have been ftruck with
inexpreffible delight upon hearing this account:
and the perfon, who gave it me, happening
to underftand the *Balnibarbian* language, which
I fpoke very well, I could not forbear breaking out into expreffions perhaps a little too
extravagant. I cried out, as in a rapture :
Happy nation, where every child hath at leaft
a chance for being immortal ! Happy people,
who enjoy fo many living examples of ancient virtue, and have mafters ready to inftruct
them in the wifdom of all former ages ! but,
happieft beyond all comparifon, are thofe excellent *firuldbrugs*, who being born exempt
from that univerfal calamity of human nature,
have their minds free and difengaged, without the weight and depreffion of fpirits caufed
by the continual apprehenfion of death. I
difcovered my admiration, that I had not
obferved any of thefe illuftrious perfons at-
court ; the black fpot on the forehead being

ſo remarkable a diſtinction, that I could not have eaſily overlooked it : and it was impoſſible that his majeſty, a moſt judicious prince, ſhould not provide himſelf with a good number of ſuch wiſe and able counſellors. Yet perhaps the virtue of thoſe reverend ſages was too ſtrict for the corrupt and libertine manners of a court. And we often find by experience, that young men are too opinionative and volatile to be guided by the ſober dictates of their ſeniors. However, ſince the king was pleaſed to allow me acceſs to his royal perſon, I was reſolved, upon the very firſt occaſion, to deliver my opinion to him on this matter freely and at large by the help of my interpreter; and whether he would pleaſe to take my advice or no, yet in one thing I was determined, that, his majeſty having frequently offered me an eſtabliſhment in this country, I would with great thankfulneſs accept the favour, and paſs my life here in the converſation of thoſe ſuperior beings, the *ſtruldbrugs*, if they would pleaſe to admit me.

The gentleman, to whom I addreſſed my diſcourſe, becauſe (as I have already obſerved) he ſpoke the language of *Balnibarbi*, ſaid to me with a ſort of a ſmile, which uſually ariſeth from pity to the ignorant, that he was glad of any occaſion to keep me among them, and deſired my permiſſion to explain to the company what I had ſpoke. He did ſo, and they talked together for ſome time in their own language, whereof I underſtood not a

5 ſyllable,

fyllable, neither could I obferve by their countenances, what impreffion my difcourfe had
made on them.   After a fhort filence the fame
perfon told me, that his friends and mine (fo
he thought fit to exprefs himfelf) were very
much pleafed with the judicious remarks I had
made on the great happinefs and advantages
of immortal life, and they were defirous to
know in a particular manner, what fcheme
of living I fhould have formed to myfelf, if
it had fallen to my lot to have been born a
ftruldbrug.

I anfwered, it was eafy to be eloquent on fo
copious and delightful a fubject, efpecially to
me, who had been often apt to amufe myfelf
with vifions of what I fhould do, if I were
a king, a general, or a great lord : and,
upon this very cafe, I had frequently run over
the whole fyftem how I fhould employ myfelf, and pafs the time, if I were fure to live
for ever.

That, if it had been my good fortune to
come into the world a *ftruldbrug*, as foon as I
could difcover my own happinefs by underftanding the difference between life and death,
I would firft refolve by all arts and methods
whatfoever to procure myfelf riches.   In the
purfuit of which by thrift and management,
I might reafonably expect in about two hundred years to be the wealthieft man in the
kingdom.   In the fecond place, I would from
my earlieft youth apply myfelf to the ftudy of
arts and fciences, by which I fhould arrive in

T 4   time

time to excel all others in learning. Laftly, I
would carefully record every action and event
of confequence that happened in the public,
impartially draw the characters of the feveral
fucceffions of princes and great minifters of
ftate, with my own obfervations on every
point. I would exactly fet down the feveral
changes in cuftoms, language, fafhions of drefs,
diet, and diverfions. By all which acquire-
ments I fhould be a living treafury of knowledge and wifdom, and certainly become the
oracle of the nation.

I would never marry after threefcore, but
live in an hofpitable manner, yet ftill on the
faving fide. I would entertain myfelf in forming and directing the minds of hopeful young
men, by convincing them from my own remembrance, experience and obfervation, forti-
fied by numerous examples, of the ufefulnefs
of virtue in public and private life. But my
choice and conftant companions fhould be a
fett of my own immortal brotherhood, among
whom I would elect a dozen from the moft
ancient down to my own contemporaries.
Where any of thefe wanted fortunes, I would
provide them with convenient lodges round my
own eftate, and have fome of them always at
my table, only mingling a few of the moft valuable among you mortals, whom length of
time would harden me to lofe with little or no
reluctance, and treat your pofterity after the
fame manner; juft as a man diverts himfelf
with the annual fucceffion of pinks and tulips

in

in his garden, without regretting the loss of those, which withered the preceding year.

These *ftruldbrugs* and I would mutually communicate our obfervations, and memorials through the courfe of time; remark the feveral gradations by which corruption fteals into the world, and oppofe it in every ftep by giving perpetual warning and inftruction to mankind; which, added to the ftrong influence of our own example, would probably prevent that continual degeneracy of human nature fo juftly complained of in all ages.

Add to all this the pleafure of feeing the various revolutions of ftates and empires; the changes in the lower and upper world; ancient cities in ruins, and obfcure villages become the feats of kings; famous rivers leffening into fhallow brooks; the ocean leaving one coaft dry, and overwhelming another; the difcovery of many countries yet unknown. Barbarity overrunning the politeft nations, and the moft barbarous become civilized. I fhould then fee the difcovery of the *longitude*, the *perpetual motion*, the *univerfal medicine*, and many other great inventions brought to the utmoft perfection.

What wonderful difcoveries fhould we make in aftronomy by out-living and confirming our own predictions, by obferving the progrefs and returns of comets, with the changes of motion in the fun, moon, and ftars.

I enlarged upon many other topics, which the natural defire of endlefs life and fublunary hap-

happineſs could eaſily furniſh me with. When I had ended, and the ſum of my diſcourſe had been interpreted, as before, to the reſt of the company, there was a good deal of talk among them in the language of the country, not without ſome laughter at my expence. At laſt the ſame gentleman, who had been my interpreter, ſaid he was deſired by the reſt to ſet me right in a few miſtakes, which I had fallen into through the common imbecillity of human nature, and upon that allowance was leſs anſwerable for them. That this breed of *ſtruldbrugs* was peculiar to their country, for there were no ſuch people either in *Balnibarbi* or *Japan*, where he had the honour to be ambaſſador from his majeſty, and found the natives in both thoſe kingdoms very hard to believe, that the fact was poſſible; and it appeared from my aſtoniſhment, when he firſt mentioned the matter to me, that I received it as a thing wholly new, and ſcarcely to be credited. That in the two kingdoms above mentioned, where during his reſidence he had converſed very much, he obſerved long life to be the univerſal deſire and wiſh of mankind. That whoever had one foot in the grave, was ſure to hold back the other as ſtrongly as he could. That the oldeſt had ſtill hopes of living one day longer, and looked on death as the greateſt evil, from which nature always prompted him to retreat; only in this iſland of *Luggnagg* the appetite for living was not ſo eager,

from

from the continual example of the *ſtruldbrugs* before their eyes.

That the ſyſtem of living contrived by me was unreaſonable and unjuſt; becauſe it ſuppoſed a perpetuity of youth, health, and vigour, which no man could be ſo fooliſh to hope, however extravagant he may be in his wiſhes [a]. That the queſtion therefore was not, whether a man would chuſe to be always in the prime of youth, attended with proſperity and health; but how he would paſs a perpetual life under all the uſual diſadvantages, which old age brings along with it. For although few men will avow their deſires of being immortal upon ſuch hard conditions, yet in the two kingdoms before mentioned, of *Balnibarbi* and *Japan*, he obſerved that every man deſired to put off death for ſome time longer, let it approach ever ſo late; and he rarely heard of any man who died willingly, except he were incited by the extremity of grief or torture. And he appealed to me, whether in thoſe countries I had travelled, as well as my own, I had not obſerved the ſame general diſpoſition [b].

After

[a] To this it may poſſibly be objected, that the perpetuity of youth, health, and vigour would be leſs a prodigy than the perpetuity of life in a body ſubject to gradual decay, and might therefore be hoped without greater extravagance of folly; but the ſentiment here expreſſed, is that of a being to whom immortality though not perpetual youth was familiar, and in whom the wiſh of perpetual youth only would have been extravagant, becauſe that only appeared from facts to be impoſſible.

[b] If it be ſaid, that although the folly of deſiring life to be prolonged under the diſadvantages of old age is here finely ex-

After this preface he gave me a particular account of the *ſtruldbrugs* among them. He ſaid, they commonly acted like mortals, till about thirty years old, after which by degrees they grew melancholy and dejected, encreaſing in both till they came to fourſcore. This he learned from their own confeſſion ; for otherwiſe, there not being above two or three of that ſpecies born in an age, they were too few to form a general obſervation by. When they came to fourſcore years, which is reckoned the extremity of living in this country, they had not only all the follies and infirmities of other old men, but many more, which aroſe from the dreadful proſpect of never dying. They were not only opinionative, peeviſh, covetous, moroſe, vain, talkative ; but incapable of friendſhip, and dead to all natural affection, which never deſcended below their grandchildren. Envy and impotent deſires are their prevailing paſſions. But thoſe objects, againſt which their envy ſeems principally directed, are the vices of the younger ſort, and the

expoſed ; yet the deſire of terreſtrial immortality upon terms, on which alone in the nature of things it is poſſible, an exemption from diſeaſe, accident and decay, is tacitly allowed. It may be anſwered, that as we grow old by imperceptible degrees, ſo for the moſt part we grow old without repining, and every man is ready to profeſs himſelf willing to die, when he ſhall be overtaken by the

decripitude of age in ſome future period ; yet when every other eye ſees that this period is arrived, he is ſtill tenacious of life, and murmurs at the condition upon which he received his exiſtence : to reconcile old age therefore to the thoughts of a diſſolution appears to be all that was neceſſary in a moral writer for practical purpoſes.

deaths

deaths of the old.   By reflecting on the former they find themfelves cut off from all pof-
fibility of pleafure; and whenever they fee a
funeral, they lament and repine that others
are gone to an harbour of reft, to which they
themfelves never can hope to arrive.   They
have no remembrance of any thing, but what
they learned and obferved in their youth and
middle age, and even that is very imperfect.
And for the truth or particulars of any fact it
is fafer to depend on common tradition, than
upon their beft recollections.   The leaft miferable among them appear to be thofe, who
turn to dotage, and intirely lofe their memories; thefe meet with more pity and affiftance,
becaufe they want many bad qualities, which
abound in others.

   If a *ftruldbrug* happen to marry one of his
own kind, the marriage is diffolved of courfe
by the courtefy of the kingdom, as foon as
the younger of the two comes to be fourfcore.
For the law thinks it a reafonable indulgence,
that thofe, who are condemned without any
fault of their own to a perpetual continuance
in the world, fhould not have their mifery
doubled by the load of a wife.

   As foon as they have compleated the term
of eighty years, they are looked on as dead in
law; their heirs immediately fucceed to their
eftates, only a fmall pittance is referved for
their fupport; and the poor ones are maintained at the public charge.   After that period
they are held incapable of any employment of

3   truft

truft or profit; they cannot purchafe lands, or take leafes; neither are they allowed to be wit- neffes in any caufe, either civil or criminal, not even for the decifion of meers and bounds.

At ninety they lofe their teeth and hair; they have at that age no diftinction of tafte, but eat and drink whatever they can get with- out relifh or appetite. The difeafes they were fubject to ftill continue, without encreafing or diminifhing. In talking they forget the com- mon appellation of things, and the names of perfons, even of thofe who are their neareft friends and relations. For the fame reafon they never can amufe themfelves with read- ing, becaufe their memory will not ferve to carry them from the beginning of a fentence to the end; and by this defect they are de- prived of the only entertainment, whereof they might otherwife be capable.

The language of this country being always upon the flux, the *ftruldbrugs* of one age do not underftand thofe of another; neither are they able after two hundred years to hold any converfation (farther than by a few general words) with their neighbours, the mortals; and thus they lie under the difadvantage of living like foreigners in their own country.

This was the account given me of the *ftruld- brugs*, as near as I can remember. I afterwards faw five or fix of different ages, the young- eft not above two hundred years old, who were brought to me at feveral times by fome of my friends; but although they were told, that I

was

was a great traveller, and had feen all the world, they had not the leaft curiofity to afk me a queftion; only defired I would give them *ſlumſkudaſk*, or a token of remembrance; which is a modeft way of begging, to avoid the law, that ftrictly forbids it, becaufe they are provided for by the public, although indeed with a very fcanty allowance.

They are defpifed and hated by all forts of people; when one of them is born, it is reckoned ominous, and their birth is recorded very particularly; fo that you may know their age by confulting the regifter; which however hath not been kept above a thoufand years paft, or at leaft hath been deftroyed by time or public difturbances. But the ufual way of computing how old they are, is, by afking them what kings or great perfons they can remember, and then confulting hiftory; for infallibly the laft prince in their mind did not begin his reign after they were fourfcore years old.

They were the moft mortifying fight I ever beheld; and the women more horrible than men. Befides the ufual deformities in extreme old age, they acquired an additional ghaftlinefs in proportion to their number of years, which is not to be defcribed; and among half a dozen I foon diftinguifhed, which was the eldeft, although there was not above a century or two between them.

The reader will eafily believe, that from what I had heard and feen, my keen appetite

for

for perpetuity of life was much abated. I grew heartily afhamed of the pleafing vifions I had formed; and thought no tyrant could invent a death, into which I would not run with plea-fure from fuch a life. The king heard of all that had paffed between me and my friends upon this occafion, and rallied me very plea-fantly; wifhing I could fend a couple of *ftruld-brugs* to my own country to arm our people againft the fear of death *, but this it feems is forbidden by the fundamental laws of the kingdom, or elfe I fhould have been well con-tent with the trouble and expence of tranf-porting them.

I could not but agree, that the laws of this kingdom relating to the *ftruldbrugs* were found-ed upon the ftrongeft reafons, and fuch as any other country would be under the neceffity of enacting in the like circumftances. Otherwife as avarice is the neceffary confequent of old age, thofe immortals would in time become proprietors of the whole nation, and engrofs the civil power; which for want of abilities to manage, muft end in the ruin of the public.

---

* Perhaps it may not be wholly ufelefs to remark, that the fight of a *Struldbrug* would no otherwife arm thofe againft the fear of death, who have no hope beyond it, than a man is armed againft the fear of breaking his limbs, who jumps out of a window when his houfe is on fire.

C H A P.

CHAP. XI.

The author leaves Luggnagg, *and sails to* Japan. *From thence he returns in a* Dutch *ship to* Amsterdam, *and from* Amsterdam *to* England.

I Thought this account of the *struldbrugs* might be some entertainment to the reader, because it seems to be a little out of the common way; at least I do not remember to have met the like in any book of travels, that hath come to my hands: and if I am deceived my excuse must be, that it is necessary * for travellers, who describe the same country, very often to agree in dwelling on the same particulars, without deserving the censure of having borowed or transcribed from those who wrote before them.

There is indeed a perpetual commerce between this kingdom and the great empire of *Japan*; and it is very probable, that the *Japanese* authors may have given some account of the *struldbrugs*; but my stay in *Japan* was so short, and I was so intirely a stranger to the language, that I was not qualified to make any

---

* The word *necessary* is here used in the same manner, as when by the idiom of our language it means *convenient*, though it is to be understood in its proper and original significa-tion. "Travellers who describe the same country very often *necessarily* agree in dwelling on the same particulars, and therefore *do not deserve* the censure of having borrowed, &c."

enquiries. But I hope the *Dutch* upon this notice will be curious and able enough to supply my defects.

His majesty having often pressed me to accept some employment in his court, and finding me absolutely determined to return to my native country, was pleased to give me his licence to depart, and honoured me with a letter of recommendation under his own hand to the emperor of *Japan*. He likewise presented me with four hundred forty-four large pieces of gold (this nation delighting in even numbers) and a red diamond, which I sold in *England* for eleven hundred pounds.

On the 6th day of *May*, 1709, I took a solemn leave of his majesty and all my friends. This prince was so gracious, as to order a guard to conduct me to *Glanguenstald*, which is a royal port to the *south-west* part of the island. In six days I found a vessel ready to carry me to *Japan*, and spent fifteen days in the voyage. We landed at a small port-town called *Xamoschi*, situated on the *south-east* part of *Japan*; the town lies on the *western* point, where there is a narrow streight leading *northward* into a long arm of the sea, upon the *north-west* part of which *Yedo* the metropolis stands. At landing I shewed the custom-house officers my letter from the king of *Luggnagg* to his imperial majesty. They knew the seal perfectly well; it was as broad as the palm of my hand. The impression was *A king lifting up a lame beggar from the earth.* The magis-
trates

trates of the town, hearing of my letter, received me as a public minifter; they provided
me with carriages and fervants and bore my
charges to *Yedo*, where I was admitted to an
audience, and delivered my letter, which was
opened with great ceremony, and explained to
the emperor by an interpreter, who then gave
me notice by his majefty's order, that I fhould
fignify my requeft, and whatever it were, it
fhould be granted for the fake of his royal brother of *Luggnagg*. This interpreter was a
perfon employed to tranfact affairs with the
hollanders; he foon conjectured by my countenance, that I was an *european*, and therefore
repeated his majefty's commands in *low-dutch*,
which he fpoke perfectly well. I anfwered (as
I had before determined) that I was a *dutch*
merchant fhipwrecked in a very remote country, from whence I had travelled by fea and
land to *Luggnagg*, and then took fhipping for
Japan, where I knew my countrymen often
traded, and with fome of thefe I hoped to get
an opportunity of returning into *Europe*: I
therefore moft humbly entreated his royal favour to give order, that I fhould be conducted
in fafety to *Nangafac*: to this I added another
petition, that for the fake of my patron the
king of *Luggnagg*, his majefty would condefcend to excufe my performing the ceremony
impofed on my countrymen, of *trampling upon
the crucifix*; becaufe I had been thrown into
his kingdom by my misfortunes, without any
intention of trading. When this latter peti-

tion was interpreted to the emperor, he feemed a little furprifed; and faid, he believed I was the firft of my countrymen, who ever made any fcruple in this point; and that he began to doubt, whether I was a real *hollander*, or no; but rather fufpected I muft be a *chriftian*. However, for the reafons I had offered, but chiefly to gratify the king of *Luggnagg* by an uncommon mark of his favour, he would comply with the *fingularity* of my humour; but the affair muft be managed with dexterity, and his officers fhould be commanded to let me pafs as it were by forgetfulnefs. For he affured me, that if the fecret fhould be difcovered by my countrymen the *Dutch*, they would cut my throat in the voyage. I returned my thanks by the interpreter for fo unufual a favour; and fome troops being at that time on their march to *Nangafac*, the commanding officer had orders to convey me fafe thither with particular inftructions about the bufinefs of the *crucifix*.

On the 9th day of *June*, 1709, I arrived at *Nangafac* after a very long and troublefome journey. I foon fell into company of fome *dutch* failors belonging to the *Amboyna* of *Amfterdam*, a ftout fhip of 450 tons. I had lived long in *Holland*, purfuing my ftudies at *Leyden*, and I fpoke *dutch* well. The feamen foon knew from whence I came laft; they were curious to enquire into my voyages, and courfe of life. I made up a ftory as fhort and probable as I could, but concealed the greateft part.

I knew

I knew many perfons in *Holland;* I was able to invent names for my parents, whom I pretended to be obfcure people in the province of *Gelderland.* I would have given the captain (one *Theodorus Vangrult*) what he pleafed to afk for my voyage to *Holland;* but underftanding I was a furgeon, he was contented to take half the ufual rate, on condition that I would ferve him in the way of my calling. Before we took fhipping, I was often afked by fome of the crew, whether I had performed the ceremony above-mentioned? I evaded the queftion by general anfwers, that I had fatisfied the emperor and court in all particulars. However, a malicious rogue of a fkipper went to an officer, and pointing to me told him, I had not yet *trampled on the crucifix:* but the other who had received inftructions to let me pafs, gave the rafcal twenty ftrokes on the fhoulders with a bamboo; after which I was no more troubled with fuch queftions.

Nothing happened worth mentioning in this voyage. We failed with a fair wind to the *cape of Good Hope,* where we ftaid only to take in frefh water. On the 10th of *April,* 1710, we arrived fafe at *Amfterdam,* having loft only three men by ficknefs in the voyage, and a fourth who fell from the fore-maft into the fea not far from the coaft of *Guinea.* From *Amfterdam* I foon after fet fail for *England* in a fmall veffel belonging to that city.

On the 16th of *April* we put in at the *Downs.* I landed next morning, and faw

once

once more my native country after an abfence of five years and fix months compleat. I went ftrait to *Redriff*, where I arrived the fame day at two in the afternoon, and found my wife and family in good health.

Nuyts Land

Edels Land

Lewins Land   I. S! Francois

I. S! Pieter

HOUYHNHNMS

LAND

Discover'd
A.D.1711.

Sneeers I.
I. Maelsuyker
De Wits I.

A
VOYAGE

To the Country of the

HOUYHNHNMS.

CHAP. I.

The author sets out as captain of a ship. His men conspire against him, confine him a long time to his cabbin. Set him on shore in an unknown land. He travels up into the country. The Yahoos, a strange sort of animal, described. The author meets two Houyhnhnms.

I Continued at home with my wife and children about five months in a very happy condition, if I could have learned the lesson of knowing when I was well. I left my poor wife big with child, and accepted an advantageous offer made me to be captain of the *Adventure*, a stout merchant-man of 350 tons: for I understood navigation well, and being grown weary of a surgeon's employment at sea, which however I could exercise upon occasion, I took a skilful young man of that calling, one *Robert Purefoy*, into my ship. We set sail from *Portsmouth* upon the 7th day of *September*, 1710; on the 14th, we met with cap-

tain

tain *Pocock* of *Briſtol* at *Tenariff*, who was going to the bay of *Campechy* to cut logwood.
On the 16th, he was parted from us by a
ſtorm; I heard ſince my return, that his ſhip
foundered, and none eſcaped, but one cabbin-
boy. He was an honeſt man, and a good
ſailor, but a little too poſitive in his own opinions, which was the cauſe of his deſtruction,
as it hath been of ſeveral others. For if he
had followed my advice, he might have been
ſafe at home with his family at this time, as
well as myſelf.

I had ſeveral men died in my ſhip of calen-
tures, ſo that I was forced to get recruits out
of *Barbadoes* and the *Leeward Iſlands*, where I
touched by the direction of the merchants,
who employed me; which I had ſoon too
much cauſe to repent; for I found afterwards,
that moſt of them had been *bucaneers**. I
had fifty hands on board, and my orders
were, that I ſhould trade with the *Indians* in
the *South-ſea*, and make what diſcoveries I
could. Theſe rogues, whom I had picked up,
debauched my other men, and they all formed
a conſpiracy to ſeize the ſhip, and ſecure me;
which they did one morning, ruſhing into my
cabbin, and binding me hand and foot, threa-
tening to throw me over-board, if I offered to
ſtir. I told them, I was their priſoner, and
would ſubmit. This they made me ſwear to
do, and then they unbound me, only faſten-

* Certain pyrates, that infeſted the *Weſt-Indies*, were ſo called.

ing

ing one of my legs with a chain near my bed, and placed a centry at my door with his piece charged, who was commanded to shoot me dead, if I attempted my liberty. They sent me down victuals and drink, and took the government of the ship to themselves. Their design was to turn pyrates, and plunder the *Spaniards,* which they could not do, till they got more men. But first they resolved to sell the goods in the ship, and then go to *Madagascar* for recruits, several among them having died since my confinement. They sailed many weeks, and traded with the *Indians*; but I knew not what course they took, being kept a close prisoner in my cabbin, and expecting nothing less than to be murdered, as they often threatened me.

Upon the 9th day of *May*, 1711, one *James Welch* came down to my cabbin, and said he had orders from the captain to set me a-shore. I expostulated with him, but in vain; neither would he so much as tell me, who their new captain was. They forced me into the long-boat, letting me put on my best suit of cloaths, which were as good as new, and take a small bundle of linnen, but no arms, except my hanger; and they were so civil as not to search my pockets, into which I conveyed what money I had with some other little necessaries. They rowed about a league; and then set me down on a strand. I desired them to tell me, what country it was. They all swore, they knew no more than myself, but said, that the captain

tain

tain (as they called him) was refolved, after they had fold the lading, to get rid of me in the firft place, where they could difcover land. They pufhed off immediately, advifing me to make hafte for fear of being overtaken by the tide, and fo bad me farewel.

In this defolate condition I advanced forward, and foon got upon firm ground, where I fat down on a bank to reft myfelf and confider what I had beft do. When I was a little refrefhed, I went up into the country, refolving to deliver myfelf to the firft favages I fhould meet, and purchafe my life from them by fome bracelets, glafs rings, and other toys, which failors ufually provide themfelves with in thofe voyages, and whereof I had fome about me. The land was divided by long rows of trees not regularly planted, but naturally growing; there was great plenty of grafs, and feveral fields of oats. I walked very circumfpectly for fear of being furprifed, or fuddenly fhot with an arrow from behind, or on either fide. I fell into a beaten road, where I faw many tracks of human feet, and fome of cows, but moft of horfes. At laft I beheld feveral animals in a field, and one or two of the fame kind fitting in trees. Their fhape was very fingular and deformed, which a little difcompofed me, fo that I lay down behind a thicket to obferve them better. Some of them coming forward near the place where I lay, gave me an opportunity of diftinctly marking their form. Their heads and breafts were covered

3 with

with a thick hair, some frizled, and others
lank; they had beards like goats, and a long
ridge of hair down their backs, and the fore-
parts of their legs and feet; but the rest of
their bodies were bare, so that I might see
their skins, which were of a brown buff colour. They had no tails, nor any hair at all
on their buttocks, except about the *anus*;
which, I presume, nature had placed there to
defend them, as they sat on the ground; for this
posture they used, as well as lying down, and
often stood on their hind feet. They climbed
high trees as nimbly as a squirrel, for they had
strong extended claws before and behind, ter-
minating in sharp points, and hooked. They
would often spring, and bound, and leap with
prodigious agility. The females were not so
large as the males; they had long lank hair on
their heads, but none on their faces, nor any
thing more than a sort of down on the rest
of their bodies, except about the *anus* and
pudenda. Their dugs hung between their fore-
feet, and often reached almost to the ground
as they walked. The hair of both sexes was
of several colours, brown, red, black, and yellow. Upon the whole, I never beheld in all
my travels so disagreeable an animal, or one
against which I naturally conceived so strong
an antipathy. So that thinking I had seen e-
nough, full of contempt and aversion, I got
up, and pursued the beaten road, hoping it
might direct me to the cabbin of some *Indian*.
I had not got far, when I met one of these

creatures

creatures full in my way, and coming up directly to me. The ugly monster, when he
saw me, distorted several ways every feature of
his visage, and stared as at an object he had
never seen before; then approaching nearer
lifted up his fore-paw, whether out of curiosity or mischief, I could not tell: but I drew
my hanger, and gave him a good blow with
the flat side of it, for I durst not strike with
the edge, fearing the inhabitants might be
provoked against me, if they should come to
know, that I had killed or maimed any of
their cattle. When the beast felt the smart,
he drew back, and roared so loud, that a herd
of at least forty came flocking about me from
the next field, howling and making odious
faces; but I ran to the body of a tree, and
leaning my back against it kept them off by
waving my hanger. Several of this cursed
brood getting hold of the branches behind
leapt up into the tree, from whence they began to discharge their excrements on my head:
however, I escaped pretty well by sticking close
to the stem of the tree, but was almost stifled
with the filth, which fell about me on every
side.

In the midst of this distress, I observed them
all to run away on a sudden as fast as they
could, at which I ventured to leave the tree,
and pursue the road, wondering what it was
that could put them into this fright. But looking on my left hand I saw a horse walking
softly in the field; which my persecutors having

ing fooner difcovered, was the caufe of their
flight.   The horfe ftarted a little, when he
came near me, but foon recovering himfelf
looked full in my face with manifeft tokens of
wonder : he viewed my hands and feet, walking round me feveral times. I would have purfued my journey, but he placed himfelf directly in the way, yet looking with a very mild
afpect, never offering the leaft violence.   We
ftood gazing at each other for fome time ; at
laft I took the boldnefs to reach my hand towards his neck with a defign to ftroak it, ufing the common ftyle and whiftle of jockies,
when they are going to handle a ftrange horfe.
But this animal feemed to receive my civilities with difdain, fhook his head, and bent
his brows, foftly raifing up his right fore-foot
to remove my hand.   Then he neighed three
or four times, but in fo different a cadence,
that I almoft began to think he was fpeaking to
himfelf in fome language of his own.

While he and I were thus employed, another horfe came up ; who applying himfelf to
the firft in a very formal manner, they gently
ftruck each other's right hoof before, neighing feveral times by turns, and varying the
found, which feemed to be almoft articulate.
They went fome paces off, as if it were to
confer together, walking fide by fide, back-
ward and forward, like perfons deliberating
upon fome affair of weight, but often turning
their eyes towards me, as it were to watch
that I might not efcape.   I was amazed to
fee

fee fuch actions and behaviour in brute beafts;
and concluded with myfelf, that if the inhabitants of this country were endued with a proportionable degree of reafon, they muft needs be the
wifeft people upon earth. This thought gave me
fo much comfort, that I refolved to go forward,
until I could difcover fome houfe or village,
or meet with any of the natives, leaving the
two horfes to difcourfe together as they pleafed.
But the firft, who was a dapple grey, obferving me to fteal off, neighed after me in fo ex-
preffive a tone, that I fancied myfelf to underftand what he meant; whereupon I turned
back, and came near him to expect his farther
commands; but concealing my fear as much
as I could; for I began to be in fome pain,
how this adventure might terminate; and the
reader will eafily believe, I did not much like
my prefent fituation.

The two horfes came up clofe to me, looking with great earneftnefs upon my face and
hands. The grey fteed rubbed my hat all
round with his right fore-hoof, and difcompofed it fo much, that I was forced to adjuft it
better by taking it off, and fettling it again;
whereat both he and his companion (who was
a brown bay) appeared to be much furprifed;
the latter felt the lappet of my coat, and finding it to hang loofe about me, they both looked with new figns of wonder. He ftroaked
my right hand, feeming to admire the foftnefs
and colour; but he fqueefed it fo hard between
his hoof and his paftern, that I was forced to
roar;

roar; after which they both touched me with all possible tenderness. They were under great perplexity about my shoes and stockings, which they felt very often, neighing to each other, and using various gestures, not unlike those of a philosopher, when he would attempt to solve some new and difficult phænomenon.

Upon the whole, the behaviour of these animals was so orderly and rational, so acute and judicious, that I at last concluded, they must needs be magicians, who had thus metamorphosed themselves upon some design, and seeing a stranger in the way resolved to divert themselves with him; or perhaps were really amazed at the sight of a man so very different in habit, feature, and complexion, from those who might probably live in so remote a climate. Upon the strength of this reasoning I ventured to address them in the following manner: gentlemen, if you be conjurers, as I have good cause to believe, you can understand any language; therefore I make bold to let your worships know that I am a poor distressed *englishman* driven by his misfortunes upon your coast, and I entreat one of you to let me ride upon his back, as if he were a real horse, to some house or village, where I can be relieved. In return of which favour I will make you a present of this knife and bracelet (taking them out of my pocket.) The two creatures stood silent while I spoke, seeming to listen with great attention; and when I had ended, they neighed frequently towards each
.other,

other, as if they were engaged in ſerious converſation. I plainly obſerved, that their language expreſſed the paſſions very well, and
the words might with little pains be reſolved
into an alphabet more eaſily than the *chineſe*.

I could frequently diſtinguiſh the word *yaboo*, which was repeated by each of them ſeveral times; and although it was impoſſible
for me to conjecture what it meant, yet while
the two horſes were buſy in converſation, I endeavoured to practiſe this word upon my tongue;
and as ſoon as they were ſilent, I boldly pronounced *yaboo* in a loud voice, imitating at the
ſame time as near as I could the neighing of a
horſe; at which they were both viſibly ſurpriſed, and the grey repeated the ſame word
twice, as if he meant to teach me the right
accent, wherein I ſpoke after him as well as I
could, and found myſelf perceivably to improve
every time, though very far from any degree
of perfection. Then the bay tried me with a ſe-
cond word much harder to be pronounced;
but reducing it to the *engliſh* orthography,
may be ſpelt thus, *Houyhnhnm*. I did not ſuc-
ceed in this ſo well as the former; but after
two or three farther trials I had better fortune;
and they both appeared amazed at my capacity.

After ſome farther diſcourſe, which I then
conjectured might relate to me, the two friends
took their leaves with the ſame compliment of
ſtriking each other's hoof; and the grey made
me

me figns that I fhould walk before him; wherein I thought it prudent to comply, till I could
find a better director. When I offered to flack-
en my pace, he would cry *bhuun, bhuun;* I gueffed his meaning, and gave him to underftand,
as well as I could, that I was weary, and not
able to walk fafter; upon which he would ftand
a-while to let me reft.

CHAP. II.

The author conducted by a Houyhnhnm to his
houfe. The houfe defcribed. The author's re-
ception. The food of the Houyhnhnms. The
author in diftrefs for want of meat, is at laft
relieved. His manner of feeding in this coun-
try.

HAving travelled about three miles, we
came to a long kind of building made of
timber ftuck in the ground, and wattled a-
crofs; the roof was low, and covered with
ftraw. I now began to be a little comforted;
and took out fome toys, which travellers ufually carry for prefents to the favage *indians* of
america and other parts, in hopes the people of
the houfe would be thereby encouraged to receive me kindly. The horfe made me a fign
to go in firft; it was a large room with a
fmooth clay floor, and a rack and manger, extending the whole length on one fide. There
were three nags, and two mares not eating,
but fome of them fitting down upon their

hams, which I very much wondered at; but wondered more to fee the reft employed in domeftic bufinefs, thefe feemed but ordinary cattle; however this confirmed my firft opinion, that a people, who could fo far civilize brute animals, muft needs excel in wifdom all the nations of the world. The grey came in juft after, and thereby prevented any ill treatment, which the others might have given me. He neighed to them feveral times in a ftyle of authority, and received anfwers.

Beyond this room there were three others reaching the length of the houfe, to which you paffed through three doors, oppofite to each other, in the manner of a vifta; we went through the fecond room towards the third; here the grey walked in firft, beckoning me to attend: I waited in the fecond room, and got ready my prefents for the mafter and miftrefs of the houfe: they were two knives, three bracelets of falfe pearl, a fmall lookingglafs, and a bead necklace. The horfe neighed three or four times, and I waited to hear fome anfwers in a human voice, but I heard no other returns, than in the fame dialect, only one or two a little fhriller than his. I began to think, that this houfe muft belong to fome perfon of great note among them, becaufe there appeared fo much ceremony, before I could gain admittance. But, that a man of quality fhould be ferved all by horfes, was beyond my comprehenfion. I feared my brain was difturbed by my fufferings and misfortunes: I
                                                        roufed

roufed myfelf, and looked about me in the room where I was left alone; this was fur-nifhed like the firft, only after a more ele-gant manner. I rubbed my eyes often, but the fame objects ftill occurred. I pinched my arms and fides to awake myfelf, hoping I might be in a dream. I then abfolutely con-cluded, that all thofe appearances could be no-thing elfe but necromancy and magic. But I had no time to purfue thefe reflections; for the grey horfe came to the door, and made me a fign to follow him into the third room; where I faw a very comely mare, together with a colt and fole, fitting on their haunches upon matts of ftraw not unartfully made and perfectly neat and clean.

The mare foon after my entrance rofe from her matt, and coming up clofe, after having nicely obferved my hands and face, gave me a moft contemptuous look; and turning to the horfe, I heard the word *yaboo* often repeated betwixt them; the meaning of which word I could not then comprehend, although it were the firft I had learned to pronounce; but I was foon better informed to my everlafting morti-fication: for the horfe beckoning to me with his head, and repeating the word *bbuun, bbuun,* as he did upon the road, which I underftood was to attend him, led me out into a kind of court, where was another building at fome diftance from the houfe. Here we entered, and I faw three of thofe deteftable creatures, which I firft met after my landing, feeding upon roots and the flesh of some animals, which I afterwards found to be that of asses and dogs, and now and then a cow dead by accident or disease. They were all tied by the neck with strong wyths fastened to a beam; they held their food between the claws of their fore-feet, and tore it with their teeth.

The master horse ordered a sorrel nag, one of his servants, to untie the largest of these a-nimals, and take him into the yard. The beast and I were brought close together; and our countenances diligently compared both by master and servant, who thereupon repeated several times the word *yaboo*. My horror and astonishment are not to be described, when I observed in this abominable animal a perfect human figure : the face of it indeed was flat and broad, the nose depressed, the lips large, and the mouth wide : but these differences are common to all savage nations, where the linea-ments of the countenance are distorted by the natives suffering their infants to lie grovelling on the earth, or by carrying them on their backs nuzzling with their face against the mo-ther's shoulders. The fore-feet of the *yaboo* differed from my hands in nothing else, but the length of the nails, the coarseness and brownness of the palms, and the hairi-ness on the backs. There was the same re-semblance between our feet, with the same differences, which I knew very well, though the horses did not because of my shoes and stockings; the same in every part of our bo-dies,

dies, except as to hairinefs and colour, which I have already defcribed.

The great difficulty, that feemed to ftick with the two horfes, was, to fee the reft of my body fo very different from that of a ya-hoo, for which I was obliged to my cloaths, whereof they had no conception. The forrel nag offered me a root, which he held (after their manner, as we fhall defcribe in its pro-per place) between his hoof and paftern; I took it in my hand, and having fmelt it re-turned it to him again as civilly as I could. He brought out of the *yahoo*'s kennel a piece of afs's flefh, but it fmelt fo offenfively, that I turned from it with loathing; he then threw it to the *yahoo*, by whom it was greedily devoured ª. He afterwards fhewed me a whifp of hay and a fetlock full of oats; but I fhook my head to fignify, that neither of thefe were food for me. And indeed I now apprehended, that I muft abfolutely ftarve, if I did not get to fome of my own fpecies; for as to thofe filthy *yahoos*, al-though there were few greater lovers of man-kind at that time, than myfelf; yet I confefs, I never faw any fenfitive being fo deteftable on all accounts; and the more I came near them, the more hateful they grew, while I ftayed in

ª Whoever is difgufted with this picture of a *yahoo*, would do well to reflect, that it be-comes his own in exact pro-portion as he deviates from virtue, for virtue is the perfec-tion of reafon: the appetites of thofe abandoned to vice are not lefs brutal and fordid than that of a *yahoo* for affes flefh, nor is their life a ftate of lefs abject fervility.

tha

that country. This the mafter horfe obferved by my behaviour, and therefore fent the *yaboo* back to his kennel. He then put his fore-hoof to his mouth, at which I was much fur-prifed, although he did it with eafe, and with a motion that appeared perfectly natural; and made other figns to know what I would eat; but I could not return him fuch an anfwer as he was able to apprehend; and if he had un-derftood me, I did not fee how it was poffible to contrive any way for finding myfelf nou-rifhment. While we were thus engaged, I obferved a cow paffing by, whereupon I point-ed to her, and expreffed a defire to go and milk her. This had its effect; for he led me back into the houfe, and ordered a mare-fer-vant to open a room, where a good ftore of milk lay in earthen and wooden veffels after a very orderly and cleanly manner. She gave me a large bowl full, of which I drank very heartily, and found myfelf well refrefhed.

About noon I faw coming towards the houfe a kind of vehicle drawn like a fledge by four *yaboos*. There was in it an old fteed, who feemed to be of quality; he alighted with his hind-feet forward, having by accident got a hurt in his left fore-foot. He came to dine with our horfe, who received him with great civility. They dined in the beft room, and had oats boiled in milk for the fecond courfe, which the old horfe eat warm, but the reft cold. Their mangers were placed circular in the middle of the room, and divided into fe-

veral

veral partitions, round which they sat on their haunches upon bosses of straw. In the middle was a large rack, with angles answering to every partition of the manger. So that each horse and mare eat their own hay, and their own mash of oats and milk, with much decency and regularity. The behaviour of the young colt and fole appeared very modest; and that of the master and mistress extremely chearful and complaisant to their guest. The grey ordered me to stand by him; and much discourse passed between him and his friend concerning me, as I found by the stranger's often looking on me, and the frequent repetition of the word *yahoo*.

I happened to wear my gloves, which the master-grey observing, seemed perplexed, discovering signs of wonder what I had done to my fore-feet; he put his hoof three or four times to them, as if he would signify, that I should reduce them to their former shape, which I presently did, pulling off both my gloves, and putting them into my pocket. This occasioned farther talk, and I saw the company was pleased with my behaviour, whereof I soon found the good effects. I was ordered to speak the few words I understood; and while they were at dinner, the master taught me the names for oats, milk, fire, water, and some others; which I could readily pronounce after him, having from my youth a great facility in learning languages.

X 4

When

When dinner was done, the master horse took me aside, and by signs and words made me understand the concern he was in, that I had nothing to eat. Oats in their tongue are called *blunnh*. This word I pronounced two or three times; for although I had refused them at first, yet upon second thoughts I considered, that I could contrive to make of them a kind of bread, which might be sufficient with milk to keep me alive, till I could make my escape to some other country, and to creatures of my own species. The horse immediately ordered a white mare-servant of his family to bring me a good quantity of oats in a sort of wooden tray. These I heated before the fire, as well as I could, and rubbed them till the husks came off, which I made a shift to winnow from the grain; I ground and beat them between two stones, then took water, and made them into a paste or cake, which I toasted · at the fire; and eat warm with milk. It was at first a very insipid diet, though common enough in many parts of *Europe*, but grew tolerable by time; and having been often reduced to hard fare in my life, this was not the first experiment I had made, how easily nature is satisfied. And I cannot but observe, that I never had one hour's sickness, while I staid in this island. It is true, I sometimes made a shift to catch a rabbit, or bird, by springes made of *yahoo*'s hairs; and I often gathered wholesome herbs, which I boiled, or eat as salads with my bread; and now and then for a rarity I made a
little

little butter, and drank the whey. I was at firſt at a great loſs for ſalt; but cuſtom ſoon reconciled me to the want of it; and I am confident, that the frequent uſe of ſalt among us is an effect of luxury, and was firſt intro-duced only as a provocative to drink; except where it is neceſſary for preſerving of fleſh in long voyages, or in places remote from great markets. For we obſerve no animal to be fond of it but man : and as to myſelf, when I left this country, it was a great while before I could endure the taſte of it in any thing that I eat.

This is enough to ſay upon the ſubject of my diet, wherewith other travellers fill their books, as if the readers were perſonally con-cerned, whether we fare well or ill. How-ever it was neceſſary to mention this matter, leſt the world ſhould think it impoſſible, that I could find ſuſtenance for three years in ſuch a country and among ſuch inhabi-tants.

When it grew towards evening, the ma-ſter horſe ordered a place for me to lodge in; it was but ſix yards from the houſe, and ſepa-rated from the ſtable of the *yahoos*. Here I got ſome ſtraw, and covering myſelf with my own cloaths ſlept very ſound. But I was in a ſhort time better accommodated, as the rea-der ſhall know hereafter, when I come to treat more particularly about my way of liv-ing.

CHAP.

C H A P. III.

The author studious to learn the language; the
Houyhnhnm, his master, assists in teaching
him. The language described. Several Houyhn-
hnms of quality came out of curiosity to see the
author. He gives his master a short account of
his voyage.

MY principal endeavour was to learn the
language, which my master (for so I
shall henceforth call him) and his children,
and every servant of his house were desirous to
teach me. For they looked upon it as a prodigy, that a brute animal should discover such
marks of a rational creature. I pointed to e-
very thing, and enquired the name of it, which
I wrote down in my *journal-book* when I was
alone, and corrected my bad accent by desiring those of the family to pronounce it often.
In this employment a sorrel nag, one of the
under servants, was very ready to assist me.
   In speaking they pronounce through the nose
and throat, and their language approaches
nearest to the *high-dutch*, or *german*, of any I
know in *Europe*; but is much more graceful and
significant. The emperor *Charles* V. made almost the same observation, when he said, That
if he were to speak to his horse, it should be
in *high-dutch*.
   The curiosity and impatience of my master
were so great, that he spent many hours of his
                                        leisure

leifure to inftruct me. He was convinced (as he afterwards told me) that I muft be a *yahoo*; but my teachablenefs, civility, and cleanlinefs, aftonifhed him; which were qualities altogether oppofite to thofe animals. He was moft perplexed about my cloaths, reafoning sometimes with himfelf, whether they were a part of my body; for I never pulled them off till the family were afleep, and got them on before they waked in the morning. My mafter was eager to learn from whence I came; how I acquired thofe appearances of reafon, which I difcovered in all my actions; and to know my ftory from my own mouth, which he hoped he fhould foon do by the great proficiency I made in learning and pronouncing their words and fentences. To help my memory I formed all I learned into the *englifh* alphabet, and writ the words down with the tranflations. This laft after fome time I ventured to do in my mafter's prefence. It coft me much trouble to explain to him what I was doing; for the inhabitants have not the leaft idea of books or literature.

In about ten weeks time I was able to underftand moft of his queftions; and in three months could give him fome tolerable anfwers. He was extremely curious to know from what part of the country I came, and how I was taught to imitate a rational creature; becaufe the *yahoos* (whom he faw I exactly refembled in my head, hands, and face, that were only vifible) with fome appearance of cunning, and the

the ftrongeft difpofition to mifchief, were obferved to be the moft unteachable of all brutes.
I anfwered, that I came over the fea from a
far place with many others of my own kind in
a great hollow veffel made of the bodies of
trees; that my companions forced me to land
on this coaft, and then left me to fhift for myfelf. It was with fome difficulty, and by the
help of many figns, that I brought him to underftand me. He replied, that I muft needs
be miftaken, or that I *faid the thing which was
not* (for they have no word in their language to
exprefs lying or falfhood.) He knew it was
impoffible, that there could be a country beyond the fea, or that a parcel of brutes could
move a wooden veffel whither they pleafed
upon water. He was fure no *Houyhnhnm* alive
could make fuch a veffel, nor would truft *yahoos* to manage it.

The word *Houyhnhnm* in their tongue fignifies a *horfe*, and in its etymology, *the perfection
of nature*. I told my mafter that I was at a
lofs for expreffion, but would improve as faft
as I could; and hoped in a fhort time I fhould
be able to tell him wonders: he was pleafed
to direct his own mare, his colt and fole, and
the fervants of the family, to take all opportunities of inftructing me; and every day for
two or three hours he was at the fame pains
himfelf: feveral horfes and mares of quality in
the neighbourhood came often to our houfe,
upon the report fpread of a wonderful *yaboo* that could fpeak like a *Houyhnhnm*, and
seemed

feemed in his words and actions to difcover
fome glimmerings of reafon.   Thefe delighted.
to converfe with me; they put many queftions,
and received fuch anfwers as I was able to return.   By all thefe advantages I made fo great
a progrefs, that in five months from my arrival I underftood whatever was fpoken, and could.
exprefs myfelf tolerably well.

The *Houyhnhnms* who came to vifit my mafter out of a defign of feeing and talking with
me, could hardly believe me to be a right *yahoo*, becaufe my body had a different covering
from others of my kind.   They were aftonifhed to obferve me without the ufual hair on
fkin, except on my head, face, and hands;
but I difcovered that fecret to my mafter upon
an accident, which happened about a fortnight
before.

I have already told the reader, that every
night, when the family were gone to bed, it
was my cuftom to ftrip, and cover myfelf with
my cloaths: it happened one morning early,
that my mafter fent for me by the forrel nag,
who was his valet; when he came, I was faft
afleep, my cloaths fallen off on one fide, and
my fhirt above my waift.   I awaked at the
noife he made, and obferved him to deliver his
meffage in fome diforder; after which he went
to my mafter, and in a great fright gave him
a very confufed account of what he had feen:
this I prefently difcovered; for going as foon
as I was dreffed to pay my attendance upon
his honour, he afked me the meaning of what
his

his servant had reported; that I was not the same thing when I slept, as I appeared to be at other times; that his valet assured him, some part of me was white, some yellow, at least not so white, and some brown.

I had hitherto concealed the secret of my dress in order to distinguish myself, as much as possible, from that cursed race of *yahoos*; but now I found it in vain to do so any longer. Besides I considered, that my cloaths and shoes would soon wear out, which already were in a declining condition, and must be supplied by some contrivance from the hides of *yahoos*, or other brutes; whereby the whole secret would be known: I therefore told my master, that in the country from whence I came those of my kind always covered their bodies with the hairs of certain animals prepared by art, as well for decency, as to avoid the inclementies of air both hot and cold; of which, as to my own person, I would give him immediate conviction, if he pleased to command me; only desiring his excuse, if I did not expose those parts that nature taught us to conceal. He said my discourse was all very strange, but especially the last part; for he could not understand, why nature should teach us to conceal what nature had given: that neither himself nor family were ashamed of any parts of their bodies; but however I might do as I pleased. Whereupon I first unbuttoned my coat, and pulled it off. I did the same with my waist-coat; I drew off my shoes, stockings, and breeches.

breeches. I let my shirt down to my waist, and drew up the bottom, fastening it like a girdle about my middle to hide my nakedness.

My master observed the whole performance with great signs of curiosity and admiration. He took up all my cloaths in his pastern one piece after another, and examined them diligently; he then stroaked my body very gently, and looked round me several times, after which he said, it was plain I must be a perfect *yahoo*; but that I differed very much from the rest of my species in the softness, whiteness, and smoothness of my skin, my want of hair in several parts of my body, the shape and shortness of my claws behind and before, and my affectation of walking continually on my two hinder feet. He desired to see no more; and gave me leave to put on my cloaths again, for I was shuddering with cold.

I expressed my uneasiness at his giving me so often the appellation of *yahoo*, an odious animal, for which I had so utter an hatred and contempt: I begged he would forbear applying that word to me, and take the same order in his family, and among his friends, whom he suffered to see me. I requested likewise, that the secret of my having a false covering to my body might be known to none but himself, at least as long as my present cloathing should last; for as to what the sorrel nag his valet had observed, his honour might command him to conceal it.

AN

All this my mafter very gracioufly confented to, and thus the fecret was kept till my cloaths began to wear out, which I was forced to fupply by feveral contrivances, that fhall hereafter be mentioned. In the mean time he defired I would go on with my utmoft diligence to learn their language, becaufe he was more aftonifhed at my capacity for fpeech and reafon, than at the figure of my body, whether it were covered or no; adding, that he waited with fome impatience to hear the wonders, which I promifed to tell him.

From thenceforward he doubled the pains he had been at to inftruct me; he brought me into all company, and made them treat me with civility, becaufe, as he told them privately, this would put me into good humour, and make me more diverting.

Every day, when I waited on him, befide the trouble he was at in teaching, he would afk me feveral queftions concerning myfelf, which I anfwered as well as I could; and by thefe means he had already received fome general ideas, though very imperfect. It would be tedious to relate the feveral fteps, by which I advanced to a more regular converfation : but the firft account I gave of myfelf in any order and length was to this purpofe:

That I came from a very far country, as I already had attempted to tell him, with about fifty more of my own fpecies; that we travelled upon the feas in a great hollow veffel made of wood, and larger than his honour's
house.

houfe. I defcribed the fhip to him in the
beft terms I could, and explained by the help
of my handkerchief difplayed, how it was
driven forward by the wind. That upon a
quarrel among us I was fet on fhore on this
coaft, where I walked forward, without knowing whither, till he delivered me from the per-
fecution of thofe execrable *yaboos*. He afked
me, who made the fhip, and how it was poffible that the *Houyhnhnms* of my country would
leave it to the management of brutes? My
anfwer was, that I durft proceed no farther in
my relation, unlefs he would give me his word
and honour that he would not be offended,
and then I would tell him the wonders I had
fo often promifed. He agreed; and I went
on by affuring him, that the fhip was made
by creatures like myfelf, who in all the countries I had travelled, as well as in my own,
were the only governing, rational animals; and
that upon my arrival hither I was as much a-
ftonifhed to fee the *Houyhnhnms* act like rational beings, as he or his friends could be in
finding fome marks of reafon in a creature he
was pleafed to call a *yaboo*; to which I owned my refemblance in every part, but could
not account for their degenerate and brutal nature. I faid farther, that if good fortune ever
reftored me to my native country to relate my
travels hither, as I refolved to do, every body
would believe, that I *faid the thing that was
not*; that I invented the ftory out of my own
head; and (with all poffible refpect to himfelf,

VOL. II.   Y   his

his family, and friends, and under his promise
of not being offended) our countrymen would
hardly think it probable, that a *Houybnbnm*
should be the presiding creature of a nation,
and a *yaboo* the brute.

C H A P. IV.

The Houyhnhnms *notion of truth and falshood.
The author's discourse disapproved by his master. The author gives a more particular account of himself, and the accidents of his voyage.*

MY master heard me with great appearances of uneasiness in his countenance;
because *doubting*, or *not believing*, are so little
known in this country, that the inhabitants
cannot tell how to behave themselves under
such circumstances. And I remember, in frequent discourses with my master concerning
the nature of manhood in other parts of the
world, having occasion to talk of *lying* and
false representation, it was with much difficulty
that he comprehended what I meant; although he had otherwise a most acute judgment. For he argued thus : that the use of
speech was to make us understand one another, and to receive information of facts ; now,
if any one *said the thing which was not*, these
ends were defeated; because I cannot properly
be said to understand him; and I am so far
from receiving information, that he leaves me
worse

worfe than in ignorance; for I am led to believe a thing *black* when it is *white*, and *fhort*
when it is *long*. And thefe were all the notions he had concerning that faculty of *lying*,
fo perfectly well underftood, and fo univerfally practifed, among human creatures.

To return from this digreffion; when I afferted that the *yahoos* were the only governing
animals in my country, which my mafter faid,
was altogether paft his conception, he defired
to know, whether we had *Houyhnhnms* among
us, and what was their employment : I told
him, we had great numbers; that in fummer
they grazed in the fields, and in winter were
kept in houfes with hay and oats, where *yahoo-*
fervants were employed to rub their fkins
fmooth, comb their manes, pick their feet,
ferve them with food, and make their beds.
I underftand you well, faid my mafter; it is
now very plain from all you have fpoken, that,
whatever fhare of reafon the *yahoos* pretend to,
the *Houyhnhnms* are your mafters; I heartily
wifh our *yahoos* would be fo tractable. I begged his honour would pleafe to excufe me from
proceeding any farther, becaufe I was very certain that the account he expected from me
would be highly difpleafing. But he infifted
in commanding me to let him know the beft
and the worft : I told him he fhould be obey-
ed. I owned, that the *Houyhnhnms* among us,
whom we called *horfes*, were the moft generous and comely animal we had; that they
excelled in ftrength and fwiftnefs; and when

Y 2   they

they belonged to perfons of quality, were employed in travelling, racing, or drawing cha-
riots, they were treated with much kindnefs
and care, till they fell into difeafes, or became
foundered in the feet; but then they were
fold, and ufed to all kind of drudgery, till
they died; after which their fkins were ftripped, and fold for what they were worth, and
their bodies left to be devoured by dogs and
birds of prey. But the common race of horfes
had not fo good fortune, being kept by farmers and carriers and other mean people who
put them to greater labour, and fed them
worfe. I defcribed, as well as I could, our
way of riding; the fhape and ufe of a bridle,
a faddle, a fpur, and a whip; of harnefs and
wheels. I added, that we faftened plates of
a certain hard fubftance, called *iron*, at the
bottom of their feet to preferve their hoofs
from being broken by the ftony ways, on which
we often travelled.

My mafter, after fome expreffions of great
indignation, wondered how we dared to venture upon a *Houyhnhnm*'s back; for he was
fure, that the weakeft fervant in his houfe
would be able to fhake off the ftrongeft *yaboo*;
or by lying down, and rolling on his back,
fqueefe the brute to death. I anfwered, that
our horfes were trained up from three or four
years old to the feveral ufes we intended them
for; that, if any of them proved intolerably
vicious, they were employed for carriages;
that they were feverely beaten, while they
were

were young, for any mifchievous tricks : that the
males, defigned for the common ufe of riding
or draught, were generally *caftrated* about two
years after their birth to take down their fpirits and make them more tame and gentle;
that they were indeed fenfible of rewards and
punifhments ; but his honour would pleafe to
confider, that they had not the leaft tincture
of reafon, any more than the *yaboos* in this
country.

It put me to the pains of many circumlocutions to give my mafter a right idea of what I
fpoke ; for their language doth not abound in
variety of words, becaufe their wants and paffions are fewer than among us. But it is impoffible to exprefs his noble refentment at our
favage treatment of the *Houyhnhnm* race; particularly after I had explained the manner and
ufe of *caftrating* horfes among us to hinder
them from propagating their kind, and to render them more fervile. He faid, if it were
poffible there could be any country, where *yahoos* alone were endued with reafon, they certainly muft be the governing animal; becaufe
reafon will in time always prevail againft brutal ftrength. But, confidering the frame of
our bodies, and efpecially of mine, he thought
no creature of equal bulk was fo ill contrived for
employing that reafon in the common offices
of life; whereupon, he defired to know, whether thofe, among whom I lived, refembled
me or the *yaboos* of his country. I affured
him, that I was as well fhaped as moft of my

age : but the younger, and the females, were much more soft and tender, and the skins of the latter generally as white as milk. He said, I differed indeed from other *yaboos*, being much more cleanly, and not altogether so deformed; but in point of real advantage he thought I differed for the worse. That my nails were of no use either to my fore or hinder-feet; as to my fore-feet, he could not properly call them by that name, for he never observed me to walk upon them; that they were too soft to bear the ground; that I generally went with them uncovered, neither was the covering I sometimes wore on them of the same shape, or so strong as that on my feet behind. That I could not walk with any security, for if either of my hinder-feet slipped, I must inevitably fall. He then began to find fault with other parts of my body: the flatness of my face, the prominence of my nose, mine eyes placed directly in front, so that I could not look on either side without turning my head: that I was not able to feed myself without lifting one of my fore-feet to my mouth: and therefore nature had placed those joints to answer that necessity. He knew not, what could be the use of those several clefts and divisions in my feet behind; that these were too soft to bear the hardness and sharpness of stones without a covering made from the skin of some other brute; that my whole body wanted a fence against heat and cold, which I was forced to put on and off every
day

day with tedioufnefs and trouble. And laftly, that he obferved every animal in this country naturally to abhor the *yahoos*, whom the weaker avoided, and the ftronger drove from them. So that, fuppofing us to have the gift of reafon, he could not fee how it were poffible to cure that natural antipathy, which every creature difcovered againft us; nor confequently, how we could tame and render them ferviceable. However, he would (as he faid) debate the matter no farther, becaufe he was more defirous to know my own ftory, the country where I was born, and the feveral actions and events of my life before I came hither.

I affured him, how extremely defirous I was, that he fhould be fatisfied in every point; but I doubted much, whether it would be poffible for me to explain myfelf on feveral fubjects, whereof his honour could have no conception; becaufe I faw nothing in his country, to which I could refemble them. That however I would do my beft, and ftrive to exprefs myfelf by fimilitudes, humbly defiring his affiftance, when I wanted proper words; which he was pleafed to promife me.

I faid, my birth was of honeft parents in an ifland called *England*, which was remote from this country as many days journey, as the ftrongeft of his honour's fervants could travel in the annual courfe of the fun. That I was bred a furgeon, whofe trade it is to cure wounds and hurts in the body gotten by accident or violence; that my country was go-

verned

verned by a female man, whom we called *queen*. That I left it to get riches, whereby I might maintain myself and family when I should return. That in my last voyage I was commander of the ship, and had about fifty *yahoos* under me, many of which died at sea, and I was forced to supply them by others picked out from several nations. That our ship was twice in danger of being sunk; the first time by a great storm, and the second by striking against a rock. Here my master interposed, by asking me, how I could persuade strangers out of different countries to venture with me, after the losses I had sustained, and the hazards I had run. I said, they were fellows of desperate fortunes, forced to fly from the places of their birth on account of their poverty or their crimes. Some were undone by law-suits; others spent all they had in drinking, whoring, and gaming; others fled for treason; many for murder, theft, poysoning, robbery, perjury, forgery, coining false money, for committing rapes or sodomy; for flying from their colours, or deserting to the enemy, and most of them had broken prison; none of these durst return to their native countries for fear of being hanged, or of starving in a jail; and therefore they were under a necessity of seeking a livelihood in other places.

During this discourse, my master was pleased to interrupt me several times; I had made use of many circumlocutions in describing to

him

him the nature of the feveral crimes, for which moft of our crew had been forced to fly their country. This labour took up feveral days converfation, before he was able to comprehend me. He was wholly at a lofs to know, what could be the ufe or neceffity of practifing thofe vices. To clear up which, I endeavoured to give him fome ideas of the defire of power and riches; of the terrible effects of luft, intemperance, malice, and envy. All this I was forced to define and defcribe by putting cafes and making fuppofitions. After which, like one whofe imagination was ftruck with fomething never feen or heard of before, he would lift up his eyes with amazement and indignation. Power, government, war, law, punifhment, and a thoufand other things had no terms, wherein that language could exprefs them; which made the difficulty almoft infuperable to give my mafter any conception of what I meant. But being of an excellent underftanding, much improved by contemplation and converfe, he at laft arrived at a competent knowledge of what human nature in our parts of the world is capable to perform, and defired I would give him fome particular account of that land, which we call *Europe*, but efpecially of my own country.

C H A P.

C H A P. V.

The author, at his master's commands, informs
him of the state of England. *The causes of*
war among the princes of Europe. *The au-*
thor begins to explain the English *constitu-*
tion.

THE reader may please to observe, that
the following extract of many conversations I had with my master, contains a sum-
mary of the most material points, which were
discoursed at several times for above two years;
his honour often desiring fuller satisfaction, as
I farther improved in the *Houyhnhnm* tongue.
I laid before him, as well as I could, the whole
state of *Europe*; I discoursed of trade and manufactures, of arts and sciences; and the answers I gave to all the questions he made as
they arose upon several subjects, were a fund
of conversation not to be exhausted. But I
shall here only set down the substance of what
passed between us concerning my own country, reducing it into order as well as I can,
without any regard to time or other circumstances, while I strictly adhere to truth. My
only concern is, that I shall hardly be able to
do justice to my master's arguments and ex-
pressions, which must needs suffer by my want
of capacity, as well as by a translation into our
barbarous *English*.

In

In obedience therefore to his honour's commands, I related to him the *revolution* under
the prince of *Orange*; the long war with
France entered into by the said prince and re-
newed by his successor the present queen,
wherein the greatest powers of *Christendom* were
engaged, and which still continued : I computed, at his request, that about a million of
yahoos might have been killed in the whole
progress of it; and perhaps a hundred or more
cities taken, and five times as many ships burnt
or sunk.

He asked me, what were the usual causes
or motives that made one country go to war
with another. I answered they were innumerable; but I should only mention a few of
the chief. Sometimes the ambition of princes, who never think they have land or people enough to govern. Sometimes the corruption of ministers, who engage their master in
a war in order to stifle or divert the clamour of
the subjects against their evil administration.
Difference in opinions hath cost many millions of lives : for instance, whether *flesh* be
bread, or *bread* be *flesh*; whether the juice of a
certain *berry* be *blood* or *wine* [a]; whether *whist-
ling* be a vice or a virtue [b]; whether it be better to *kiss a post,* or throw it into the fire [c];
what is the best colour for a *coat,* whether
black, white, red, or *grey*; and whether it should
be *long* or *short, narrow* or *wide, dirty* or *clean,*

---

[a] Transubstantiation.   [b] Church-music.   [c] Kissing a
cross.

3

with

with many more ª. Neither are any wars fo furious and bloody, or of fo long continuance, as thofe occafioned by difference in opinion, efpecially if it be in things indifferent.

Sometimes the quarrel between two princes is to decide, which of them fhall difpoffefs a third of his dominions, where neither of them pretend to any right. Sometimes one prince quarrelleth with another, for fear the other fhould quarrel with him. Sometimes a war is entered upon becaufe the enemy is too *ftrong*; and fometimes becaufe he is too *weak*. Sometimes our neighbours *want* the *things* which we *have*, or *have* the things which we *want*; and we both fight, till they take ours, or give us theirs. It is a very juftifiable caufe of a war, to invade a country after the people have been wafted by famine, deftroyed by peftilence, or embroiled by factions among themfelves. It is juftifiable to enter into war againft our neareft ally, when one of his towns lie convenient for us, or a territory of land, that would render our dominions round and compact. If a prince fends forces into a nation, where the people are poor and ignorant, he may lawfully put half of them to death, and make flaves of the reft, in order to civilize and reduce them from their barbarous way of living. It is a very kingly, honourable, and frequent practice, when one prince defires the affiftance of another to fecure him againft an

ª The colour and make of facred veftments, and different orders of popifh ecclefiaftics.

invafion,

invafion, that the affiftant, when he hath driven out the invader, fhould feize on the dominions himfelf, and kill, imprifon, or banifh
the prince he came to relieve. Alliance by
blood, or marriage, is a frequent caufe of war
between princes; and the nearer the kindred
is, the greater is their difpofition to quarrel :
poor nations are *hungry*, and *rich* nations are
proud; and pride and hunger will ever be at
variance. For thefe reafons, the trade of a
foldier is held the moft honourable of all others:
becaufe a *foldier* is a *yahoo* hired to kill in cold
blood as many of his own fpecies, who have
never offended him, as poffibly he can.

There is likewife a kind of beggarly princes
in *Europe*, not able to make war by themfelves, who hire out their troops to richer nations, for fo much a day to each man; of
which they keep three-fourths to themfelves,
and it is the beft part of their maintenance;
fuch are thofe in many *northern* parts of Europe.

What you have told me (faid my mafter)
upon the fubject of war, does indeed difcover
moft admirably the effects of that reafon you
pretend to : however it is happy that the *fhame*
is greater than the *danger*; and that nature
hath left you utterly incapable of doing much
mifchief. For, your mouths lying flat with
your faces, you can hardly bite each other to
any purpofe, unlefs by confent. Then as to
the claws upon your feet before and behind,
they are fo fhort and tender, that one of

our

our *yahoos* would drive a dozen of yours before him. And therefore in recounting the numbers of thofe who have been killed in battle, I cannot but think you have *faid the thing which is not*.

I could not forbear fhaking my head, and fmiling a little at his ignorance. And being no ftranger to the art of war, I gave him a defcription of cannons, culverins, mufquets, carabines, piftols, bullets, powder, fwords, bayonets, battles, fieges, retreats, attacks, undermines, countermines, bombardments, fea-fights, fhips funk with a thoufand men, twenty-thoufand killed on each fide, dying groans, limbs flying in the air, fmoke, noife, confufion, trampling to death under horfes feet; flight, purfuit, victory; fields ftrewed with carcafes, left for food to dogs and wolves, and birds of prey; plundering, ftripping, ravifhing, burning and deftroying. And to fet forth the valour of my own dear countrymen, I affured him, that I had feen them blow up a hundred enemies at once in a fiege, and as many in a fhip; and beheld the dead bodies drop down in pieces from the clouds, to the great diverfion of the fpectators *.

I was

---

* It would perhaps be impoffible, by the moft laboured argument or forcible eloquence, to fhew the abfurd injuftice and horrid cruelty of war fo effectually, as by this fimple exhibition of them in a new light: with war, including every fpecies of iniquity and every art of deftruction, we become familiar by degrees under fpecious terms, which are feldom examined, becaufe they are learned at an age, in which the mind implicitly receives and retains whatever is impreft: thus it happens, that when

I was going on to more particulars, when my mafter commanded me filence. He faid, whoever underftood the nature of *yaboos*, might eafily believe it poffible for fo vile an animal to be capable of every action I had named, if their ftrength and cunning equalled their malice. But as my difcourfe had increafed his abhorrence of the whole fpecies, fo he found it gave him a difturbance in his mind, to which he was wholly a ftranger before. He thought his ears, being ufed to fuch abominable words, might by degrees admit them with lefs deteftation. That although he hated the *yaboos* of this country, yet he no more blamed them for their odious qualities, than he did a *gnnayh* (a bird of prey) for its cruelty, or a fharp ftone for cutting his hoof. But when a creature, pretending to reafon, could be capable of fuch enormities, he dreaded, left the corruption of that faculty might be worfe than brutality itfelf. He feemed therefore confident, that inftead of reafon we were only pof-

when one man murders another to gratify his luft, we fhudder; but when one man murders a million to gratify his vanity, we approve and we admire, we envy and we applaud. If, when this and the preceding pages are read, we difcover with aftonifhment, that when the fame events have occurred in hiftory we felt no emotion, and acquiefced in wars which we could not but know to have been commenced for fuch caufes, and carried on by fuch means; let not him be cenfured for too much debafing his fpecies, who has contributed to their felicity and prefervation by ftripping off the veil of cuftom and prejudice, and holding up in their native deformity the vices by which they become wretched, and the arts by which they are deftroyed.

feffed

feſſed of ſome quality fitted to encreaſe our natural vices; as the reflection from a troubled
ſtream returns the image of an ill-ſhapen body
not only *larger* but more *diſtorted*.

He added, that he had heard too much upon
the ſubject of war both in this, and ſome former diſcourſes. There was another point,
which a little perplexed him at preſent. I had
informed him, that ſome of our crew left their
country on account of being ruined by *law*;
that I had already explained the meaning of
the word; but he was at a loſs, how it
ſhould come to paſs, that the *law*, which was
intended for every man's preſervation, ſhould
be any man's ruin. Therefore he deſired to
be farther ſatisfied what I meant by *law*, and
the *diſpenſers* thereof, according to the preſent
practice in my own country: becauſe he
thought *nature* and *reaſon* were ſufficient guides
for a reaſonable animal, as we pretended to
be, in ſhewing us what we ought to do, and
what to avoid.

I aſſured his honour, that *law* was a ſcience,
in which I had not much converſed, further
than by employing advocates in vain upon
ſome injuſtices, that had been done me; however I would give him all the ſatisfaction I was
able.

I ſaid, there was a ſociety of men among
us bred up from their youth in the art of
proving by words multiplied for the purpoſe,
that *white* is *black*, and *black* is *white* accord-

ing

ing as they are paid *. To this fociety all the reft of the people are *flaves*. For example, if my neighbour hath a mind to my *cow*, he hires a *lawyer* to prove that he ought to have my *cow* from me. I muft then hire another to defend my right, it being againft all rules of *law*, that any man fhould be allowed to fpeak for himfelf. Now in this cafe I, who am the right owner, lie under two great dif-advantages; *firft*, my *lawyer*, being practifed almoft from his cradle in defending falfhood, is quite out of his element, when he would be an advocate for juftice, which is an unnatural office he always attempts with great awkward-nefs, if not with ill will. The *fecond* difad-vantage is, that my *lawyer* muft proceed with great caution, or elfe he will be reprimanded by the *judges*, and abhorred by his brethren as one that would leffen the practice of the *law*. And therefore I have but two methods to preferve my *cow*. The firft is, to gain over my adverfary's *lawyer* with a double fee; who will then betray his client by infinuating, that he hath *juftice* on his fide. The fecond way is, for my *lawyer* to make my caufe appear as *unjuft* as he can by allowing the *cow* to belong to my adverfary; and this, if it be fkilfully done, will certainly befpeak the fa-vour of the bench. Now your honour is to know, that thefe *judges* are perfons appointed to decide all controverfies of property, as well

* As in every caufe council be pretended, that this account are fee'd on both fides, it cannot is much exaggerated.

as for the tryal of criminals, and picked out
from the moſt dextrous lawyers who are grown
old or lazy ; and having been byaſſed all
their lives againſt truth and equity, lie under
ſuch a fatal neceſſity of favouring fraud, perjury, and oppreſſion, that I have known ſome
of them ·refuſe a large bribe from the ſide
where juſtice lay, rather than injure the faculty by doing any thing unbecoming their
nature or their office.

It is a maxim among theſe lawyers, that
whatever hath been done before, may legally
be done again : and therefore they take ſpecial
care to record all the deciſions formerly made
againſt common juſtice, and the general reaſon
of mankind. Theſe, under the name of *precedents,* they produce as authorities to juſtify
the moſt iniquitous opinions, and the judges
·never fail of directing accordingly.

In pleading they ſtudiouſly avoid entering
into the *merits* of the cauſe; but are loud, violent, and tedious, in dwelling upon all *circum-
ſtances* which are not to the purpoſe. For in-
ſtance, in the caſe already mentioned : they
never deſire to know what claim or title my
adverſary hath to my *cow*; but whether the
ſaid *cow* were red or black ; her horns long or
ſhort; whether the field l graze her in be
round or ſquare ; whether ſhe was milked at
home or abroad ; what diſeaſes ſhe is ſubject
to, and the like ; after which they conſult *precedents,* adjourn the cauſe from time to time,
and

and in ten, twenty, or thirty years come to an iſſue.

It is likewiſe to be obſerved, that this ſociety hath a peculiar cant and jargon of their own, that no other mortal can underſtand, and wherein all their laws are written, which they take ſpecial care to multiply; whereby they have wholly confounded the very eſſence of truth and falſhood, of right and wrong; ſo that it will take thirty years to decide, whether the field left me by my anceſtors for ſix generations belongs to me or to a ſtranger three hundred miles off.

In the trial of perſons accuſed for crimes againſt the ſtate, the method is much more ſhort and commendable: the judge firſt ſends to found the diſpoſition of thoſe in power, after which he can eaſily hang or ſave a criminal, ſtrictly preſerving all due forms of *law*.

Here my maſter interpoſing, ſaid it was a pity, that creatures endowed with ſuch prodigious abilities of mind, as theſe *lawyers*, by the deſcription I gave of them, muſt certainly be, were not rather encouraged to be inſtructors of others in wiſdom and knowledge. In anſwer to which I aſſured his honour, that in all points out of their own trade they were uſually the moſt ignorant and ſtupid generation among us, the moſt deſpicable in common converſation, avowed enemies to all knowledge and learning, and equally diſpoſed to pervert the general reaſon of mankind in every other

Z 2   ſubject

tants are able to confume, as well as liquors extracted from grain, or preffed out of the fruit of certain trees, which made excellent drink; and the fame proportion in every other convenience of life. But in order to feed the luxury and intemperance of the males, and the vanity of the females, we fent away the greateft part of our neceffary things to other countries, from whence in return we brought the materials of difeafes, folly, and vice, to fpend among ourfelves. Hence it follows of neceffity, that vaft numbers of our people are compelled to feek their livelihood by begging, robbing, ftealing, cheating, pimping, flattering, fuborning, forfwearing, forging, gaming, lying, fawning, hectoring, voting, fcribling, ftar-gazing, poyfoning, whoring, canting, libelling, freethinking, and the like occupations : every one of which terms I was at much pains to make him underftand.

That *Wine* was not imported among us from foreign countries to fupply the want of water, or other drinks, but becaufe it was a fort of liquid, which made us merry by putting us out of our fenfes, diverted all melancholy thoughts, begat wild extravagant imaginations in the brain, raifed our hopes, and banifhed our fears; fufpended every office of reafon for a time, and deprived us of the ufe of our limbs, till we fell into a profound fleep; although it muft be confeffed, that we always awaked fick and difpirited; and that the ufe of

this

this liquor filled us with diseases, which made our lives uncomfortable and short [*].

But beside all this, the bulk of our people supported themselves by furnishing the necessities or conveniencies of life to the rich, and to each other. For instance, when I am at home, and dressed as I ought to be, I carry on my body the workmanship of an hundred tradesmen; the building and furniture of my house employ as many more, and five times the number to adorn my wife.

I was going on to tell him of another sort of people, who get their livelihood by attending the sick, having upon some occasions informed his honour, that many of my crew had died of diseases. But here it was with the utmost difficulty, that I brought him to apprehend what I meant. He could easily conceive, that a *Houybnhnm* grew weak and heavy a few days before his death, or by some accident might hurt a limb: but that nature, who works all things to perfection, should suffer any pains to breed in our bodies, he thought impossible, and desired to know the reason of so unaccountable an evil. I told him, we fed on a thousand things, which operated contrary to each other; that we eat when we were not hungry, and drank without the provocation of thirst; that we sat whole nights drinking strong liquors without eating a bit, which disposed us to

[*] This account excites ideas of drunkenness very different from those, which are conceived under the terms by which it is generally expressed.

sloth,

floth, enflamed our bodies, and precipitated
or prevented digeftion.   That proftitute female *yaboos* acquired a certain malady, which
bred rottennefs in the bones of thofe who fell
into their embraces; that this and many o-
ther difeafes were propagated from father to
fon; fo that great numbers come into the world .
with complicated maladies upon them : that it
would be endlefs to give him a catalogue of
all difeafes incident to human bodies; for they
could not be fewer than five or fix hundred
fpread over every limb and joint; in fhort,
every part, external and inteftine, having difeafes appropriated to itfelf.   To remedy which
there was a fort of people bred up among us
in the profeffion, or pretence, of curing the
fick.   And becaufe I had fome fkill in the faculty, I would in gratitude to his honour let
him know the whole myftery and method, by
which they proceed.

Their fundamental is, that all difeafes a-
rife from *repletion*; from whence they conclude, that a great *evacuation* of the body is
neceffary either through the natural paffage,
or upwards at the mouth.   Their next bufinefs is from herbs, minerals, gums, oyls,
fhells, falts, juices, fea-weed, excrements,
barks of trees, ferpents, toads, frogs, fpiders,
dead mens flefh and bones, birds, beafts, and
fifhes to form a compofition for fmell and tafte
the moft abominable, naufeous, and deteftable, they can poffibly contrive, which the ftomach immediately rejects with loathing; and
                                        this

this they call a *vomit:* or elfe from the fame
ftore-houfe, with fome other poyfonous additions, they command us to take in at the orifice *above*.or *below* (juft as the phyfician then
happens to be difpofed) a medicine equally an-
noying and difguftful to the bowels; which
relaxing the belly, drives down all before it;
and this they call a *purge,* or a *clyfter.* For
nature (as the phyficians alledge) having intended the fuperior anterior orifice only for the
intromiffion of folids and liquids, and the inferior pofterior for ejection; thefe artifts inge-
nioufly confidering that in all difeafes nature is
forced out of her feat, therefore to replace her
in it, the body muft be treated in a manner
directly contrary, by interchanging the ufe of
each orifice; forcing folids and liquids in at
the *anus,* and making evacuations at the
mouth.

But befides real difeafes, we are fubject to
many that are only imaginary, for which the
phyficians have invented imaginary cures; thefe
have their feveral names, and fo have the drugs
that are proper for them; and with thefe our
female *yaboos* are always infefted.

One great excellency in this tribe is their
fkill at *prognofticks,* wherein they feldom fail;
their predictions in real difeafes, when they rife
to any degree of malignity, generally portend-
ing *death,* which is always in their power,
when recovery is not: and therefore upon any
unexpected figns of amendment after they have
pronounced their fentence, rather than be accufed

cufed as falfe prophets, they know how to approve their fagacity to the world by a feafonable dofe.

They are likewife of fpecial ufe to hufbands and wives, who are grown weary of their mates; to eldeft fons, to great minifters of ftate, and often to princes.

I had formerly upon occafion difcourfed with my mafter upon the nature of *government* in general, and particularly of our own *excellent conftitution*, defervedly the wonder and envy of the whole world. But having here accidentally mentioned a *minifter of ftate*; he commanded me fome time after to inform him, what fpecies of *yaboo* I particularly meant by that appellation.

I told him, that a firft or chief minifter of ftate, who was the perfon I intended to defcribe, was a creature wholly exempt from joy and grief, love and hatred, pity and anger; at leaft, makes ufe of no other paffions, but a violent defire of wealth, power, and titles; that he applies his words to all ufes, except to the indication of his mind; that he never tells a *truth* but with an intent that you fhould take it for a *lye*; nor a *lye*, but with a defign that you fhould take it for a *truth*; that thofe he fpeaks worft of behind their backs are in the fureft way of preferment; and whenever he begins to praife you to others, or to yourfelf, you are from that day forlorn. The worft mark you can receive is a *promife*, efpecially when it is confirmed with an oath; after which
which

which every wife man retires, and gives over all hopes.

There are three methods, by which a man may rife to be chief minifter. The firft is by knowing how with prudence to difpofe of a wife, a daughter, or a fifter: the fecond by betraying or undermining his predeceffor: and the third is, by a *furious Zeal* in public affemblies againft the corruptions of the court. But a wife prince would rather choofe to employ thofe, who practife the laft of thefe methods; becaufe fuch zealots prove always the moft obfequious and fubfervient to the will and paffions of their mafter. That thefe *Minifters*, having all employments at their difpofal, preferve themfelves in power by bribing the majority of a fenate or great council; and at laft by an expedient called an *act of indemnity* (whereof I defcribed the nature to him) they fecure themfelves from after reckonings, and retire from the public laden with the fpoils of the nation.

The palace of a *chief minifter* is a feminary to breed up others in his own trade: the pages, lacquies, and porter by imitating their mafter become *minifters of ftate* in their feveral diftricts, and learn to excel in the three principal *ingredients*, of *infolence*, *lying*, and *bribery*. Accordingly they have a *fubaltern* court paid to them by perfons of the beft rank; and fometimes, by the force of dexterity and impudence, arrive through feveral gradations to be fucceffors to their lord.

5

He

He is ufually governed by a decayed wench, or favourite footman, who are the tunnels through which all graces are conveyed, and may properly be called, *in the laſt reſort*, the governors of the kingdom.

One day in difcourſe my maſter, having heard me mention the *nobility* of my country, was pleaſed to make me a compliment, which I could not pretend to deſerve : that he was ſure I muſt have been born of ſome noble family, becauſe I far exceeded in ſhape, colour, and cleanlineſs all the *yaboos* of his nation, although I ſeemed to fail in ſtrength and agility, which muſt be imputed to my different way of living from thoſe other brutes ; and befides, I was not only endowed with the faculty of ſpeech, but likewiſe with ſome rudiments of reaſon, to a degree, that with all his acquaintance I paſſed for a prodigy.

He made me obſerve, that among the *Houybnhnms*, the *white*, the *ſorrel*, and the *iron-grey*, were not ſo exactly ſhaped as the *bay*, the *dapple-grey*, and the *black* ; nor born with equal talents of mind, or a capacity to improve them; and therefore continued always in the condition of ſervants, without ever aſpiring to match out of their own race, which in that country would be reckoned monſtrous and unnatural.

I made his honour my moſt humble acknowledgments for the good opinion he was pleaſed to conceive of me ; but aſſured him at the ſame time, that my birth was of the lower ſort, having-been born of plain honeſt parents,

rents, who were juft able to give me a tolerable education : that *nobility* among us was altogether a different thing from the idea he had of it ; that our young noblemen are bred from their childhood in idlenefs and luxury ; that as foon as years will permit, they confume their vigour, and contract odious difeafes among lewd females ; and when their fortunes are almoft ruined, they marry fome woman of mean birth, difagreeable perfon, and unfound conftitution, merely for the fake of money, whom they hate and defpife. That the productions of fuch marriages are generally fcrophulous, ricketty, or deformed children ; by which means the family feldom continues above three generations, unlefs the wife takes care to provide a healthy father among her neighbours or domeftics in order to improve and continue the breed. That a weak difeafed body, a meagre countenance, and fallow complexion are the true marks of *noble blood* ; and a healthy robuft appearance is fo difgraceful in a man of quality, that the world concludes his real father to have been a *groom*, or a *coachman*. The imperfections of his mind run parallel with thofe of his body, being a compofition of fpleen, dulnefs, ignorance, caprice, fenfuality, and pride.

Without the confent of this illuftrious body no law can be enacted, repealed, or altered ; and thefe *nobles* have likewife the decifions of all our poffeffions, without appeal.

C H A P.

C H A P. VII.

The author's great love of his native country.
His master's, observations upon the constitution
and administration of England, *as described by*
the author, with parallel cases and compari-
sons. His master's observations upon human
nature.

THE reader may be disposed to wonder,
how I could prevail on myself to give so
free a representation of my own species among
a race of mortals, who are already too apt to
conceive the vilest opinion of human kind from
that intire congruity betwixt me and their *ya-*
hoos. But I must freely confess, that the many virtues of those excellent *quadrupeds,* placed
in opposite view to human corruptions, had so
far opened my eyes, and enlarged. my understanding, that I began to view the actions and
passions of man in a very different light; and
to think the honour of my own kind not worth
managing; which besides it was impossible for
me to do before a person of so acute a judgment as my master, who daily convinced me
of a thousand faults in myself, whereof I had
not the least perception before, and which
with us would never be numbered even among
human infirmities. I had likewise learned from
his example an utter detestation of all falshood
or disguise ; and *truth* appeared so amiable to
me,

me, that I determined upon sacrificing every thing to it.

Let me deal so candidly with the reader as to confess, that there was yet a much stronger motive for the freedom I took in my representation of things. I had not been a year in this country, before I contracted such a love and veneration for the inhabitants, that I entered on a firm resolution never to return to human kind, but to pass the rest of my life among these admirable *houyhnhnms* in the contemplation and practice of every virtue; where I could have no example or incitement to vice. But it was decreed by fortune, my perpetual enemy, that so great a felicity should not fall to my share. However it is now some comfort to reflect, that in what I said of my countrymen, I *extenuated* their faults as much as I durst before so strict an examiner; and upon every article gave as *favourable* a turn, as the matter would bear. For indeed who is there alive, that will not be swayed by his byass and partiality to the place of his birth?

I have related the substance of several conversations I had with my master, during the greatest part of the time I had the honour to be in his service; but have indeed for brevity sake omitted much more than is here set down.

When I had answered all his questions, and his curiosity seemed to be fully satisfied; he sent for me one morning early, and commanding me to sit down at some distance (an honour which

which he had never before conferred upon me)
he faid, he had been very ferioufly confidering
my whole ftory as far as it related both to
myfelf and my country : that he looked upon
us as a fort of animals, to whofe fhare, by what
accident he could not conjecture, fome fmall
pittance of *reafon* had fallen, whereof we made
no other ufe, than by its affiftance to aggravate
our *natural* corruptions, and to acquire new
ones, which nature had not given us : that
we difarmed ourfelves of the few abilities fhe
had beftowed ; had been very fuccefsful in
multiplying our original wants, and feemed to
fpend our whole lives in vain endeavours to
fupply them by our own inventions.   That as
to myfelf it was manifeft, I had neither the
ftrength or agility of a common *yaboo* ; that I
walked infirmly on my hinder feet ; had found
out a contrivance to make my claws of no ufe
or defence, and to remove the hair from my
chin, which was intended as a fhelter from the
fun and the weather.   Laftly, That I could
neither run with fpeed, nor climb trees like
my *bretbren*, (as he called them) the *yaboos* in
this country.

That our inftitutions of *government* and *law*
were plainly owing to our grofs defects in *reafon*, and by confequence in *virtue*; becaufe
reafon alone is fufficient to govern a *rational*
creature ; which was therefore a character we
had no pretence to challenge, even from the
account I had given of my own people ; although he manifeftly perceived, that in order

to favour them I had concealed many particulars, and often *said the thing which was not.*

He was the more confirmed in this opinion, becaufe he obferved, that as I agreed in every feature of my body with other *yahoos,* except where it was to my real difadvantage, in point of ftrength, fpeed, and activity, the fhortnefs of my claws, and fome other particulars where nature had no part; fo from the reprefentation I had given him of our lives, our manners and our actions, he found as near a refemblance in the difpofition of our minds. He faid the *yahoos* were known to hate one another, more than they did any different fpecies of animals; and the reafon ufually affigned was, the odioufnefs of their own fhapes, which all could fee in the reft but not in themfelves.   He had therefore begun to think it not unwife in us to *cover* our bodies, and by that invention conceal many of our deformities from each other, which would elfe be hardly fupportable.   But he now found he had been miftaken, and that the diffentions of thofe brutes in his country were owing to the fame caufe with ours, as I had defcribed them. For if (faid he) you throw among five *yahoos* as much food as would be fufficient for fifty, they will, inftead of eating peaceably, fall together by the ears, each fingle one impatient to *have all to itfelf;* and therefore a fervant was ufually employed to ftand by, while they were feeding abroad, and thofe kept at home were tied at a diſtance from each other; that if a cow died of age or accident, before a *Houyhnhnm* could ſecure it for his own *yahoos*, thoſe in the neighbourhood would come in herds to ſeize it, and then would enſue ſuch a battle as I had deſcribed, with terrible wounds made by their claws on both ſides, although they ſeldom were able to kill one another for want of ſuch convenient inſtruments of death as we had invented. At other times the like battles have been fought between the *yahoos* of ſeveral neighbourhoods without any viſible cauſe: thoſe of one diſtrict watching all opportunities to ſurpriſe the next, before they are prepared. But if they find their project hath miſcarried, they return home, and for want of enemies engage in what I call a civil war among themſelves.

That in ſome fields of his country there are certain *ſhining ſtones* of ſeveral colours, whereof the *yahoos* are violently fond; and when part of theſe *ſtones* is fixed in the earth, as it ſometimes happeneth, they will dig with their claws for whole days to get them out; then carry them away and hide them by heaps in their kennels; but ſtill looking round with great caution for fear their comrades ſhould find out their treaſure. My maſter ſaid he could never diſcover the reaſon of this unnatural appetite, or how theſe *ſtones* could be of any uſe to a *yahoo*; but now he believed it might proceed from the ſame principle of a-varice, which I had aſcribed to mankind:

That

That he had once, by way of experiment, privately removed a heap of these *stones* from the place, where one of his *yahoos* had buried it: whereupon the sordid animal, missing his treasure, by his loud lamenting brought the whole herd to the place, there miserably howled, then fell to biting and tearing the rest; began to pine away, would neither eat, nor sleep, nor work, till he ordered a servant privately to convey the *stones* into the same hole, and hide them as before; which when his *yahoo* had found, he presently recovered his spirits, and good humour, but took care to remove them to a better hiding-place, and hath ever since been a very serviceable brute [*].

My master farther assured me, which I also observed myself, that in the fields where the *shining stones* abound, the fiercest and most frequent battles are fought, occasioned by perpetual inroads of the neighbouring *yahoos*.

He said, it was common, when two *yahoos* discovered such a *stone* in a field, and were contending which of them should be the proprietor, a third would take the advantage, and carry it away from them both; which my master would needs contend to have some kind of resemblance with our *suits at law*; wherein I thought it for our credit not to undeceive him; since the decision he mentioned was much more equitable than many decrees among us:

[*] Nothing can be said to make avarice a greater reproach to mankind, except that it is a vice, which this description will not cure.

because

becaufe the plaintiff and defendant there loft nothing befide the *ftone* they contended for, whereas our *courts of equity* would never have difmiffed the caufe, while either of them had any thing left.

My mafter continuing his difcourfe faid, there was nothing that rendered the *yaboos* more odious, than their undiftinguifhing appetite to devour every thing that came in their way, whether herbs, roots, berries, the corrupted flefh of animals, or all mingled together: and it was peculiar in their temper, that they were fonder of what they could get by rapine or ftealth at a greater diftance, than much better food provided for them at home. If their prey held out, they would eat till they were ready to burft, after which nature had pointed out to them a certain *root* that gave them a general evacuation.

There was a'fo another kind of *root* very *juicy* but fomewhat rare and difficult to be found, which the *yaboos* fought for with much eagernefs, and would fuck it with great delight; it produced in them the fame effects, that wine hath upon us. It would make them fometimes hug, and fometimes tear one another; they would howl and grin, and chatter, and reel, and tumble, and then fall afleep in the mud.

I did indeed obferve, that the *yaboos* were the only animals in this country fubject to any difeafes; which however were much fewer than horfes have among us, and contracted not by

any

any ill treatment they meet with, but by the naftinefs, and greedinefs of that fordid brute. Neither has their language any more than a general appellation for thofe maladies, which is borrowed from the name of the beaft, and called *hnea-yahoo* or the *yahoo's evil*, and the cure prefcribed is a mixture of *their own dung* and *urine*, forcibly put down the *yahoo's* throat. This I have fince often known to have been taken with fuccefs, and do here freely recommend it to my countrymen, for the public good as an admirable fpecific againft all difeafes produced by repletion.

As to learning, government, arts, manufactures, and the like, my mafter confeffed, he could find little or no refemblance between the *yahoos* of that country and thofe in ours. For he only meant to obferve, what parity there was in our natures. He had heard indeed fome curious *Houyhnhnms* obferve, that in moft herds there was a fort of ruling *yahoo* (as among us there is generally fome leading or principal ftag in a park) who was always more *deformed* in body, and *mifchievous in difpofition*, than any of the reft. That this *leader* had ufually a favourite as *like himfelf* as he could get, whofe employment was to *lick his mafter's feet and pofteriors, and drive the female* yahoos *to his kennel* [a]; for which he was now and then rewarded with a piece of afs's flefh. This *favourite* is hated by the whole herd, and there-

---

[a] Flattery and pimping.

fore

fore to protect himfelf keeps always *near the perfon of his leader*. He ufually continues in office, till a worfe can be found; but the very moment he is difcarded, his fucceffor at the head of all the *yahoos* in that diftrict, young and old, male and female, come in a body, and difcharge their excrements upon him from head to foot. But how far this might be ap-plicable to our *courts* and *favourites*, and *mini-fters of ftate*, my mafter faid I could beft de-termine.

I durft make no return to this malicious in-finuation, which debafed human underftand-ing below the fagacity of a common *hound*, who hath judgment enough to diftinguifh and follow the cry of the *ableft dog in the pack*, without being ever miftaken.

My mafter told me, there were fome quali-ties remarkable in the *yahoos*, which he had not obferved me to mention, or at leaft very flightly, in the accounts I had given him of human kind; he faid, thofe animals like other brutes had their females in common; but in this they differed, that the fhe *yahoo* would ad-mit the male, while fhe was pregnant; and that the hees would quarrel and fight with the females, as fiercely as with each other. Both which practices were fuch degrees of in-famous brutality, as no other fenfitive creature ever arrived at.

Another thing he wondered at in the *yahoos*, was their ftrange difpofition to naftinefs and dirt; whereas there appears to be a natural love

of

of cleanlinefs in all other animals. As to the two former accufations, I was glad to let them pafs without any reply, becaufe I had not a word to offer upon them in defence of my fpecies, which otherwife I certainly had done from my own inclinations. But I could have eafily vindicated human kind from the impu-tation of fingularity upon the laft article, if there had been any *fwine* in that country (as unluckily for me there were not) which, al-though it may be a *fweeter quadruped* than a *yaboo*, cannot, I humbly conceive, in juftice pretend to more cleanlinefs; and fo his ho-nour himfelf muft have owned, if he had feen their filthy way of feeding, and their cuftom of wallowing and fleeping in the mud.

My mafter likewife mentioned another qua-lity, which his fervants had difcovered in fe-veral *yaboos*, and to him was wholly unac-countable. He faid, a fancy would fometimes take a *yaboo* to retire into a corner, to lie down, and howl and groan, and fpurn away all that came near him, although he were young and fat, wanted neither food nor wa-ter: nor did the fervants imagine what could poffibly ail him. And the only remedy they found was, to fet him to hard work, after which he would infallibly come to himfelf. To this I was filent out of partiality to my own kind; yet here I could plainly difcover the true feeds of *fpleen*, which only feizeth on the *lazy*, the *luxurious*, and the *ricb*; who if they were forced to undergo the *same regimen*, I would undertake for the cure.

His honour had farther obferved, that a female *yahoo* would often ftand behind a bank or a bufh to gaze on the young males paffing by, and then appear, and hide, ufing many antic geftures and grimaces, at which time it was obferved that fhe had a moft *offenfive fmell*; and when any of the males advanced would flowly retire, looking often back, and with a counterfeit fhew of fear run off into fome convenient place, where fhe knew the male would follow her.

At other times, if a female ftranger came among them, three or four of her own fex would get about her, and ftare, and chatter, and grin, and fmell her all over; and then turn off with geftures, that feemed to exprefs contempt and difdain.

Perhaps my mafter might refine a little in thefe fpeculations, which he had drawn from what he obferved himfelf, or had been told him by others: however I could not reflect without fome amazement and much forrow, that the rudiments of *lewdnefs, coquetry, cenfure,* and *fcandal* fhould have place by inftinct in womankind.

I expected every moment, that my mafter would accufe the *yahoos* of thofe unnatural appetites in both fexes, fo common among us. But nature, it feems, hath not been fo expert a fchool-miftrefs; and thefe politer pleafures

are

are intirely the productions of art and reason on our side of the globe.

CHAP. VIII.

The author relates several particulars of the ya-hoos. *The great virtues of the* Houyhnhnms. *The education and exercise of their youth. Their general assembly.*

A S I ought to have underſtood human na-ture much better, than I ſuppoſed it poſ-ſible for my maſter to do, ſo it was eaſy to ap-ply the character he gave of the *yahoos* to my-ſelf, and my countrymen; and I believed, I could yet make farther diſcoveries from my own obſervation.   I therefore often begged his honour to let me go among the herds of *ya-boos* in the neighbourhood, to which he al-ways very graciouſly conſented, being perfectly convinced, that the hatred I bore thoſe brutes would never ſuffer me to be corrupted by them; and his honour ordered one of his ſer-vants, a ſtrong ſorrel nag, very honeſt and good-natured, to be my guard, without whoſe protection I durſt not undertake ſuch adven-tures.   For I have already told the reader, how much I was peſtered by thoſe odious animals upon my firſt arrival.   And I afterwards failed very narrowly three or four times of falling into their clutches, when I happened to ſtray at any diſtance without my hanger.   And I have reaſon to believe they had ſome imagination

nation that I was of their own species, which I often assisted myself by stripping up my sleeves, and shewing my naked arms and breast in their sight, when my protector was with me. At which times they would approach as near as they durst, and imitate my actions after the manner of monkies, but ever with great signs of hatred; as a tame *jack-daw* with cap and stockings is always persecuted by the wild ones, when he happens to be got among them.

· They are prodigiously nimble from their infancy; however I once caught a young male of three years old, and endeavoured by all marks of tenderness to make it quiet; but the little imp fell a squalling, and scratching, and biting, with such violence, that I was forced to let it go; and it was high time, for a whole troop of old ones came about us at the noise, but finding the cub was safe (for away it ran) and my sorrel nag being by, they durst not venture near us. I observed the young animal's flesh to smell very rank, and the stink was somewhat between a *weasel* and a *fox*, but much more disagreeable. I forgot another circumstance (and perhaps I might have the reader's pardon, if it were wholly omitted) ·that while I held the odious vermin in my hands, it voided its filthy excrements of a yellow liquid substance all over my cloaths; but by good fortune there was a small brook hard by, where I washed myself as clean as I could; although I durst not come into my master's presence, until I were sufficiently aired.

By

By what I could difcover, the *yahoos* appear to be the moft unteachable of all animals; their capacities never reaching higher than to draw or carry burthens. Yet I am of opinion, this defect arifeth chiefly from a perverfe, reftive difpofition. For they are cunning, malicious, treacherous, and revengeful. They are ftrong and hardy, but of a cowardly fpirit, and by confequence infolent, abject, and cruel. It is obferved, that the *red haired* of both fexes are more libidinous and mifchievous than the reft, whom yet they much exceed in ftrength and activity.

The *Houyhnhnms* keep the *yahoos* for prefent ufe in huts not far from the houfe; but the reft are fent abroad to certain fields, where they dig up roots, eat feveral kinds of herbs, and fearch about for carrion, or fometimes catch *weafels* and *lubimubs* (a fort of *wild rat*) which they greedily devour. Nature hath taught them to dig deep holes with their nails on the fide of a rifing ground, wherein they lie by themfelves; only the kennels of the females are larger, fufficient to hold two or three cubs.

They fwim from their infancy like frogs, and are able to continue long under water, where they often take fifh, which the females carry home to their young. And upon this occafion I hope the reader will pardon my relating an odd adventure.

Being one day abroad with my protector the forrel nag, and the weather exceeding hot, I
entreated

entreated him to let me bathe in a river that was near. He confented, and I immediately ftripped myfelf ftark naked, and went down foftly into the ftream. It happened that a young female *yaboo*, ftanding behind a bank, faw the whole proceeding, and enflamed by defire, as the nag and I conjectured, came running with all fpeed, and leaped into the water within five yards of the place where I bathed. I was never in my life fo terribly frighted; the nag was grazing at fome diftance, not fufpecting any harm. She embraced me after a moft fulfome manner; I roared as loud as I could, and the nag came galloping towards me, whereupon fhe quitted her grafp with the utmoft reluctancy, and leaped upon the oppo-fite bank, where fhe ftood gazing and howling all the time I was putting on my cloaths.

This was a matter of diverfion to my mafter and his family, as well as of mortification to myfelf. For now I could no longer deny, that I was a real *yaboo* in every limb and fea-ture, fince the females had a natural propen-fity to me, as one of their own fpecies : nei-ther was the hair of this brute of a red colour (which might have been fome excufe for an appetite a little irregular) but black as a floe, and her countenance did not make an appear-ance altogether fo hideous as the reft of her kind : For, I think, fhe could not be above eleven years old.

Having

Having lived three years in this country, the reader I suppose will expect that I should, like other travellers, give him some account of the manners and customs of its inhabitants, which it was indeed my principal study to learn.

As these noble *Houyhnhnms* are endowed by nature with a general disposition to all virtues, and have no conceptions or ideas of what is evil in a rational creature; so their grand maxim is, to cultivate *reason*, and to be wholly governed by it.   Neither is *reason* among them a point problematical, as with us, where men can argue with plausibility on both sides of a question; but strikes you with immediate conviction; as it must needs do, where it is not mingled, obscured, or discoloured, by passion and interest.   I remember it was with extreme difficulty, that I could bring my master to understand the meaning of the word *opinion*, or how a point could be disputable; because *reason* taught us to affirm or deny only where we are certain; and beyond our knowledge we cannot do either. So that controversies, wranglings, disputes, and positiveness, in false or dubious propositions, are evils unknown among the *Houyhnhnms*.   In the like manner, when I used to explain to him our several systems of *natural philosophy*, he would laugh, that a creature pretending to *reason* should value itself upon the knowledge of other people's conjectures, and in things where that knowledge, if it were certain, could be of no use.   Wherein he agreed intirely with the sentiments of *So-*

crates

crates as *Plato* delivers them; which I mention as the higheſt honour I can do that prince of philoſophers. I have often ſince reflected, what deſtruction ſuch a doctrine would make in the libraries of *Europe*; and how many paths to fame would be then ſhut up in the learned world.

Friendſhip and *benevolence* are the two principal virtues among the *Houyhnhnms* [a]; and theſe not confined to particular objects, but univerſal to the whole race. For a ſtranger from the remoteſt part is equally treated with the neareſt neighbour; and wherever he goes, looks upon himſelf as at home. They preſerve *decency* and *civility* in the higheſt degrees, but are altogether ignorant of *ceremony*. They have no fondneſs for their colts or foles, but the care they take in educating them proceedeth intirely from the dictates of *reaſon* [b]. And I obſerved my maſter to ſhew the ſame affection to his neighbour's iſſue, that he had for his own. They will have it that *nature* teaches them to love the whole ſpecies, and it is *reaſon* only that maketh a diſtinction of perſons, where there is a ſuperior degree of virtue [c].

When

---

[a] Their virtuous qualities are only negative. ORRERY.

[b] We here view the pure inſtincts of brutes, acting in their narrow ſphere, merely for their immediate preſervation. ORRERY.

[c] It may perhaps be thought ſomewhat ſtrange, that the ſenſe of the noble commentator ſhould appear to be directly oppoſite to that of the author, in the paſſages which theſe notes were intended to illuſtrate; but this apparent oppoſition may ariſe merely from the uſing the ſame word

When the matron *Houyhnhnms* have produced one of each fex, they no longer accompany with their conforts, except they lofe one of their iffue by fome cafualty, which very feldom happens: but in fuch a cafe they meet again; or when the like accident befals a perfon whofe wife is paft bearing, fome other couple beftow him one of their own colts, and then go together again until the mother is pregnant. This caution is neceffary to prevent the country from being over-burthened with numbers. But the race of inferior *Houyhnhnms*, bred up to be fervants, is not fo ftrictly limited upon this article; thefe are allowed to produce three of each fex to be domeftics in the noble families.

In their marriages they are exactly careful to choofe fuch colours, as will not make any difagreeable mixture in the breed. *Strength* is chiefly valued in the male, and *comelinefs* in the female; not upon the account of *love*, but to preferve the race from degenerating; for where a female happens to excel in *ftrength*, a confort is chofen with regard to *comelinefs*.

Courtfhip, love, prefents, jointures, fettlements, have no place in their thoughts; or terms whereby to exprefs them in their language. The young couple meet and are joined,

---

word in an oppofite fenfe; as by the word *candour*, his lordfhip always means a quality which inclines a man to put the worft conftruction upon the words and actions of another, and by *candour*, the dean always means juft the contrary.

Compare *Orrery*, fmall edit. p. 100. large edit. p. 146. laft paragraph, with *Swift's* apology for the *Tale of a Tub*, p. 3.

merely

merely becaufe it is the determination of their parents and friends: it is what they fee done every day, and they look upon it as one of the neceffary actions of a reafonable being. But the violation of marriage, or any other un-chaftity, was never heard of: And the married pair pafs their lives with the fame friend-fhip, and mutual benevolence, that they bear to all others of the fame fpecies, who come in their way; without jealoufy, fondnefs, quar-relling, or difcontent.

In educating the youth of both fexes their method is admirable, and highly deferveth our imitation. Thefe are not fuffered to tafte a grain of *oats*, except upon certain days, till eighteen years old; nor *milk*, but very rarely; and in fummer they graze two hours in the morning, and as many in the evening, which their parents likewife obferve; but the fervants are not allowed above half that time, and a great part of their grafs is brought home, which they eat at the moft convenient hours, when they can be beft fpared from work.

Temperance, induftry, exercife, and *cleanlinefs*, are the leffons equally enjoined to the young ones of both fexes: and my mafter thought it monftrous in us to give the females a different kind of education from the males, except in fome articles of domeftic management; whereby, as he truly obferved, one half of our natives were good for nothing but bringing children into the world: and to truft the care

of

of our children to such useless animals; he said, was yet a greater instance of brutality.

But the *Houyhnhnms* train up their youth to strength, speed, and hardiness by exercising them in running races up and down steep hills, and over hard stony grounds, and when they are all in a sweat, they are ordered to leap over head and ears into a pond or river. Four times a year the youth of a certain district meet to shew their proficiency in running and leaping, and other feats of strength and agility; where the victor is rewarded, with a song in his or her praise. On this festival the servants drive a herd of *yahoos* into the field laden with hay, and oats, and milk, for a repast to the *Houyhnhnms*; after which these brutes are immediately driven back again, for fear of being noisome to the assembly.

Every fourth year, at the *vernal equinox*, there is a representative council of the whole nation, which meets in a plain about twenty miles from our house, and continueth about five or six days. Here they enquire into the state and condition of the several districts; whether they abound, or be deficient in hay or oats, or cows or *yahoos*? and wherever there is any want (which is but seldom) it is immediately supplied by unanimous consent and contribution. Here likewise the regulation of children is settled: as for instance, if a *Houyhnhnm* hath two males, he changeth one of them with another that hath two females: and when a child hath been lost by any casualty, where

the mother is paſt breeding, it is determined
what family in the diſtrict ſhall breed another
to ſupply the loſs.

C H A P. IX.

A grand debate at the general aſſembly of the
Houyhnhnms, *and how it was determined.*
The learning of the Houyhnhnms. *Their build-*
ings. Their manner of burials. The defective-
neſs of their language.

ONE of theſe grand aſſemblies was held
in my time, about three months before
my departure, whither my maſter went as the
repreſentative of our diſtrict.   In this council
was reſumed their old debate, and indeed the
only debate that ever happened in their country; whereof my maſter after his return gave
me a very particular account.

The queſtion to be debated was, whether
the *yahoos* ſhould be exterminated from the
face of the earth.   One of the *members* for the
affirmative offered ſeveral arguments of great
ſtrength and weight; alledging, that as the
yahoos were the moſt filthy, noiſome, and deformed animal which nature ever produced, ſo
they were the moſt reſtive and indocible, miſ-
chievous and malicious : they would privately
ſuck the teats of the *Houyhnhnms* cows; kill
and devour their cats, trample down their oats
and graſs, if they were not continually watch-
ed, and commit a thouſand other extravagan-
cies.

cies. He took notice of a general tradition,
that *yahoos* had not been always in their country; but that many ages ago two of thefe
brutes appeared together upon a mountain;
whether produced by the heat of the fun upon
corrupted mud and flime, or from the ooze
and froth of the fea, was never known: that
thefe *yahoos* engendered, and their brood in a
fhort time grew fo numerous as to over-run
and infeft the whole nation: that the *Houyhnhnms* to get rid of this evil made a general
hunting, and at laft enclofed the whole herd;
and deftroying the elder, every *Houyhnhnm*
kept two young ones in a kennel, and brought
them to fuch a degree of tamenefs, as an animal fo favage by nature can be capable of acquiring; ufing them for draught and carriage:
that there feemed to be much truth in this tradition, and that thofe creatures could not be
Ylnhniamfhy (or *aborigines* of the land) becaufe
of the violent hatred the *Houyhnhnms*, as well
as all other animals, bore them; which, although their evil difpofition fufficiently deferv-
ed, could never have arrived at fo high a degree, if they had been *Aborigines*; or elfe they
would have long fince been rooted out: that
the inhabitants, taking a fancy to ufe the fervice of the *yahoos*, had very imprudently neglected to cultivate the breed of *affes*, which
are a comely animal, eafily kept, more tame
and orderly, without any offenfive fmell, ftrong
enough for labour, although they yield to the
other in agility of body; and, if their braying

be no agreeable found, it is far preferable to the horrible howlings of the *yahoos*.

Several others declared their sentiments to the same purpose, when my master proposed an expedient to the assembly, whereof he had indeed borrowed the hint from me. He approved of the tradition mentioned by the *honourable member*, who spoke before ; and affirmed, that the two *yahoos*, said to be first seen· among them, had been driven thither over the sea; that coming to land, and being forsaken by their companions, they retired to the mountains, and' degenerating by degrees, became in process of time much more savage, than those of their own species in the country from whence these two originals came. The reason of this assertion was, that he had now in his possession a certain wonderful *yahoo* (meaning myself) which most of them had heard of and many of them had seen. He then related to them, how he first found me ; that my body was all covered with an artificial composure of the skins and hairs of other animals : that I spoke in a language of my own, and had thoroughly learned theirs : that I had related to him the accidents, which brought me thither ; that, when he saw me without my covering, I was an exact *yahoo* in every part, only of a whiter colour, less hairy, and with shorter claws. He added, how I had endeavoured to persuade him, that in my own and other countries the *yahoos* acted as the governing, rational animal, and held the *Houyhnhnms* in servitude : that he observed in me all the qualities of a *yahoo*, only a little

more

more civilized by fome tincture of reafon; which however was in a degree as far inferior to the *Houyhnhnm* race, as the *yahoos* of their country were to me : that, among other things, I mentioned a cuftom we had of *caſtrating Houyhnhnms* when they were young in order to render them tame; that the operation was eafy and fafe; that it was no fhame to learn wifdom from brutes, as induftry is taught by the ant, and building by the fwallow (for fo I tranflate the word *lyhannh*, although it be a much larger fowl :) that this invention might be practifed upon the younger *yahoos* here, which, befides rendering them tractable and fitter for ufe, would in an age put an end to the whole fpecies without deftroying life: that in the mean time the *Houyhnhnms* fhould be *exhorted* to cultivate the breed of affes, which as they are in all refpects more valuable brutes, fo they have this advantage, to be fit for fervice at five years old, which the others are not till twelve.

This was all my mafter thought fit to tell me at that time, of what paffed in the grand council. But he was pleafed to conceal one particular, which related perfonally to myfelf, whereof I foon felt the unhappy effect, as the reader will know in its proper place, and from whence I date all the fucceeding misfortunes of my life.

The *Houyhnhnms* have no letters, and confequently their knowledge is all traditional. But there happening few events of any mo-

ment.

ment among a people fo well united, naturally
difpofed to every virtue, wholly governed by
reafon, and cut off from all commerce with
other nations; the hiftorical part is eafily preferved without burthening their memories. I
have already obferved that they are fubject to
no difeafes, and therefore can have no need of
phyficians. However, they have excellent medicines compofed of herbs to cure accidental
bruifes and cuts in the paftern or frog of the
foot by fharp ftones, as well as other maims
and hurts in the feveral parts of the body.

They calculate the year by the revolution of
the fun and the moon, but ufe no fubdivifions
into weeks. They are well enough acquainted
with the motions of thofe two luminaries, and
underftand the nature of *eclipfes*; and this is
the utmoft progrefs of their *aftronomy*.

In *poetry* they muft be allowed to excel all
other mortals; wherein the juftnefs of their fi-
milies, and the minutenefs as well as exactnefs
of their defcriptions, are indeed inimitable.
Their verfes abound very much in both of
thefe; and ufually contain either fome exalted
notions of friendfhip and benevolence, or the
praifes of thofe, who were victors in races and
other bodily exercifes. Their buildings, although very rude and fimple, are not inconve-
nient, but well contrived to defend them from
all injuries of cold and heat. They have a
kind of tree, which at forty years old loofens
in the root, and falls with the firft ftorm; it
grows very ftrait, and being pointed like
ftakes,

ftakes, with a fharp ftone (for the *Houyhnhnms*
know not the ufe of iron) they ftick them
erect in the ground about ten inches afunder,
and then weave in oat-ftraw, or fometimes
wattles, betwixt them.   The roof is made after the fame manner, and fo are the doors.

The *Houyhnhnms* ufe the hollow part, between the paftern and the hoof, of their fore-
feet, as we do our hands, and this with greater
dexterity, than I could at firft imagine.   I
have feen a white mare of our family thread a
needle (which I lent her on purpofe) with that
joint.   They milk their cows, reap their oats,
and do all the work which requires hands in
the fame manner.   They have a kind of hard
flints, which by grinding againft other ftones
they form into inftruments, that ferve inftead
of wedges, axes, and hammers.   With tools
made of thefe flints they likewife cut their
hay, and reap their oats, which there grow
naturally in feveral fields: the *yahoos* draw
home the fheaves in carriages, and the fervants
tread them in certain covered hutts to get out
the grain, which is kept in ftores.   They
make a rude kind of earthen and wooden veffels, and bake the former in the fun.

If they can avoid cafualties, they die only
of old-age, and are buried in the obfcureft
places that can be found, their friends and relations expreffing neither joy nor grief at their
departure; nor does the dying perfon difcover
the leaft regret that he is leaving the world,
any more than if he were upon returning home

from

from a visit to one of his neighbours. I remember my master having once made an ap-
pointment with a friend and his family to come
to his house upon some affair of importance,
on the day fixed the mistress and her two children came very late; she made two excuses, first
for her husband, who, as she said, happened that
very morning to *lhnuwnh*. The word is strongly
expressive in their language, but not easily rendered into *english*; it signifies, *to retire to his
first mother*. Her excuse for not coming soon-
er was, that her husband dying late in the
morning, she was a good while consulting her
servants about a convenient place where his
body should be laid; and I observed, she behaved herself at our house as chearfully as the
rest : she died about three months after.

They live generally to seventy, or seventy-
five years, very seldom to fourscore : some
weeks before their death they feel a gradual
decay; but without pain. During this time
they are much visited by their friends, because
they cannot go abroad with their usual ease and
satisfaction. However, about ten days before
their death, which they seldom fail in computing, they return the visits that have been
made them by those, who are nearest in the
neighbourhood, being carried in a convenient
sledge drawn by *yahoos*; which vehicle they
use, not only upon this occasion, but when
they grow old, upon long journies, or when
they are lamed by any accident. And therefore when the dying *Houyhnhnms* return those
visits,

visits, they take a solemn leave of their friends, as if they were going to some remote part of the country, where they designed to pass the rest of their lives.

I know not whether it may be worth observing, that the *Houyhnhnms* have no word in their language to express any thing that is *evil*, except what they borrow from the deformities, or ill qualities of the *yahoos*. Thus they denote the folly of a servant, an omission of a child, a stone that cuts their feet, a continuance of foul or unseasonable weather, and the like, by adding to each the epithet of *yahoo*. For instance, *hhnm yahoo, whnaholm yahoo, ynlhmndwihlma yahoo*, and an ill contrived house, *ynholmhnmrohlnw yahoo*.

I could with great pleasure enlarge farther upon the manners and virtues of this excellent people; but intending in a short time to publish a volume by itself expresly upon that subject, I refer the reader thither. And in the mean time, proceed to relate my own sad catastrophe.

CHAP.

CHAP. X.

*The author's oeconomy, and happy life, among the
Houyhnhnms. His great improvement in virtue by conversing with them. Their conversations. The author hath notice given him
by his master, that he must depart from the
country. He falls into a swoon for grief; but
submits. He contrives and finishes a canoo by
the help of a fellow servant, and puts to sea at
a venture.*

I Had settled my little oeconomy to my own
heart's content. My master had ordered a
room to be made for me after their manner a-
bout six yards from the house; the sides and
floors of which I plaistered with clay, and covered with rush-matts of my own contriving;
I had beaten hemp, which there grows wild,
and made of it a sort of ticking: this I filled
with the feathers of several birds I had taken
with springes made of *yahoos* hairs, and were
excellent food. I had worked two chairs with
my knife, the sorrel nag helping me in the
grosser and more laborious part. When my
cloaths were worn to rags, I made myself o-
thers with the skins of rabbets, and of a certain beautiful animal about the same size, called *nnubnoh*, the skin of which is covered with
a fine down. Of these I also made very tolerable stockings. I soaled my shoes with wood,
which I cut from a tree, and fitted to the up-

per-

per-leather; and when this was worn out ,I
fupplied it with the fkins of *yaboos* dried in the
fun. I often got honey out of hollow trees,
which I mingled with water, or eat with my
bread. No man could more verify the truth
of thefe two maxims, *That nature is very eafily
fatisfied*; and, *That neceffity is the mother of invention.* I enjoyed perfect health of body, and
tranquillity of mind; I did not feel the treachery or inconftancy of a friend, nor the injuries
of a fecret or open enemy. I had no occafion
of bribing, flattering, or pimping, to procure
the favour of any great man, or of his minion.
I wanted no fence againft fraud or oppreffion;
here was neither phyfician to deftroy my body, nor lawyer to ruin my fortune; no in-
former to watch my words and actions, or
forge accufations againft me for hire: here
were no gibers, cenfurers, backbiters, pick-
pockets, highway-men, houfe-breakers, attor-
nies, bawds, buffoons, gamefters, politicians,
wits, fplenatics, tedious talkers, controvertifts,
ravifhers, murderers, robbers, virtuofoes; no
leaders or followers of party and faction; no
encouragers to vice by feducement or examples; no dungeon, axes, gibbets, whipping-
pofts, or pillories; no cheating fhopkeepers or
mechanics; no pride, vanity, or affectation;
no fops, bullies, drunkards, ftrolling whores,
or poxes; no ranting, lewd, expenfive wives;
no ftupid, proud pedants; no importunate,
over-bearing, quarrelfome, noify, roaring, empty, conceited, fwearing companion; no fcoun-
drels

drels raifed from the duſt upon the merit of their vices, or nobility thrown into it on account of their virtues; no lords, fidlers, judges, or dancing-maſters.

I had the favour of being admitted to ſeveral *Houyhnhnms,* who came to viſit or dine with my maſter; where his honour gracioufly fuffered me to wait in the room, and liſten to their diſcourfe. Both he and his company would often defcend to aſk me queſtions, and receive my anfwers. I had alfo ſometimes the honour of attending my maſter in his viſits to others. I never prefumed to ſpeak, except in anfwer to a queſtion; and then I did it with inward regret, becaufe it was a lofs of ſo much time for improving myfelf: but I was infinitely delighted with the ſtation of an humble auditor in ſuch converfations, where nothing paſſed but what was ufeful, expreffed in the feweſt and moſt fignificant words: where (as I have already ſaid) the greateſt *decency* was obferved without the leaſt degree of ceremony; where no perfon ſpoke without being pleafed himſelf, and pleafing his companions; where there was no interruption, tedioufnefs, heat, or difference of fentiments. They have a notion, that, when people are met together, a ſhort filence doth much improve converfation: this I found to be true; for during thofe little intermiſſions of talk new ideas would arife in their minds, which very much enlivened the diſcourfe. Their ſubjeɛts are generally on friendſhip and benevolence, on order and oeconomy;

nomy ; fometimes upon the vifible operations
of nature, or ancient traditions ; upon the
bounds and limits of virtue ; upon the uner-
ring rules of reafon, or upon fome determinations to be taken at the next great affembly; and often upon the various excellencies of *poetry*. I may add without vanity,
that my prefence often gave them fufficient
matter for difcourfe, becaufe it afforded my
mafter an occafion of letting his friends into
the hiftory of me and my country, upon which
they were all pleafed to defcant in a manner
not very advantageous to human kind; and
for that reafon I fhall not repeat what they
faid : only I may be allowed to obferve, that
his honour to my great admiration appeared
to underftand the nature of *yahoos*, much better than myfelf. He went through all our
vices and follies, and difcovered many, which
I had never mentioned to him, by only fop-
pofing what qualities a *yahoo* of their country
with a fmall proportion of reafon might be
capable of exerting; and concluded, with too
much probability, how vile as well as miferable fuch a creature muft be.

I freely confefs, that all the little knowledge
I have of any value, was acquired by the lectures I received from my mafter, and from
hearing the difcourfes of him and his friends;
to which I fhould be prouder to liften, than
to dictate to the greateft and wifeft affembly in
Europe. I admired the ftrength, comelinefs,
and fpeed of the inhabitants ; and fuch a con-

ftellation

ftellation of virtues, in fuch amiable perfons, produced in me the higheft veneration. At firft indeed I did not feel that natural awe, which the *yaboos* and all other animals bear to-wards them ; but it grew upon me by degrees, much fooner than I imagined, and was ming-led with a refpectful love and gratitude, that they would condefcend to diftinguifh me from the reft of my fpecies.

When I thought of my family, my friends, my countrymen, or human race in general, I confidered them as they really were, *yaboos* in fhape and difpofition, perhaps a little more ci-vilized, and qualified with the gift of fpeech; but making no other ufe of reafon, than to improve and multiply thofe vices, whereof their brethren in this country had only the fhare that nature allotted them. When I hap-pened to behold the reflection of my own form in a lake or a fountain, I turned away my face in horror and deteftation of myfelf; and could better endure the fight of a common *yaboo*, than of my own perfon. By converfing with the *Houyhnhnms*, and looking upon them with delight, I fell to imitate their gait and gefture, which is now grown into an habit; and my friends often tell me in a blunt way, that *I trot like a horfe*; which however I take for a great compliment : neither fhall I difown, that in fpeaking I am apt to fall into the voice and manner of the *Houyhnhnms*, and hear myfelf ridiculed on that account without the leaft mortification.

In

In the midft of all this happinefs, and when I looked upon myfelf to be fully fettled for life, my mafter fent for me one morning a little earlier than his ufual hour.   I obferved by his countenance that he was in fome perplexity, and at a lofs how to begin what he had to fpeak.   After a fhort filence, he told me, he did not know how I would take what he was going to fay; that in the laft general affembly, when the affair of the *yahoos* was entered upon, the reprefentatives had taken offence at his keeping a *yahoo* (meaning myfelf) in his family, more like a *Houyhnhnm*, than a brute animal.   That he was known frequently to converfe with me, as if he could receive fome advantage or pleafure in my company : that fuch a practice was not agreeable to reafon or nature, or a thing ever heard of before among them.   The affembly did therefore *exhort* him either to employ me like the reft of my fpecies, or command me to fwim back to the place from whence I came.   That the firft of thefe expedients was utterly rejected by all the *Houyhnhnms*, who had ever feen me at his houfe or their own : for they alledged, that becaufe I had fome rudiments of reafon, added to the natural pravity of thofe animals, it was to be feared, I might be able to feduce them into the woody and mountainous parts of the country, and bring them in troops by night to deftroy the *Houyhnhnms* cattle, as being naturally of the ravenous kind, and averfe from labour.

My

My mafter added, that he was daily preffed by the *Houybnbnms* of the neighbourhood to have the affembly's *exhortation* executed, which he could not put off much longer. He doubted it would be impoffible for me to fwim to another country; and therefore wifhed I would contrive fome fort of vehicle refembling thofe I had defcribed to him, that might carry me on the fea; in which work I fhould have the affiftance of his own fervants, as well as thofe of his neighbours. He concluded, that for his own part he could have been content to keep me in his fervice as long as I lived; becaufe he found I had cured myfelf of fome bad habits and difpofitions by endeavouring, as far as my inferior nature was capable, to imitate the *Houyhnbnms*.

I fhould here obferve to the reader, that a decree of the general affembly in this country is expreffed by the word *bnbloayn*, which fignifies an *exhortation*, as near as I can render it: for they have no conception how a rational creature can be *compelled*, but only advifed, or *exhorted*; becaufe no perfon can difobey reafon without giving up his claim to be a rational creature.

I was ftruck with the utmoft grief and defpair at my mafter's difcourfe; and being unable to fupport the agonies I was under, I fell into a fwoon at his feet: when I came to myfelf, he told me, that he concluded I had been dead (for thefe people are fubjeĉt to no fuch imbecillities of nature.) I anfwered in a faint voice,

voice, that death would have been too great an happiness; that although I could not blame the affembly's *exhortation*, or the urgency of his friends; yet in my weak and corrupt judgment, I thought it might confift with reafon to have been lefs rigorous: that I could not fwim a league, and probably the neareft land to theirs might be diftant above an hundred: that many materials, neceffary for making a fmall veffel to carry me off, were wholly wanting in this country, which however I would attempt in obedience and gratitude to his honour, although I concluded the thing to be impoffible, and therefore looked on myfelf as already devoted to deftruction: that the certain profpect of an unnatural death was the leaft of my evils: for fuppofing I fhould efcape with life by fome ftrange adventure, how could I think with temper of paffing my days among *yaboos*, and relapfing into my old corruptions for want of examples to lead and keep me within the paths of virtue: that I knew too well upon what folid reafons all the determinations of the wife *Houyhnhnms* were founded, not to be fhaken by arguments of mine, a miferable *yaboo*; and therefore, after prefenting him with my humble thanks for the offer of his fervants affiftance in making a veffel, and defiring a reafonable time for fo difficult a work, I told him I would endeavour to preferve a wretched being; and if ever I returned to *England*, was not without hopes of being ufeful to my own fpecies by celebrating the praifes of the renowned *Houyhnhnms,* and propofing their virtues to the imitation of mankind.

My mafter in a few words made me a very gracious reply, allowed me the fpace of two *months* to finifh my boat; and ordered the forrel nag, my fellow-fervant (for fo at this diftance I may prefume to call him) to follow my inftructions; becaufe I told my mafter, that his help would be fufficient, and I knew he had a tendernefs for me.

In his company, my firft bufinefs was to go to that part of the coaft, where my rebellious crew had ordered me to be fet on fhore. I I got upon a heighth, and looking on every fide into the fea, fancied I faw a fmall ifland towards the *north-eaft :* I took out my pocketglafs, and could then clearly diftinguifh it about five leagues off, as I computed; but it appeared to the forrel nag to be only a blue cloud : for as he had no conception of any country befide his own, fo he could not be as expert in diftinguifhing remote objects at fea, as we who fo much converfe in that element.

After I had difcovered this ifland, I confidered no farther; but refolved, it fhould, if poffible, be the firft place of my banifhment, leaving the confequence to fortune.

I returned home, and confulting with the forrel nag, we went into a copfe at fome diftance, where I with my knife, and he with a fharp flint faftened very artificially after their manner to a wooden handle, cut down feveral oak wattles, about the thicknefs of a walking-ftaff, ſtaff, and ſome larger pieces. But I ſhall not trouble the reader with a particular deſcription of my own mechanics; let it ſuffice to ſay, that in ſix weeks time with the help of the ſorrel nag, who performed the parts that required moſt labour, I finiſhed a ſort of indian canoo, but much larger, covering it with the ſkins of *yahoos* well ſtitched together with hempen threads of my own making. My ſail was likewiſe compoſed of the ſkins of the ſame animal; but I made uſe of the youngeſt I could get, the older being too tough and thick; and I likewiſe provided myſelf with four paddles. I laid in a ſtock of boiled fleſh, of rabbets and fowls; and took with me two veſſels, one filled with milk, and the other with water.

I tried my canoo in a large pond near my maſter's Houſe, and then corrected in it what was amiſs; ſtopping all the chinks with *yahoo* tallow, till I found it ſtanch; and able to bear me and my freight. And, when it was as compleat as I could poſſibly make it, I had it drawn on a carriage very gently by *yahoos* to the ſea-ſide, under the conduct of the ſorrel nag, and another ſervant.

When all was ready, and the day came for my departure, I took leave of my maſter and lady and the whole family, my eyes flowing with tears, and my heart quite ſunk with grief. But his honour out of curioſity, and perhaps (if I may ſpeak it without vanity) partly out of kindneſs, was determined to ſee

me

me in my canoo; and got feveral of his neighbouring friends to accompany him. I was
forced to wait above an hour for the tide, and
then obferving the wind very fortunately bearing towards the ifland, to which I intended
to fteer my courfe, I took a fecond leave of
my mafter: but, as I was going to proftrate
myfelf to kifs his hoof, he did me the honour
to raife it gently to my mouth. I am not ignorant how much I have been cenfured for
mentioning this laft particular. Detractors are
pleafed to think it improbable, that fo illuftrious a perfon fhould defcend to give fo great
a mark of diftinction to a creature fo inferior
as I. Neither have I forgotten how apt fome
travellers are to boaft of extraordinary favours
they have received. But, if thefe cenfurers
were better acquainted with the noble and
courteous difpofition of the *Houyhnhnms*, they
would foon change their opinion.

I paid my refpects to the reft of the *Houyhnhnms* in his honour's company; then getting
into my canoo I pufhed off from fhore.

CHAP.

CHAP. XI.

The author's dangerous voyage. He arrives at New-Holland, hoping to settle there. Is wounded with an arrow by one of the natives. Is seized and carried by force into a portugueze *ship. The great civilities of the captain. The author arrives at* England.

I Began this desperate voyage on *February* 15, 1714-15, at 9 o'clock in the morning. The wind was very favourable; however I made use at first only of my paddles; but considering I should soon be weary, and that the wind might chop about, I ventured to set up my little sail; and thus with the help of the tide I went at the rate of a league and a half an hour, as near as I could guess. My master and his friends continued on the shore, till I was almost out of sight; and I often heard the forrel nag (who always loved me) crying out, *bnuy illa nyba majah yahoo,* Take care of thyself gentle *yahoo.*

My design was, if possible, to discover some small island uninhabited, yet sufficient by my labour to furnish me with the necessaries of life, which I would have thought a greater happiness, than to be first minister in the politest court of *europe*; so horrible was the idea I conceived of returning to live in the society and under the government of *yahoos.* For, in such a solitude as I desired, I could at least en-

joy

joy my own thoughts, and reflect with delight on the virtues of those inimitable *Houyhnhnms* without any opportunity of degenerating into the vices and corruptions of my own species.

The reader may remember what I related, when my crew conspired against me, and confined me to my cabbin. How I continued there several weeks without knowing what course we took; and when I was put a-shoar in the long-boat, how the sailors told me with oaths, whether true or false, that they knew not in what part of the world we were. However, I did then believe us to be about ten degrees *southward* of the *Cape of Good-Hope*, or about 45 degrees *southern* latitude, as I gathered from some general words I overheard among them, being I supposed to the *south-east* in their intended voyage to *Madagascar*. And although this were but little better than conjecture, yet I resolved to steer my course *eastward*, hoping to reach the *south-west* coast of *New-Holland*, and perhaps some such island as I desired lying *westward* of it. The wind was full *west*, and by six in the evening I computed I had gone *eastward* at least eighteen leagues; when I spied a very small island about half a league off, which I soon reached. It was nothing but a rock with one creek naturally arched by the force of tempests. Here I put in my canoo, and climbing a part of the rock I could plainly discover land to the *east*, extending from *south* to *north*. I lay all night

in

in my canoo; and repeating my voyage early in the morning, I arrived in seven hours to the *south-east* point of *New-Holland*. This confirmed me in the opinion I have long entertained, that the *maps* and *charts* place this country at least three degrees more to the *east,* than it really is; which thought I communicated many years ago to my worthy friend, Mr. *Herman Moll*, and gave him my reasons for it, although he hath rather chosen to follow other authors.

I saw no inhabitants in the place where I landed, and being unarmed I was afraid of venturing far into the country. I found some shell-fish on the shore, and eat them raw, not daring to kindle a fire for fear of being discovered by the natives. I continued three days feeding on oysters and limpits to save my own provisions; and I fortunately found a brook of excellent water, which gave me great relief.

On the fourth day venturing out early a little too far, I saw twenty or thirty natives upon a heighth not above five hundred yards from me. They were stark naked, men, women, and children round a fire, as I could discover by the smoke. One of them spied me, and gave notice to the rest; five of them advanced towards me, leaving the women and children at the fire. I made what haste I could to the shore, and getting into my canoo shoved off: the savages observing me retreat ran after me; and, before I could get far enough into the

C c 4 sea,

sea, difcharged an arrow which wounded me deeply on the infide of my left knee (I fhall carry the mark to my grave.) I apprehended the arrow might be poifoned, and paddling out of the reach of their darts (being a calm day) I made a fhift to fuck the wound, and drefs it as well as I could.

I was at a lofs what to do, for I durft not return to the fame landing-place, but ftood to the *north*, and was forced to paddle; for the wind, though very gentle, was againft me, blowing *north-weft*. As I was looking about for a fecure landing-place, I faw a fail to the *north-north-eaft*, which appearing every minute more vifible, I was in fome doubt, whether I fhould wait for them or no; but at laft my deteftation of the *yaboo* race prevailed; and turning my canoo I failed and paddled together to the *fouth*, and got into the fame creek, from whence I fet out in the morning, chufing ra- ther to truft myfelf among thefe *barbarians*, than live with *European yaboos*. I drew up my canoo as clofe as I could to the fhore, and hid myfelf behind a ftone by the little brook, which, as I have already faid, was excellent water.

The fhip came within half a league of this creek, and fent out her long-boat with veffels to take in frefh water (for the place, it feems, was very well known) but I did not obferve it, till the boat was almoft on fhore; and it was too late to feek another hiding-place. The feamen at their landing obferved my canoo, and rummaging

rummaging it all over, eafily conjectured that
the owner could not be far off. Four of them,
well armed, fearched every cranny and lurking-
hole, till at laft they found me flat on my face
behind the ftone.   They gazed a while in admiration at my ftrange uncouth drefs ; my coat
made of fkins, my wooden foaled fhoes, and
my furred ftockings ; from whence however
they concluded, I was not a native of the
place, who all go naked.   One of the feamen,
in *portugueze*, bid me rife, and afked who I
was.   I underftood that language very well, and
getting upon my feet faid I was a poor *yaboo* banifhed from the *Houybnbnms*, and defired they
would pleafe to let me depart.   They admired
to hear me anfwer them in their own tongue,
and faw by my complexion, I muft be an *European* ; but were at a lofs to know what I
meant by *yaboos*, and *Houybnbnms*, and at the
fame time fell a laughing at my ftrange tone
in fpeaking, which refembled the neighing of a
horfe.   I trembled all the while betwixt fear
and hatred : I again defired leave to depart,
and was gently moving to my canoo ; but they
laid hold on me, defiring to know, what country I was of ? whence I came ? with many
other queftions.   I told them I was born in
England, from whence I came about five years
ago, and then their country and ours were at
peace.   I therefore hoped they would not treat
me as an enemy, fince I meant them no harm,
but was a poor *yaboo*, feeking fome defolate
                                        place

place where to pafs the remainder of his unfortunate life.

When they began to talk, I thought I never
heard or faw any thing fo unnatural; for it
appeared to me as monftrous, as if a dog or a
cow fhould fpeak in *England*, or a *yaboo* in
Houybnbnm-land. The honeft *Portugueze* were
equally amazed at my ftrange dreſs, and the
odd manner of delivering my words, which
however they underftood very well. They
fpoke to me with great humanity, and faid
they were fure the captain would carry me
gratis to *Liſbon*, from whence I might return
to my own country; that two of the feamen
would go back to the fhip, inform the captain
of what they had feen, and receive his orders;
in the mean time, unlefs I would give my folemn oath not to fly, they would fecure me
by force. I thought it beft to comply with
their propofal. They were very curious to
know my ftory, but I gave them very little
fatisfaction; and they all conjectured, that my
misfortunes had impaired my reafon. In two
hours the boat, which went loaden with veffels of water, returned with the captain's command to fetch me on board. I fell on my
knees to preferve my liberty; but all was in
vain, and the men having tied me with cords
heaved me into the boat, from whence I was
taken into the fhip, and from thence into the
captain's cabbin.

His name was *Pedro de Mendez*; he was a
very courteous and generous perfon; he en-

treated

treated me to give some account of myself, and desired to know what I would eat or drink; said, I should be used as well as himself, and spoke so many obliging things, that I wondered to find such civilities from a *yaboo*. However, I remained silent and sullen; I was ready to faint at the very smell of him and his men. At last I desired something to eat out of my own canoo; but he ordered me a chicken, and some excellent wine, and then directed that I should be put to bed in a very clean cabbin. I would not undress myself, but lay on the bed-cloaths, and in half an hour stole out, when I thought the crew was at dinner, and getting to the side of the ship was going to leap into the sea, and swim for my life, rather than continue among *yaboos*. But one of the seamen prevented me, and having informed the captain, I was chained to my cabbin.

After dinner *Don Pedro* came to me, and desired to know my reason for so desperate an attempt; assured me, he only meant to do me all the service he was able, and spoke so very movingly, that at last I descended to treat him like an animal, which had some little portion of reason. I gave him a very short relation of my voyage; of the conspiracy against me by my own men; of the country where they set me on shore, and of my five years residence there. All which he looked upon, as if it were a dream or a vision; whereat I took great offence; for I had quite forgot the faculty of lying so peculiar to *yaboos* in all countries where they

they preside, and consequently the disposition of suspecting truth in others of their own species. I asked him whether it were the custom in his country to *say the thing which was not?* I assured him, I had almost forgot what he meant by falsehood, and, if I had lived a thousand years in *Houyhnhnm-land*, I should never have heard a lye from the meanest servant; that I was altogether indifferent whether he believed me or no; but however in return for his favours, I would give so much allowance to the corruption of his nature, as to answer any objection he would please to make, and then he might easily discover the truth.

The captain, a wise man, after many endeavours to catch me tripping in some part of my story, at last began to have a better opinion of my veracity. But he added, that, since I professed so inviolable an attachment to truth, I must give him my word and honour to bear him company in this voyage without attempting any thing against my life, or else he would continue me a prisoner till we arrived at *Lisbon*. I gave him the promise he required; but at the same time protested, that I would suffer the greatest hardships, rather than return to live among *yahoos*.

Our voyage passed without any considerable accident. In gratitude to the captain I sometimes sat with him at his earnest request, and strove to conceal my antipathy against human kind, although it often broke out; which he suffered to pass without observation. But the

greatest

greateft part of the day I confined myfelf to
my cabbin to avoid feeing any of the crew.
The captain had often entreated me to ftrip myfelf of my favage drefs, and offered to lend me
the beft fuit of cloaths he had. This I would
not be prevailed on to accept, abhorring to cover myfelf with any thing that had been on the
back of a *yahoo*. I only defired he would lend
me two clean fhirts, which, having been wafhed fince he wore them, I believed would not
fo much defile me. Thefe I changed every
fecond day, and wafhed them myfelf.

We arrived at *Lifbon*, *Nov.* 5, 1715. At
our landing the captain forced me to cover myfelf with his cloak to prevent the rabble from
crouding about me. I was conveyed to his
own houfe; and at my earneft requeft he led me
up to the higheft room backwards. I conjured
him to conceal from all perfons what I had
told him of the *Houyhnhnms*; becaufe the leaft
hint of fuch a ftory would not only draw numbers of people to fee me, but probably put me
in danger of being imprifoned or burnt by
the *inquifition*. The captain perfuaded me to
accept a fuit of cloaths newly made; but I
would not fuffer the taylor to take my meafure;
however, *Don Pedro* being almoft of my fize,
they fitted me well enough. He accoutred me
with other neceffaries, all new, which I aired
for twenty-four hours, before I would ufe
them.

The captain had no wife, nor above three
fervants, none of which were fuffered to attend

tend at meals ; and his whole deportment was
so obliging, added to very good *human* understanding, that I really began to tolerate his
company. He gained so far upon me, that I
ventured to look out of the back window. By
degrees I was brought into another room, from
whence I peeped into the street, but drew my
head back in a fright. In a week's time he
seduced me down to the door. I found my
terror gradually lessened, but my hatred and
contempt seemed to encrease. I was at last
bold enough to walk the street in his company,
but kept my nose well stopped with rue, or
sometimes with tobacco.

In ten days *Don Pedro*, to whom I had given
some account of my domestic affairs, put it
upon me as a matter of honour and conscience,
that I ought to return to my native country,
and live at home with my wife and children.
He told me, there was an *english* ship in the
port just ready to sail, and he would furnish
me with all things necessary. It would be tedious to repeat his arguments, and my contra-
dictions. He said it was altogether impossible
to find such a solitary island as I had desired to
live in; but I might command in my own
house, and pass my time in a manner as recluse
as I pleased.

I complied at last, finding I could not do
better. I left *Lisbon* the 24th day of *November*
in an *english* merchant-man, but, who was the
master, I never enquired. *Don Pedro* accompanied me to the ship, and lent me twenty
pounds.

pounds. He took kind leave of me, and embraced me at parting, which I bore as well as I could. During this last voyage I had no commerce with the master, or any of his men; but pretending I was sick kept close in my cabbin. On the 5th of *December*, 1715, we cast anchor in the *Downs* about nine in the morning, and at three in the afternoon I got safe to my house at *Rotherhith*.

My wife and family received me with great surprize and joy, because they concluded me certainly dead; but I must freely confess the sight of them filled me only with hatred, disgust, and contempt; and the more by reflecting on the near alliance I had to them. For although, since my unfortunate exile from the *Houyhnbnm* country, I had compelled myself to tolerate the sight of *yahoos*, and to converse with *Don Pedro de Mendez*; yet my memory and imagination were perpetually filled with the virtues and ideas of those exalted *Houyhnhnms*. And when I began to consider, that by copulating with one of the *yahoo*-species I had become a parent of more, it struck me with the utmost shame, confusion, and horror.

As soon as I entered the house, my wife took me in her arms, and kissed me; at which, having not been used to the touch of that odious animal for so many years, I fell into a swoon for almost an hour. At the time I am writing, it is five years since my last return to *England*: during the first year I could not endure my wife or children in my presence; the very

very ſmell of them was intolerable; much leſs. could I ſuffer them to eat in the ſame room. To this hour they dare not preſume to touch my bread, or drink out of the ſame cup; neither was I ever able to let one of them take me by the hand. The firſt money I laid out was to buy two young ſtone-horſes, which I keep in a good ſtable, and next to them the groom is my greateſt favourite; for I feel my ſpirits revived by the ſmell he contracts in the ſtable. My horſes underſtand me tolerably well; I converſe with them at leaſt four hours every day. They are ſtrangers to bridle or ſaddle; they live in great amity with me, and friendſhip to each other.

C H A P.

C H A P. XII.

The author's veracity. His design in publishing this work. His censure of those travellers who swerve from the truth. The author clears himself from any sinister ends in writing. An objection answered. The method of planting colonies. His native country commended. The right of the crown to those countries described by the author, is justified. The difficulty of conquering them. The author takes his last leave of the reader; proposeth his manner of living for the future; gives good advice and concludeth.

THUS gentle reader, I have given thee a faithful history of my travels for sixteen years and above seven months; wherein I have not been so studious of ornament as of truth. I could perhaps, like others, have astonished thee with strange improbable tales; but I rather chose to relate plain matter of fact in the simplest manner and style, because my principal design was to inform, and not to amuse thee.

It is easy for us who travel into remote countries, which are seldom visited by *englishmen* or other *europeans*, to form descriptions of wonderful animals both at sea and land. Whereas a traveller's chief aim should be to make men wiser and better, and to improve their minds by the bad, as well as good example, of what they deliver concerning foreign places.

I could heartily wish a law was enacted, that every traveller, before he were permitted to publish his voyages, should be obliged to make oath before the *lord high Chancellor*, that all he intended to print was absolutely true to the best of his knowledge; for then the world would no longer be deceived, as it usually is; while some writers, to make their works pass the better upon the public, impose the grossest falsities on the unwary reader. I have perused several books of travels with great delight in my younger days; but having since gone over most parts of the globe, and been able to contradict many fabulous accounts from my own observation, it hath given me a great disgust against this part of reading, and some indignation to see the credulity of mankind so impudently abused. Therefore, since my acquaintance were pleased to think my poor endeavours might not be unacceptable to my country, I imposed on myself as a maxim never to be swerved from, that I would *strictly adhere to truth*; neither indeed can I be ever under the least temptation to vary from it, while I retain in my mind the lectures and example of my noble master, and the other illustrious *Houyhnhnms*, of whom I had so long the honour to be an humble hearer.

———*Nec*

—— Nec fi miferum Fortuna Sinonem
Finxit, vanum etiam, mendacemque improbæ
finget.

I know very well, how little reputation is to be got by writings, which require neither genius nor learning, nor indeed any other talent, except a good memory, or an exact *journal.* I know likewife, that writers of travels, like *dictionary*-makers, are funk into oblivion by the weight and bulk of thofe, who come laft, and therefore lie uppermoft. And it is highly probable, that fuch travellers, who fhall hereafter vifit the countries defcribed in this work of mine, may by detecting my errors (if there be any) and adding many new difcoveries of their own, juftle me out of vogue and ftand in my place, making the world forget that ever I was an author. This indeed would be too great a mortification, if I wrote for fame : but as my fole intention was the *public good,* I cannot be altogether difappointed. For who can read of the virtues I have mentioned in the glorious *Houyhnhnms* without being afhamed of his own vices, when he confiders himfelf as the reafoning, governing animal of his country ? I fhall fay nothing of thofe remote nations, where *yahoos* prefide ; amongft which the leaft corrupted are the *Brobdingnagians,* whofe wife maxims in morality and govern-

ment

ment it would be our happineſs to obſerve. But I forbear deſcanting farther, and rather leave the judicious reader to his own remarks and applications.

I am not a little pleaſed, that this work of mine can poſſibly meet with no cenſurers: for what objections can be made againſt a writer, who relates only plain facts, that happened in ſuch diſtant countries, where we have not the leaſt intereſt with reſpect either to trade or negotiations? I have carefully avoided every fault, with which common writers of travels are often too juſtly charged. Beſides, I med-dle not the leaſt with any *party*, but write without paſſion, prejudice, or ill-will againſt any man, or number of men whatſoever. I write for the nobleſt end, to inform and in-ſtruct mankind, over whom I may, without breach of modeſty, pretend to ſome ſuperi-ority from the advantages I received by con-verſing ſo long among the moſt accompliſhed *Houyhnhnms*. I write without any view to-wards profit or praiſe. I never ſuffer a word to paſs, that may look like reflection, or poſ-ſibly give the leaſt offence, even to thoſe who are moſt ready to take it. So that I hope, I may with juſtice pronounce myſelf an au-thor perfectly blameleſs; againſt whom the tribes of anſwerers, conſiderers, obſervers, re-flecters, detecters, remarkers, will never be able to find matter for exerciſing their ta-lents.

I confeſs,

I confeſs, it was whiſpered to me, that I was bound in duty, as a ſubject of *England*, to have given in a memorial to a ſecretary of ſtate at my firſt coming over; becauſe, whatever lands are diſcovered by a ſubject, belong to the crown. But I doubt whether our conqueſts, in the countries I treat of, would be as eaſy as thoſe of *Ferdinando Cortez* over the naked *Americans*. The *Lilliputians*, I think, are hardly worth the charge of a fleet and army to reduce them; and I queſtion whether it might be prudent or ſafe to attempt the *Brobdingnagians*. Or whether an *engliſh* army would be much at their eaſe with the flying iſland over their heads. The *Houyhnhnms* indeed appear not to be ſo well prepared for war, a ſcience to which they are perfect ſtrangers, and eſpecially againſt miſſive weapons. However, ſuppoſing myſelf to be a miniſter of ſtate, I could never give my advice for invading them. Their prudence, unanimity, unacquaintedneſs with fear, and their love of their country, would amply ſupply all defects in the military art. Imagine twenty thouſand of them breaking into the midſt of an *european* army, confounding the ranks, overturning the carriages, battering the warriors faces into mummy by terrible yerks from their hinder hoofs; for they would well deſerve the character given to *Auguſtus* : *Recalcitrat undique tutus*. But inſtead of propoſals for conquering that magnanimous nation, I rather wiſh they were in a capacity, or diſpoſition,

to fend a fufficient number of their inhabitants for civilizing *Europe*, by teaching us the
firft principles of honour, juftice, truth, temperance, public fpirit, fortitude,. chaftity,
friendfhip, benevolence, and fidelity. The
names of all which virtues are ftill retained a-
mong us in moft languages, and are to be met
with in modern, as well as ancient authors;
which I am able to affert from my own fmall
reading.

But I had another reafon, which made me
lefs forward to enlarge his majefty's dominions by my difcoveries. To fay the truth, I
had conceived a few fcruples with relation to
the diftributive juftice of princes upon thofe
occafions. For inftance, a crew of pyrates are
driven by a ftorm they know not whither; at
length a boy difcovers land from the top-
maft; they go on fhore to rob and plunder;
they fee an harmlefs people, are entertained
with kindnefs; they give the country a new
name; they take formal poffeffion of it for
their king; they fet up a rotten plank or a
ftone for a memorial; they murder two or
three dozen of the natives, bring away a couple more by force for a fample, return home,
and get their pardon. Here commences a
new·dominion acquired with a title by *divine
right*. Ships are fent with the firft opportunity; the natives driven·out or deftroyed; their
princes tortured to difcover their gold; a free
licence given to all acts of inhumanity and
luft, the earth reeking with the blood of its
inhabi-

inhabitants : and this execrable crew of butch-
ers employed in so pious an expedition, is a
modern colony, sent to convert and civilize an
idolatrous and barbarous people.

But this description, I confess, doth by no
means affect the *British* nation, who may be
an example to the whole world for their wis-
dom, care, and justice in planting colonies;
their liberal endowments for the advancement
of religion and learning; their choice of de-
vout and able pastors to propagate *christianity*;
their caution in stocking their provinces with
people of sober lives and conversations from
this the mother kingdom; their strict regard
to the distribution of justice, in supplying the
civil administration through all their colonies
with officers of the greatest abilities, utter
strangers to corruption; and to crown all, by
sending the most vigilant and virtuous governors, who have no other views than the happiness of the people over whom they preside,
and the honour of the king their master.

But as those countries, which I have described, do not appear to have any desire of
being conquered, and enslaved, murdered or
driven out by colonies; nor abound either in
gold, silver, sugar, or tobacco; I did humbly
conceive, they were by no means proper objects of our zeal, our valour, or our interest.
However, if those, whom it more concerns,
think fit to be of another opinion, I am ready
to depose, when I shall be lawfully called,
that no *European* did ever visit these countries
before

before me. I mean, if the inhabitants ought to be believed, unlefs a difpute may arife concerning the two *yaboos* faid to have been feen many ages ago upon a mountain in *Houybnbnm-land*.

But, as to the formality of taking poffef-fion in my fovereign's name, it never came once into my thoughts ; and if it had, yet, as my affairs then ftood, I fhould perhaps in point of prudence and felf-prefervation have put it off to a better opportunity.

Having thus anfwered the only objection, that can ever be raifed againft me as a travel-ler ; I here take a final leave of all my cour-teous readers, and return to enjoy my own fpeculations in my little garden at *Reddriff*; to apply thofe excellent leffons of virtue, which I learned among the *Houybnbnms*; to in-ftruct the *yaboos* of my own family, as far as I fhall find them docible animals ; to behold my figure often in a glafs, and thus, if poffi-ble, habituate myfelf by time to tolerate the fight of a human creature : to lament the bru-tality of *Houybnbnms* in my own country, but always treat their perfons with refpect for the fake of my noble mafter, his family, his friends, and the whole *Houybnbnm* race, whom thefe of ours have the honour to refemble in all their lineaments, however their intellectu-als came to degenerate.

I began laft week to permit my wife to fit at dinner with me at the fartheft end of a long table ; and to anfwer (but

with the utmoſt brevity) the few queſtions I
aſked her. Yet, the ſmell of a *yaboo* continuing very offenſive, I always keep my noſe well
ſtopped with rue, lavender, or tobacco-leaves.
And, although it be hard for a man late in
life to remove old habits, I am not altogether
out of hopes in ſome time to ſuffer a neighbour *yaboo* in my company, without the ap-
prehenſions I am yet under of his teeth or his
claws.

My reconcilement to the *yaboo* kind in general might not be ſo difficult, if they would
be content with thoſe vices and follies only,
which nature hath intitled them to. I am not in
the leaſt provoked at the ſight of a lawyer, a
pickpocket, a colonel, a fool, a lord, a game-
ſter, a politician, a whore-monger, a phyſician,
an evidence, a ſuborner, an attorney, a traitor,
or the like: this is all according to the due
courſe of things : but when I behold a lump
of deformity and diſeaſes both in body and
mind ſmitten with *pride*, it immediately breaks
all the meaſures of my patience; neither ſhall
I be ever able to comprehend how ſuch an
animal, and ſuch a vice, could tally together.
The wiſe and virtuous *Houybnhnms,* who a-
bound in all excellencies that can adorn a rational creature, have no name for this vice in
their language, which hath no terms to expreſs any thing that is evil, except thoſe whereby they deſcribe the deteſtable qualities of their
yahoos, among which they were not able to
diſtinguiſh this of pride for want of thoroughly

ly underſtanding human nature, as it ſheweth itſelf in other countries, where that animal preſides. But I, who had more experience, could plainly obſerve ſome rudiments of it a-mong the wild *yahoos.*

But the *Houybnhnms,* who live under the go-vernment of reaſon, are no more proud of the good qualities they poſſeſs, than I ſhould be for not wanting a leg or an arm, which no man in his wits would boaſt of, although he muſt be miſerable without them. I dwell the longer upon this ſubject, from the deſire I have to make the ſociety of an *engliſh yahoo* by any means not inſupportable; and therefore I here entreat thoſe, who have any tincture of this abſurd vice, that they will not preſume to come in my ſight.

' To mortify pride, which in-deed was not made for man, and produces not only the moſt ridiculous follies, but the moſt extenſive calamity, appears to have been one general view of the author in every part of theſe travels. Perſonal ſtrength and beauty, the wiſdom and the vir-tue of mankind, become objects not of pride but of humility, in the diminutive ſtature and con-temptible weakneſs of the *Lil-liputians*; in the horrid defor-mity of the *Brobdingnagians*; in the learned folly of the *Lapu-tians*, and in the parallel drawn between our manners and thoſe of the *Houybubnms.*

F I N I S.